The Dating Bible

Ty Adams

The Dating Bible

© Copyright 2014 Ty Adams

Heaven Enterprises
20318 Grand River Detroit, MI 48219
www.iTy.TV

www.TyAdamsTV.com

Printed in the United States of America

ALL RIGHTS RESERVED

This book is protected under the copyright laws of the United States of America. No portion of this book may be reproduced in any form or by any means--electronic, mechanical, photocopying, recording or otherwise--without the written permission of the publisher. Permission granted upon request. Unless otherwise noted, Scripture quotations are from the King James Version of the Bible.

Unless otherwise marked, Scripture quotations are from The Holy Bible, New King James Version copyright © 1979, 1980, 1982 by Thomas Nelson, Inc.

Scripture noted AMP are taken from the Amplified New Testament copyright © 1958, 1987 by The Lockman Foundation. Used by permission.

Scripture noted MSG are taken from THE MESSAGE. Copyright © by Eugene H. Peterson, 1993, 1994, 1995, 1996. Used by permission of NavPress Publishing Group.

Scripture quotation marked (NTL) are taken from the Holy Bible, New Living Translation.

Copyright © 1996. Used by permission of Tyndale Home Publishers, Inc., Wheaton, Illinois 60819. All rights reserved.

Photography and Cover: Marlon E. Hines

The Dating Bible by Ty Adams

MEET TY

Ty Adams, CEO and Founder of Heaven Enterprises and Girls Gone God.com, is a sex and relationship expert, best-selling author and life coach. She is the voice of counsel to thousands around the world through her celebrated web-based column, Ask Dr. Ty. After being both nominated for broadcast of the year and receiving more than 100,000 hits during the premiere month of her daily radio program, Ty began preparing for the launch of her captivating television show, iTy!

Ty is highly recognized as the creative pen behind the best-selling book, Single Saved and Having Sex, reaching best-seller status in its inception. As if TV personality, author and international speaker weren't enough, Ty piled on producer to that list, creating The Real Housewives Of The Bible brand. Her literary work and productions have landed her on numerous television and radio programs, including CNN, ABC News, FOX News, TBN's Praise the Lord, The 700 Club, Ebony Magazine, Heart & Soul Magazine's Sex and earmarked as an Essence Magazine bestseller and landing at number three on Amazon.com's Top 100.

Affectionately known as "Dr. Ty", she skillfully navigates through multimedia, books, television and film to help design and fashion healthy lifestyles. Dr. Ty's bold, ram's horn approach to lifestyle, sex and relationships makes her one of the most sought after speakers in the country, distinguishing her as a leading advisor and "SEXpert" in America.

Ty has been in love with love since she was a child when she laid eyes on her first crush, Bert and Ernie from Sesame Street! Since then she's been on the journey to finding, understanding and teaching on love and relationships! The most important and favorite part of her life is being mommy to her beautiful and talented daughter, Heaven. Ty is totally addicted to Welch's Black Cherry Grape Juice and her mother's hot-out-the-oven Peach Cobbler. You can learn more about Ty and hang out with her in her adventurous life at www.iTy.TV

What's Your Dating Style?

This a Dating and Sex Profile to determine/define your style of dating and relating. Please answer the following:

do you define dating? _____

personal views about dating are _____

personal views about sex and dating or sex before marriage is _____

I could have sex on my terms, I would _____

What level of intimacy or sexual expression do you think is acceptable in a dating relationship? _____

At what age did you begin dating? How did you learn/develop your concepts about dating? ___
_____

How do you typically choose a date? What criteria do you have? _____

What dating habits/patterns do you find consistent? _____
_____

What are your religious beliefs/convictions? Do you incorporate them in your dating relationships? How? _____
_____

I would describe my personal relationship with God as _____

What have you learned about love, dating, relationships? _____
_____

What have you learned from your parents about love? _____

I first learned about sex when I was ___ years old. I learned that sex is _____
_____

How has that shaped who you are today? _____
_____

If you are a Christian, how has that changed after meeting God? _____
_____

If your dating history was a genre of music, it would be:
    a) Rock N Roll
    b) Jazz
    c) Opera
    d) Country
    e) Rhythm and Blues
    f) A broken record

Explain why _____
Describe how your single life has been for the last 5 years? _____
_____

Describe one of the most memorable dates or a time you most cherished while you were dating/in a relationship _____
_____

If you could describe your dating style, what would it be?
    a) Trendy
    b) Conservative
    c) Casual
    d) After five
    e) Out of style

Explain _____
_____

I would define a healthy relationship as _____
_____

If I could describe the perfect dating relationship, it would look like this _____
_____

I define love as _____
_____

The most frustrating thing about my single and dating life is _____
_____

What I love most about my single life is _____
_____

Are You Ready To Date?

So, you think you're ready to date? Take this quiz to figure out exactly where you stand! BE HONEST WITH YOURSELF!

Answer True or False to the Following:
1. I'm tired of being single.
2. I often choose the wrong person.
3. I find it difficult to break off a relationship that seems to be no good for me.
4. I don't trust men/women.
5. I love who I'm becoming!
6. I don't know how or why it keeps happening, but I keep finding myself with men that are no good.
7. I will go as far as heavy petting and other sexual favors but not sex.
8. I feel adrift right now; at a crossroad in my life.
9. I need to have a relationship or I'll go crazy!
10. In my last 3 relationships, I was sexually involved/active.
11. I'm often concerned about how I look or compare myself to others.
12. I can't help but to think about what it would've been like if my ex and I would not have broken up.
13. Every time I think about my ex, I want to punch a hole in a wall! Uggh!
14. I think I have a lot to offer in a relationship.
15. I think sex is a good way to determine if I'm compatible with a person or not.
16. I'm frustrated about my life right now!
17. There are times that I've been in relationships that I've mistaken it for love when it was really lust.
18. I think I would be so much happier if I had a mate or significant other.
19. My social life sucks!
20. The only way you can truly know if you're compatible with someone is to be sexually intimate with them.
21. I'm at the place in my life where I can be myself.
22. I think it's acceptable to have sex if you're in a committed relationship and love the person.
23. I find it hard to commit to just one person.
24. I need to make my life more exciting.
25. I'm still kicking it with my ex.
26. I struggle with masturbation.
27. Single parent is on overload; I need help!
28. I have often compromised my beliefs in relationships in order to stay in the relationship.

29. I haven't mentally let go of my ex.
30. I'm trying to end this battle with porn.
31. I find it difficult to just be single and not dating. I can't stand the loneliness so I am often dating or in one relationship after the next.
32. My prayer life is weak.
33. I want to meet someone new but I can't help but to think about my ex and if there's still a possibility or chance of renewing that.
34. I'm so lonely; I'm just tired of being by myself.
35. I feel spiritually bankrupt and need to get my life right with God.
36. I can't eat or sleep because of a break-up.
37. There is only one true love/soul mate for me and I'm waiting for that person.
38. I have to click with the person and strongly attracted to them in order to go out on a date with them.
39. I talk myself into staying in a relationship that I know is no good and I should end it but I don't want to be alone or hurt their feelings.
40. I'm inconsistent with my prayer life.
41. I've stayed in relationships that materially sustained me but wasn't good for me.
42. I've stayed in high-end, drama relationships mistaking them for true love.
43. I've gotten my heart caught up in relationships, later realized they were the wrong one but it was too late because my heart was caught up in it.
44. I tend to give in because the sexual chemistry is so powerful.
45. For much of my life, I haven't felt that I am special to someone.
46. I don't feel right or I feel insecure if I'm not in a relationship or have sexual fulfillment.
47. My esteem suffers a low if someone rejects me that I really want to be in a relationship with.
48. At times, my career or personal success and growth in life are stunted or have suffered when I'm in a relationship or sexually fulfilled.
49. Tick tock, tick tock! My biological clock is running out of time; I'm starting to get older now and I need to find someone soon to settle down with.
50. I want to make a commitment with celibacy but I just can't seem to help myself and end up falling when I don't intend to.
51. The relationship I'm in right now is exciting! Even though I wasn't expecting them, they came along at a good time after my break-up with my ex.
52. I think it's virtually impossible to build a relationship without sex.

DO NOT PASS GO, DO NOT COLLECT $200, GO STRATIGHT TO CHAPTER ONE, If you answered TRUE to any other numbers besides 5, 14 and 20.

Table Of Contents

Single…………………………………………………………10

Single Ladies……………………………………………….23

Playing House……………………………………………..36

Fashion Statement………………………………………..46

We've Already Crossed The Line……………………………..49

Price Tag……………………………………………………58

10 Things…………………………………………………..62

There's An App For That…………………………………63

Window Shopping…………………………………………64

I Am Ready To Date………………………………………69

Tailor-Made…………………………………………………70

Seamstress…………………………………………………78

10 Commandments Of Dating…………………………………82

How To Get The One………………………………………83

How To Prepare for Marriage without Dating………………88

Shoplist……………………………………………………..89

Online Shopping…………………………………………..91

Dressed To Kill……………………………………………………95

Dating With Kids………………………………………………101

50 Things………………………………………………………105

Shoplifting………………………………………………………107

Unequally Yoked………………………………………………125

I'd Rather Be Single……………………………………………139

Breaking Up……………………………………………………140

Dating Addiction………………………………………………153

10 Things That Destroy Relationships…………………………154

Bodyguard………………………………………………………156

How Far Is Too Far……………………………………………177

Pants On Fire……………………………………………………190

Myths……………………………………………………………203

Is This The One…………………………………………………206

History…………………………………………………………207

Pizza and A Date………………………………………………214

Thank you………………………………………………………218

Chapter 1
Single

What if you came home to find that I did an extreme fashion makeover on your house and built you a walk-in closet double the size of your bedroom, filled from wall-to-wall with a brand new wardrobe? Wait, wait! Before you get all excited that's the other Ty on Extreme Makeover that does that; *not this Ty*. So let's calm down before you start hyperventilating thinking about this new wardrobe! (LOL) Ok, let's reverse that; what if I came to your home and took every piece of clothing you had in your wardrobe and left you with only one pair of clothing for the rest of your life? I know, right; the unthinkable! But that's just how many singles live their lives; it's compartmentalized and marginalized to one-square-footage of focus on dating and sex. Chasing after sex and relationships most of your single life is equivalent to having only one single garment to wear when there's an entire wardrobe of possibilities in life that go beyond dating and sex. There are so many singles that are predominately fixated on relationship, engrossed with who they're going to be with, and fulfilling their sexual desires, that they end up living in a vacuum of lust, sexual confusion, and an unfulfilled love life. The paramount problem that I see in the lives of many singles is **mismanagement.**

- Mismanagement of relationships
- Mismanagement of purpose
- Mismanagement of time
- Mismanagement of desire
- Mismanagement of sex
- Mismanagement of self

You don't have a money problem, a job problem, a loneliness problem, a dating problem or even a sexual sin problem; you have a management problem. Yes, sexual misgiving is about mismanagement. You have not learned to manage yourself or your single life. You have not learned to properly develop, manage, govern and supervise your own life. Many singles are never really single and do not know what it means to be single. They cheat themselves out of a stylish single life because they're always trying to escape it; they are distracted and consumed with dating, and meeting emotional and sexual desire is the prominent focus and ironically, are ill-prepared for dating because they have not mastered the art of being single and are not yet successful at being single. Erroneously throwing themselves in relationships, they send their emotions on a crash test, developing improper relational habits, increasing their inability to control their emotions, feelings, behavior, and desire. Many single Christians do not cultivate Christ-centered relationships because they do not exercise character, relationship integrity, or nurture and fortify their dating partners into a more fulfilling life in Christ. Hence, what you often have are two, broken Christians getting together, trying to "merge companies" in the form of a romantic relationship and the outcome is more damage and brokenness; which is the total opposite of what it means to be single. My spiritual dad, Dr. Myles Munroe, defines **single** as: separate, unique, whole and undivided.

> "At the time GOD made Earth and Heaven, before any grasses or shrubs had sprouted from the ground—GOD hadn't yet sent rain on Earth, nor was there anyone around to work the ground—GOD formed Man out of dirt from the ground and blew into his nostrils the breath of life. The Man came alive—a living soul! Then GOD planted a garden in Eden, in the east. He put the Man he had just made in it. GOD made all kinds of trees grow from the ground, trees beautiful to look at and good to eat. The Tree-of-Life was in the middle of the garden, also the Tree-of-Knowledge-of-Good-and-Evil. GOD took the Man and set him down in the Garden of Eden to work the ground and keep it in order. GOD commanded the Man, "You can eat from any tree in the garden, except from the Tree-of-Knowledge-of-Good-and-Evil. Don't eat from it. The moment you eat from that tree, you're dead." GOD said, "It's not good for the Man to be alone; I'll make him a helper, a companion. So GOD formed from the dirt of the ground all the animals of the field and all the birds of the air. He brought them to the Man to see what he would name them. Whatever the Man called each living creature, that was its name. The Man named the cattle, named the birds of the air, named the wild animals; but he didn't find a suitable companion. GOD put the Man into a deep sleep. As he slept he removed one of his ribs and replaced it with flesh. GOD then used the rib that he had taken from the Man to make Woman and presented her to the Man. The Man said, "Finally! Bone of my bone, flesh of my flesh! Name her Woman for she was made from Man." Gen. 2:5-9, 15-24 MSG

Contrary to unpopular belief, marriage is not the first institution; <u>singleness is.</u> Before there was Eve, Adam had God. The single most important aspect of your life is your relationship with God. Outside of your relationship with Him, the next most important relationship is the one that you have with yourself. Yet many see their single life as a curse so they attempt to escape it, well before they are prepared to, not realizing that the fabric of society, the moral condition of our nation, the preservation of community, family, and the world at large is the by-product of a whole, separate, unique, undivided single man or woman. It was God who made Adam aware that he was alone and then He created someone complimentary to him after Adam lived a whole and complete single life. Before God put Adam in any relationship, Adam first developed a relationship with Him where he had a consistent, open line of communication with God, an obedient life, and a surrendered abandonment to the plan God had for him. Next he was given his purpose and assignment on earth, with rest signifying his obedience and submission to God's will for his life. Not until then, was he qualified to have a relationship with Eve.

"It is not good for *that* man to be alone." Dr. Myles Munroe

The opposite is the case with many singles: they get in a relationship, long before they even determine what God's will is for their lives, attempt to establish their career or find their purpose after they are well engrossed in a relationship and then try to find God to help them fix the relationship after they find that they are not adequately equipped to sustain a career or a relationship, or realize they're in the wrong career and relationship altogether. If you cannot improve and cultivate your own life as a single, how are you going to be able to do that for someone else? If you have not surrendered your life completely to the Lord or you have not allowed Him to develop you into the man or woman that He wants you to be and to make you whole, then it is good for you to be alone, *for now*. You are not ready for a relationship with anyone until you are **SINGLE!** Totally Single! Separate, unique, whole and undivided! How do you know you're totally single? Adam did not know he was alone and needed a mate until God interrupted him and made him aware of it. You need to become so engrossed, consumed and fulfilled in your relationship with God and your purpose that God has to tap you on the shoulder and interrupt you to invite you to a relationship with someone else.

"My desire is to have you free from all anxiety and distressing care. The unmarried man is anxious about the things of the Lord--how he may please the Lord; But the married man is anxious about worldly matters--how he may please his wife--And he is drawn in diverging directions [his interests are divided and he is distracted from his devotion to God]. And the unmarried woman or girl is concerned and anxious about the matters of the Lord, **how to be wholly separated and set apart in body and spirit;** but the married woman has her cares [centered] in earthly affairs--how she may please her husband. Now I say this for your own welfare and profit, not to put [a halter of] restraint upon you, but to promote what is seemly and in good order and to secure your **undistracted and undivided devotion to the Lord."**
1 Cor. 7:32-35 AMP

(tap, tap, tap...<taps mike>) "Is this thing on? (clears throat) ATTENTION, ALL SINGLES! THERE WILL BE PLENTY OF TIME FOR SKYROCKETING, TOE-TINGLING, PASSIONATE, UNLIMITED LOVEMAKING WHEN YOU GET MARRIED! THEY'LL BE PLENTY OF TIME FOR NESLTING AND NECKING ON

THE COUCH TOGETHER! THEY'LL BE PLENTY OF TIME FOR DATING! BUT NOW IS NOT THAT TIME!"

"But I thought this was a book on dating?!"

Yes, this is a book on dating and that's exactly what I'm trying to show you. Your life is so consumed with dating and being in a relationship with someone that you have yet to cultivate the relationship you need to have in order to adequately sustain a love relationship. You've spent so much time engulfed in dating that you've never really developed a relationship with God. The common thread that I see with most single Christians and why their life and their relationships are dysfunctional is because most singles do not develop a strong foundational relationship with the Lord. A wholesome relationship is built on two healthy, whole individuals; you cannot become whole unless you build a relationship with God first. Paul said, "I'm not trying to put any restraints on you," and neither am I. And above that, God doesn't want any restraints on you; He wants you to have a love relationship where you care for the concerns of another person, to focus on the pleasure of someone you love and to enjoy the gift of sex that He created for you. And I, the person who is in love with love and enchanted by the thought of romance, is certainly not trying to put limitations on your life, throw you in a nunnery or make you become a eunuch. What I am trying to do is, "promote what is seemly and in good order and to secure your undistracted and undivided devotion to the Lord," so that it becomes the foundation of your life and, in essence, will give you the ability to
enjoy life with someone else.

Let me ask you something: when you first entered into a relationship with God did you develop a love relationship with Him, where you committed undivided time to just you and Him? Did you allow God to pour His love into you, where you developed a relationship totally dependent upon Him, independent of anyone else? Did you allow Him to remove the traces of the broken life you lived before Him, rebuilt your life in Him and the word, and went on a journey with Him to discover who you are in Him and renewed your mind to His will and purpose for your life? If you answered yes, then by all means skip to the chapter, Date Night, but for the majority of us we need to plant ourselves right here in this chapter and go on a journey to discovering that kind of relationship, where that path will eventually lead us to a love-filled relationship with someone else. Because if the *truth be told*, many of you have spent so much time fulfilling it with dating that God has not had your undivided attention and devotion because He's always had to share you with someone else. This is one of the reasons why a great majority of singles are not whole when they get in a relationship; our constant compulsion with dating hinders our spiritual growth and self-development because God does not have a chance to develop us, *because the relationship is*. Then the only thing that we carry into a relationship is our inadequate and defective relational experiences. When singles spend more time dating than focusing on how they can please the Lord, they become distracted from God's plan and purpose for their lives. Inadvertently, dating consumption distracts you from even fulfilling that purpose. Mary was engaged to Joseph and before they came together she was already impregnated with destiny! Destiny was already in her womb! That is why you have to become so consumed and engrossed with your relationship with God that it impregnates you with purpose!

"…Mary was engaged to be married to Joseph. But before the marriage took place, while she was still a virgin, she became pregnant through the power of the Holy Spirit." Matt. 1:18 NLT

"We aren't really living unless we know why we're alive." Rebecca St. James

The main reason why so many singles are sexually struggling is because they do not know God's plan. The greatest tragedy in life is not being single, not having a date, or a companion but living your life without ever discovering and living out your God-given purpose! The most important aspect of your single life is not to find a mate, but to discover who you are in God and His purpose of why you are here on earth! Purpose gives direction and it helps govern your decisions. When you know the plan of God for your life then your purpose will dictate, shape and influence your direction. It prevents you from falling into traps because purpose says, "this is not a part of the plan." It will obstruct and block you from getting in the wrong relationships or staying in one that is no good for you. My papa, Myles Munroe, says, "When the purpose of a thing is unknown, abuse is inevitable." When you don't know the purpose of your life, then abuse, or *misuse*, is imminent.

"Where there is no vision, the people perish." Prov. 29:18 KJV

In the original translation the word, perish, is actually translated, "to make naked." So it should read:

"Where there is no vision, the people become naked."

This is one of the main reasons why so many singles are living in sexual sin; they spend most of their life distracted from God's purpose and without vision they have no self-control, they throw off restraint (NIV), run wild (NLT), and become naked. They are uncovered, unprotected, exposed and living the single life in the nude! Paul was dealing with the single Christians in Corinth about their focus on sex and relationships. They were consumed with sexual immorality and indoctrinating pagan culture in their relationships and in his letter that he wrote to them, Paul gave this antidote to put an end to their inordinate behavior with sex and relationships: pour that energy and focus into your relationship with God! That's right, instead of squandering your single life in sexual relationships, with reckless abandonment, throw yourself into an unwavering committed relationship with the Lord, go on a journey to discover your God-given purpose, then serve your gift to the world; become whole in your spirit, mind, body and soul, develop discipline and integrity, get mentally and emotionally healthy, lose some weight, get fit, get your finances in order, invest in some stocks, buy a house, find a cause to get under, travel around the world, take a dancing class or a cooking course, find out what makes you happy and get busy doing it! Stop trying to escape singleness; instead of looking at it as a curse, focus on the blessings in being single, embrace it, and make the most of it! Discover ways that you can make the best of your single life before you add someone to it. This is the time for you to begin guarding your single life, protect it, and begin developing your identity without someone else's.

Me, myself & God!

When you entered into a relationship with God, did you take the time to develop a strong foundation, where you anchored yourself to Him? How do you continue to grow and maintain your relationship with the Lord? Take inventory of your relationship with Him and ask yourself, "How much of my life and my time do I give to the Lord? Do I give Him my leftovers, after the day is well spent or do I only spend time with Him when I need Him? Do I give myself to others more than I give to God?" You are not ready to date or pursue a relationship until you begin the process of becoming complete in Christ. Like any relationship, it is developed by spending time with one another. In order for your relationship to grow with God, you must begin to set aside time each day with Him in prayer and in The Word of God. Other ways that you can develop your relationship is by finding an enriching Bible Study and a Biblically-sound, teaching church to help you grow.

Perhaps you are a new Christian and can begin with devoting ten minutes in the morning before you begin your day, then make that most important ten minutes of your day. Start there and begin increasing it over time where you develop the habit of spending time in the presence of God daily. Or maybe you've been with the Lord for quite some time now and have lost your fervency and your time with God has become a chore; reach out to your mentor or spiritual leaders, change your devotional regime, upgrade your resources, and challenge your complacency; fine-tuning and enhancing your worship experience can even revitalize the heartbeat of your relationship with the Lord. Check for anything that may be depleting or diverting your focus from the Lord. You must make Him the most important part of your life and not allow anything to stand in the way of it. By ensuring that you put your relationship with God as the central focus of your life, you give Him the ability to make you *whole and a holy instrument of God*, heal you from your past, discover your purpose, and mature you in Christ, giving you the ability to live sexually pure and possess the capacity to give and receive love. When you think about all that the Lord has done for you, this is not even considered a sacrifice; it's devotion and adoration, giving back your life for the life that He has given to you; no, this is not a sacrifice, it's a mere privilege.

While other singles frown upon you because 'you are not pacifying your flesh with short-term, sex-filled relationships and you're not having any so-called fun committing your life to the Lord,' they ransack theirs, throwing it into temporal pleasure, thinking they are fulfilling it with sex and dating, they will soon find that that way of living will haunt them, and prevent them from experiencing real love; all the while you're truly fulfilling your life by surrendering it to God, serving Him while He prepares you to receive all of the promises of God that has been stored up for you. God will put you on a window display, using the relationship that He has prepared for you to be an example of an unbreakable, life-long, passionate, love infused marriage. Oh trust me, the life that you surrender to God will not be in vain; the time that you are spending learning about love while you're in a love relationship with Love Himself, will be the very thing that God will use to spill over into your relationship when you finally marry. God is not holding you back from a relationship, my dear friends; He's preparing you for it! He wants you to experience authentic love and He's *grooming* you for that time when you can enjoy it to its fullest! So don't look at like you're "missing out" or seeing it as wasted time; it's preparing you for all that *energy* you'll need in caring, nurturing, caressing, canoodling, *footsying*, spooning, and unadulterated lovemaking in marriage! Look at yourself and emphatically and unapologetically say, "My time developing a love relationship with God while I'm single is not in vain!" (insert praise here)

"The time and energy that married people spend on caring for and nurturing each other, the unmarried can spend in becoming whole and holy instruments of God. I'm trying to be helpful and make it as easy as possible for you, not make things harder. All I want is for you to be able to develop a way of life in which you can spend plenty of time together with the Master without a lot of distractions." MSG

The Bible says, "To love the Lord, Your God, with all your heart, all your heart, and with all your soul." (Matt. 22:37) In what ways can you or are you accomplishing that?
_____
_____

Meditate on 1 Corinthians 7:34, what do you think becoming whole and holy instruments of God looks like?
_____
_____

How much time do you dedicate to God now? How can you increase it or bring quality to the time you spend together?

How can you make God and spending time with Him the most important a part of your everyday life?

I was born for this!

"For I know the plan I have for you," declares the LORD, "plans to prosper you and not to harm you, plans to give you hope and a future." (Jer. 29:11 NIV) Just as sure as you see these words, be assured in knowing that God has a plan and a purpose for your life! The most important discovery in life is the original purpose of God's will and you must embark upon a relentless journey until you find it. One of the main reasons why it is difficult for many of you to discover God's will is *because you have never killed yours.* In order for you to find God's will and fulfill it is by killing your will like Jesus did in order to fulfill God's Will for you and I to be set free from sin and have eternal life. As long as your life is led by what you want, by your own will, you will never fulfill God's. You must kill it! Nail your will to the Cross. What does that mean? Annihilate it! Assassinate your plan and any options for a Plan B! You will find that your plans can't match or even come close to God's ultimate plan for your life. When you come to the place of saying, "Lord, not what I want, but what You want," you will begin to see the promises of God manifest itself in your life.

"(Jesus) saying, 'Father, if it is Your will, take this cup away from Me; nevertheless not My will, but Yours, be done.'" Luke 2:42 NKJV

I've stood in many churches and have asked the question to thousands of people, "What has God you to do? What is your God-given purpose?" I end up facing a crowd of shrugged shoulders or vague responses like, "I love to help people." Which means that you don't know what exactly is it that you're called to do. Let me begin pointing you in the direction to finding the answer.

- Visit your local bookstore or go online and order, "In Pursuit of Purpose," and "Understanding Your Potential," by Dr. Myles Munroe. And I'm not saying this because he's my dad, but this book will literally impact and change your life and equip you with the ability to begin walking in your God-given purpose.
- Set aside a quiet, private time with God. You're probably thinking, "I don't know how to hear God's voice or you've attempted this before and didn't hear "anything;" Well, go back again. This time stay long enough to hear, use your Bible as a GPS/guide, and then

specifically ask these questions while you're alone in the presence of God"
- What is Your will for my life, Lord?
- If I could wake up tomorrow morning doing what I love most, even if I couldn't get paid for it, what would it be?
- What makes me angry? I'm not talking about the slow person driving in front of you in traffic. No, what really makes you angry; what pains you to see when it's out of place or out of order? What causes you to deeply ache when you see a problem or a need that goes unmet?

When you find the answers to these questions, you will find yourself, smack dab in the middle of God's purpose for your life! Get a planner specifically for your purpose and begin setting yearly, monthly, weekly, then daily goals to help you stay focus and accomplish it. Find mentors or business coaches for training and enroll in a course that would help you cultivate your gift. List the gifts and talents that you naturally possess, find out what makes your gift unique and then serve God and the world with those gifts.

"Lord, You are immersed in every part of my life, down to every detail, even numbering every strand of hair on my head. I know that you have purposefully laid out for my life and I trust You. I trust You with my life and I trust the plan that you have for me. Reveal the plan You have for me and I will follow it. I open my ears, my heart and my spirit to hear and receive that plan, in Jesus name, Amen."

Take inventory of your time
Many times people will claim that they do not have time to focus on their discovering or developing their purpose, but I give all the Black Cherry Welch's juice in my kitchen cabinets that it has more to do with mismanagement of time. If you take inventory of your time and account for where it is spent, I can promise you that there's something in your life or schedule that can be eliminated or altered.

Am I wasting time watching too much television?
Am I wasting time hanging out with people who are going nowhere?
Am I wasting time going overboard on leisure activities?
Am I wasting time indulging myself in sinful pleasures?
Am I wasting time chasing money and not my purpose?
Am I wasting time trying to please people instead of God?
Am I wasting time in an unfruitful relationship?
Am I wasting time living in fear, regret, guilt, and condemnation?

Becoming
As we have established, all great relationships are dependent upon a whole single. The product of a any long-lasting relationship will be predicated on the quality of the individuals

that are in the relationship. Right relationships or the right people do not come in your life by osmosis. You are able to attract healthy people and a satisfying relationship by becoming that. If you don't already possess it or lack the necessary development needed for a relationship, the relationship itself will only amplify what you lack. A man/woman will not complete you, they will expose you. Your singleness is the time in which God uses to manufacture wholeness and develop integrity, trust, honesty, compassion, and self-control, to discipline you, and strengthen your capacity for love. You want to spend this time becoming the best you, so when that special someone comes into your life, you will bring value into the relationship. You will be an asset; not a liability.

There are some people who believe that they can't possibly prepare for a relationship without being in one. There are many people who erroneously think that you have to be in a dating relationship in order to train and develop for one. As I stated early, experience is not always the best teacher and some experiences can often be a detriment than a help. Dating is not the only way that God can develop and prepare you for a relationship. God can cultivate the necessary qualities you need for an intimate relationship through other personal relationships like your siblings, relatives, coworkers, and need I add church members. These relationships give the perfect opportunity for you to develop and exercise fundamental, relational qualities like patience, forgiveness, adaptability, and kindness.

A loving and fulfilling relationship is more about what we can give than what we can get. Use this time to not only become what you want in a mate but more importantly developing Godly character for personal development and becoming Christ-like, whether you enter a relationship or not. Ask yourself, "What areas do I need to change or grow in? What Godly character is dominant in my life or what areas do I need to spiritually mature in?" Place a number (from one to three, three being the highest score) in the blank, signifying the level in which you currently possess the characteristic. Add the total to find out what stage you're maturing at and the areas in which you need to focus more on.

Loving ___	Thoughtful ___	Self-control ___	Agreeable ___
Kindness ___	Compassion ___	Faithful ___	Humility ___
Generosity ___	Consideration ___	Accountable ___	Caring ___
Appreciation ___	Courteous ___	Selflessness ___	Integrity ___
Reliable ___	Happy ___	Consistent ___	Service to others ___

Patience ___	Forgiveness ___	Gentleness ___	Reliable ___
Giving ___	Virtue ___	Trust ___	Emotionally stable ___
Trust ___	Understanding ___	Thankfulness ___	Respect for Others ___

96-76 Spiritual and emotional growth
75-54 Spiritual and emotional progress
53-32 Spiritual and emotional stagnation

Single's Bucket List

I look at it like it's a Single's Shopping Spree! This is an opportunity to focus on improving, upgrading, and simply enjoying your life to the full, while you are single! Whether it's going to school to further your education, pay off debt, buy a home, open your own business, enjoy hobbies you'd like to engage in, or perhaps there's a specific area you would like to travel to; whatever it is, it is time to live your life! Make of list of goals you would like to accomplish before marriage and take action on them while you wait for God to bring that person to you. Don't focus on finding a mate, focus on developing and maintain your relationship with God, discovering and fulfilling your purpose, and do what you love and love will find you!

_____   _____   _____   _____

_____   _____   _____   _____

_____   _____   _____   _____

_____   _____   _____   _____

_____   _____   _____   _____

_____   _____   _____   _____

In what ways have you mismanaged yourself, relationships, time, your purpose, desire, and sex?
_____
_____

What have you lost? What would you like to have redeemed?
_____

What can you do now with your life to serve the Lord with it?
_____
_____

What is your vision, purpose and mission in life?
_____
_____

If you could wake up tomorrow doing what you love, what would it be?
_____

What makes you happy?
_____

What are some things you've always wanted to do or have interest in, but haven't put a plan into action to do them?
_____

How can you put more focus on this?
_____

My spiritual goal is
_____

My health goal is
_____

My career goal is
_____

My educational goal is
_____

My financial goals are
_____

On a scale from 1 to 10, how strong do you think your relationship with God is?
_____

How much time do you spend with God on a weekly basis?
_____

How often do you read your Bible? How do you incorporate the Word in your life?
_____

What ways can you develop and grow your relationship with God, to make it stronger? How will you begin making time for God daily?
_____

Take inventory of your daily schedule? Where does most of your time go? What is your time appropriated/divided to? _____
_____

What can I adjust or eliminate in my schedule to make time for God? For my career/purpose? For myself?_____
_____

What are the advantages of being single? List ten fun things about being single. _____
_____
_____

Chapter 2
Single Ladies

In the fall of 2008 recording artist, Beyonce, ignited a world-wide craze with her up tempo, pop-dancing sensation, Single Ladies (Put A Ring On It)*. It was so popular that it sparked dance parodies, where Youtube videos were popping up everywhere with people reenacting the choreography, even President Barack Obama! I mean, the song was huge, becoming the anthem for many single women around the world! The song is about a single woman who had just ended a three-year relationship and her ex is mad that a new man is interested in her, provoking a neck-rolling response, "If you liked it, then you should've put a ring on it!"

While many single women were bobbing their heads to the tune and mimicking the dance moves, they pointed to their ring finger, while lip syncing the same jingle, demanding a ring. This song became the echo for many women who wanted to send a message to the men in their lives to step up to the plate and marry them! There's a big, ogre-size problem with that; many of the women who belt out these lyrics are just like the woman in the song: you're letting him "like it." Oh, this is more than hitting the "like" button on Facebook; you're giving him taste testers, letting him "like it," allowing him to have the pleasures of sex without commitment and you spoil his appetite for marriage. Like this woman in the song, you are the one that's preventing and holding up the ring because you allow a man to park in your life while he has the liberty of making as many trips as he wants to the all-you-can-eat buffet without paying the cost to have it; you're letting him get as much sex as he wants without paying the price of commitment.

Three years and No Ring=You're being played

According to the National Marriage Report at Rutgers University, the number one reason men don't commit is that they know they can get sex without getting married. You're performing as a wife in girlfriend status and that's why you haven't gotten the ring: youreplayingyourself.com! He never should get a chance to "like it" without paying the cost to have it first: Whooaaa oh, oh! As long as you give up sex and play *wifey*, then you won't become *one*. As long as a boyfriend gets husband privileges, he will not upgrade his status or yours. While a study by the Pew Research Center and Time magazine in November 2010 noted that some believe marriage is becoming obsolete, I believe that women are *allowing* it to become obsolete. Just months before in August 2010, CNN asked the question, "Is the black church keeping women single?" No, single women are keeping themselves single.

> Demimonde: a class of women who have lost their standing in respectable society usually because of sexual promiscuity.

Some years ago, I lived in a condo where a professional basketball player lived in a unit right above me. I would venture to say that there would be many women who would define him as attractive, nicely built with a tall frame of swagger and I would imagine a fat bank account to match based upon the luxury cars he drove, the Cadillac truck with the spinning rims, and the nice furniture that was brought into his house as I stood nosey, peaking out the blinds the day he moved in. He had the gall to try and brush up on a sister, but you know I shot his advances down quick because I knew he was recruiting me to be a chick to roll around in the sheets with. How do I know? Let's just say that whoever designed those condos didn't think things through during the blueprint stages. Whoever it was had to be insane to build the units to match the bedrooms to be right under the other because he had a different chick sprinting through every other night and I had to have my Israel Houghton and Hillsong music shuffling through my earphones throughout the night; well not the whole night. I remember one late night after hearing the beginning of "wicked thunder" brewing above my head, I belted out an immediate, oh-so-frank prayer to the Lord, "Please, God, let this be two minutes." You guys, I'm not kidding; I actually prayed that prayer. I'm glad to say that I have a very close relationship with the Lord where He answers my prayers; He wouldn't want His daughter, who is a single woman living sexually pure, to be forced and subjugated to such horrific tortures and unwilling participation of sin. And wouldn't you know it, minutes later, through the thin walls, I heard the dangling noise of unbuckled straps to high-heeled shoes coming down the stairs. Though nestled in to rest, I couldn't go to sleep; lying there I couldn't help but to pray for the woman who owned those heels that didn't even have the time to buckle them because, like many women, she has become accustomed to running into a man's house to give sexual favors, making it just as normal as she would run into the gas station to pay for a fill up on pump number five.

I couldn't roll over and go to sleep and act as if I didn't know what just happened, when I knew exactly because that used to be me. Like many women who take on the girlfriend mentality where sex comes along with the dating territory, you don't even label yourself as sexually promiscuous because you become so used to having to give your body that now sex comes along with the package and it becomes the standard to have sex with the men you date. When a woman has sex with a man without him committing himself, it sends a clear message that 'I don't have to obligate myself and I can acquire and have access to you without sacrifice on my part.' With confidence, he tells himself, 'I can get *that* without cost; she's free.' Many men now expect sex and wife privileges in girlfriend status that when a woman doesn't freely give she is labeled "high and mighty." That's because we have allowed it! If he sees that you'll play hard to get, he'll pacify you with barter and exchange: you give me sex, I'll give you attention, fine dining, and pay your light bill. You then treat your life like it's commerce and stick a sign on you that says, "Open For Business." Though you're open for business, there's no increase on your life. In fact, you reduce your value and worth because many of you are playing the prostitute role, getting your hair and nails done, getting your rent and car note paid in exchange for sex and a man's attention.

Whore: a woman who engages in sexual acts for money; a promiscuous or immoral woman. Also one who compromises one's principles for personal gain. (Thefreedictionary.com)

Dear Single Ladies: don't be a doorknob where every man gets a turn.

You would think that single women would get it by now, but using your body to try and get a man to commit or marry is the prison mindset of a girlfriend that succumbs to the pressure of using sexual performance to win the attention of a man. It's like the official pageant for women competing for the crown of a man, where her body and sexual pleasure is the performing act that determines the winner; she has subconsciously come to believe that giving her body to him will make him want her more. Without many women even realizing or admitting it, in the basement of her mind she believes that she's going to have to have sex with him in order to keep him and outdo another woman in bed to win him over, so her genitalia becomes the commodity of exchange for his attention. But you can do all kinds of acrobatic positions and the fifty-two mind-blowing sex tricks listed on the front cover of a magazine on newsstands, it won't make him stay, it won't make him commit and it won't make him put a ring on it! No matter how many times this has been proven, there are so many women who still continue to use their body to try to get a man to commit or to even try to change him, but using your body will not get him to change anything but his drawers!

"He said, 'Go call your husband and then come back.'
'I have no husband," she said.
'That's nicely put: 'I have no husband.' You've had five husbands, and the man you're living with now isn't even your husband. You spoke the truth there, sure enough.'" MSG

Many single women mirror the woman that Jesus encountered at the well; she had the ability to get a man, but couldn't keep him. Resembling so many other women, she used her body to get him because she doesn't know how to get a man without sex, but as you can see, it didn't make them stay because having sex with him is not going to make him commit, otherwise many of you would still be with the men who you've slept with and many marriages would still be together if sex kept a man. Many women use sexual favors to get a man and his attention but I can tell you that if you do that you have just lost him. You've been doing it wrong this whole time; the way to get a husband is to withhold sex. Many single women would be married if they didn't stay in dead-end relationships and stop having sex with dating partners (boyfriends), but having sex with every man you date or get in a relationship with depletes your value, your substance, your flavor and your favor.

"*He who* finds a wife finds a good *thing,* And obtains favor from the LORD." Proverbs 18:22 NKJV

When you give him husband privileges in girlfriend status, you give him access to favor he hasn't qualified for. As long as you treat your boyfriend like a husband, he'll remain a boyfriend. He has no reason to upgrade when he's already getting the privileges of a husband. Until you come to know and realize that what you have to give and that your value is worth him giving you a commitment to have you, you will stay stuck in single mode, old, and used goods and still a girlfriend in your old age. A sexually promiscuous woman is like the first slice of bread in a loaf: everybody touches it *but nobody wants it.* Are you an end piece? If you continue like this, soon they'll be nothing left of you but crumbs. Don't you know that real man wants a woman that is pure? If you continue to give sexual favors and wife privileges in girlfriend status you'll further your chances of ever getting the ring! You need to act like a lady and think like a WIFE!

WIFE MENTALITY: YOU PUT A RING ON IT, THEN YOU GET SEX!

And if women would close the candy shop, he wouldn't have another sweet bed to run to. It doesn't help if I tell him, "No," but then he runs down the street and you let him have *it*! No, we have to do this together! There needs to be a panty strike, where we all keep Victoria a secret! It's an easily solution. What we allow, many men will accept. It's called supply and demand; inventory of marriage is in short supply because there is high demand for sex without commitment. When there is a low demand, where women don't require commitment of marriage for sex, there will be a high supply of single women that will remain single or in girlfriend status. Women must put the demand and the standard back and make it a requirement that sex is not available without sacrifice. If you're not willing to sacrifice your life for me, then you can't have me sexually. It's when you make a decision that you will no longer give your body without the ring, trust me, men will then step up and do what's necessary to have you. The power is completely in your hands. How you act will determine if he puts a condom on or a ring on it. God never intended for you to have to protect yourself from the person you give your body to because His plan is for you to have one man that would commit his life to you and only you. You must come to that same mindset that God has for you. You give people a blueprint on how to treat you: how you view yourself, how you let others to treat you, and by what you allow. That is why one of the most powerful things a single woman can do is close her legs. That's right; close them, cross them, and be a lady. When you do that you revolutionize relationships and restore the original order of how God designed relationships.

One way to truly know if a person wants you is if they stick around when you tell them, "No!" No is a powerful word; it will protect you. It weeds out sexual abusers and users. "…But, Ty, if I don't have sex with him, he's going to leave me or get it from some other woman." Sweetheart, then he's not yours in the first place. If sex is why he stays, then he's not there for you, he's there for the sex, and once he gets that, he's gone! If you're afraid to refrain from having sex with him because you think he'll leave, and then he does exactly what you thought he would do and he leaves, then you have just spared yourself from sexual despair, anguish and misery! He should know that it's his loss, that you won't wait around dangling your life in girlfriend status to meet his sexual needs, playing wifey. Sing it with me, "hit the road, Jack, and don't cha come back no mo, no mo, no mo, no mo!!!" Au revoir, sayonara, arrivederci, hasta la vista, baby! Or even plain English will suffice, "Boy, bye!" When you take a firm stand you let him know that I'm worth you sacrificing your life to have me. As long as you give your boyfriend husband privileges, he'll never change or upgrade his status or yours. You can't make a man out of a husband by giving him sex. The opposite is ironically the outcome because sexual promiscuity is a husband repellent.

>"Now don't worry about a thing…I will do what is necessary, for everyone in town knows you are a virtuous woman." Ruth 3:11 NLT

Women that are sexually promiscuous and have sex with men that she dates are like prostitutes; they come a dime a dozen. But a woman that is committed to the Lord knows her worth, has the highest level of standards, the epitome of grace, excellence in character, keeps herself pure, and doesn't allow a man to have easy access into her life…she's rare, priceless, and hard to find. So when a man finds a woman like that, he will pursue her with every ounce of energy in him and his possessions, his time, and everything he owns will follow, because he will do whatever is necessary to get you. He will lay down his life, before laying you down. He will wed you before he bed you! When he knows that you will not bend your standards, he will bend over backwards and do what he has to do to make sure that he meets the requirements to make you his. That man will be the corresponding compliment of who she is.

Many single women want a man like that. His name is Boaz; single, wealthy, a real estate mogul who loves the Lord and is willing to do what is necessary to have you! The question is can you attract a man like that? I'm not talking about you're beauty or money.

Ruth slept in the basement of her mother-in-law's house. She was a widow that didn't have any money and probably had a credit score of zero! So what did Ruth have that made her a magnet to Boaz? Ruth was a virtuous woman; she had the Proverbs 31 factor. If you want to attract a man like Boaz then you need to be a virtuous woman. Did you hear me? Sexual impurity is a husband repellent. The fastest way to get a man like him is to close up shop and I'm not talking about minizmiaing sin and sleeping with just your boyfriend. No, I'm talking about absolute purity. You must wear the fragrance of purity to attract him. Boaz's mother, Rahab, was a prostitute, so he knew the difference between a wife and a whore; you can't pretened to be virtuous. His mother was transformed from prostitution, so he knew what sexual purity and a true commitment to God looked like. Boaz knew the difference between wife material and a woman just looking for a man to exchange sex to get her bills paid, to wine and dine her and meet her shoe fetish.[5] Boaz knew that Ruth was coming to serve him and meet his needs and that he could trust her with his wealth. Does your reputation precede you? Does everyone in town know that you're a virtuous woman or *a woman of the night*?

So which "w" are you? Are you a wife or a whore? How you live your life will determine if you get the keys to the house or the hotel. Whores get keys to the hotel, wives get keys to the house. The house, the keys, the ring...everything! Everything Boaz owns is yours and available to you. But the only way to get that is a virtuous life. While you wait on God to present you to a man, don't let a man treat you like a hotel, check into you, roll around in your sheets, and then check out, leaving you with the mess to clean up like you're an old maid! Instead, preserve yourself for your future husband, focus on your God-given purpose, get behind a mission and serve your gifts instead of your body. You deserve a man that loves you, respects you, values you, is honest, faithful and will give you his life. See yourself through God's eyes: I'm more than just a chick that provides sexual favors but I'm worthy of love and commitment, respect, and honor. Put your validation in the worth that God has given you, not a sexual vixen that society has put on you. Refuse to allow yourself to be reduced to a sexual act and don't let a man make you common! Make a decision that you will keep yourself pure on the journey to marriage.

> "Gathered with her family and the wedding guests in her mother's cottage, the bride said to her stepbrothers, When I was a little girl, you said] We have a little sister and she has no breasts. What shall we do for our sister on the day when she is spoken for in marriage? If she is a wall [discreet and womanly], we will build upon her a turret [a dowry] of silver; but if she is a door [bold and flirtatious], we will enclose her with boards of cedar. [Well] I am a wall [with battlements], and my breasts are like the towers of it. Then was I in [the king's] eyes as one [to be respected and to be allowed] to find peace." SOS 8:8-10 AMP

When Solomon's bride was a young girl her brothers fast-forwarded to her future when she would become of age to marry. They posed two options, "If she's a wall, a woman that will keep herself sexually pure, then there's nothing she'll need or want for; but if she's a door, promiscuous, like a swinging door with different men going in and out of it, then she'll never have a husband. She will be enclosed with cedar (condemned)." I love this chick! Her response is beyond classic! She empathically responded (and probably with a neck roll accompanying it), "Not only am I still a virgin but my breast are now full, I am of age and I'm ready. I am what satisfies kings; I am what a king wants and what he is looking for. The man who gets me will be satisfied and content; when he looks at me there will be contentment in his eyes. I will be in his eyes as one that has found favor.[4] I deserve his favor, his respect, and his kingdom! Yes, I'm worthy of a king." WOW! This chick is fabulous! Let me ask you something: are you a door or a wall? Are men in-and-out of your house where the hinges are barely on it, going from one relationship to the next, and having sex with men you're not married to? Or are you one a woman that can satisfy a king: a queen in waiting that keeps her treasures locked up: a wall, guarded and protected from sexual impurity? You need to put a wall up; not just any wall, but a wall with battlements. A battlement serves two purposes: it's not only a barrier that protects you from impurity but it is secondly defined as a decoration, making you stand out above others as a noticeable attraction to a man that celebrates and honors a virtuous woman.

Don't allow failed relationship and disappointments of your past chain you there; don't give on love or lose hope because love God's way still works and it still happens! Women try to play the game and act as if it doesn't bother them, 'I don't want a relationship, I don't want to settle down right now, it doesn't faze me, or two can play that game mentality,' but it does affect us tremendously. We try to cover it up in a pretentious 'I don't care attitude," but underneath the betrayal, the let downs, the façades and the makeup, there are deep-seated wounds with pain from relational dismay because we were not made for hook-ups, uncommitted, casual sex. We try to separate our heart and emotions from sex and attempt to repress our feelings but it's impossible; God didn't make us that way. He created us to be loved, uninterrupted. Within each woman, He fearfully and wonderfully made us to be genuinely loved, honored, valued, protected, nurtured, and cared for. We're naturally designed and wired for commitment. When we connect with a man, we instinctively bond to him and we malfunction when we are forced to disconnect. We were not made to have our hearts scattered, to go from relationship-to-relationship and bed-to-bed, with multiple sex partners.

Many women have hardened their hearts because our fragile hearts have been deceived, mistreated, neglected, abused, abandoned, dropped and left broken, but even behind the seemingly toughest, disenchanted and embittered woman, she wants a man that adores her and will be faithful; one she can call her own and don't have to share, because we're hoarders when it comes to the man we love and when we're unloved, watch out! Shakespeare said, "Hell hath no fury on a woman scorned," but God said it even better, "Under three things the earth is disquieted, and under four it cannot bear up…an unloved and repugnant woman when she is married."[6] The whole earth is disturbed when women are unloved and when our hearts are damaged! We malfunction when our relationships are not in alignment with the original design of how God created us to be loved. My dear sister, there is nothing wrong you! It's a natural desire to want to be married, treasured and faithfully loved by one man. But when God's plan for love is disrupted by society, it attempts to undermine that plan, and a downward spiral of sexual and relational disorder begins to unfold in society, then finds its way into the church. Many women have taken on the roles of men, pursuing them, paying their bills, putting cars and cell phones in their name, allowing men to impregnate them without commitment, while men take the low role and women become the providers and leaders of the home. When we try to force ourselves into mere sex partners, girlfriends and babies mommas, we malfunction.

"That will be the day when seven women will gang up on one man, saying, "We'll take care of ourselves, get our own food and clothes. Just give us a child. Make us pregnant so we'll have something to live for!" Is. 4:1 MSG

"In that day so few men will be left that seven women will fight for each man, saying, "Let us all marry you! We will provide our own food and clothing. Only let us take your name so we won't be mocked as old maids." NLT

"And in that day seven women shall take hold of one man, saying, We will eat our own bread and provide our own apparel; only let us be called by your name to take away our reproach [of being unmarried]." AMP

I tell yah, the Bible has everything in it if we would just dive in it! This has become the state of our society, where marriage is scarce. There are approximately 11 million more Christian women than men. With a shortage of available, faithful, good and marriageable men, women have become desperate to the point of sharing a man, chasing after a man, fighting over a man, bearing children without marriage, taking on the responsibility of providing in the relationship…all for the sake of having a man; even a piece of a man, where many would rather share him than to have no man at all. It has become the custom for women to use and sacrifice their bodies to validate their lives, to give their life meaning and purpose, to have something to live for because the man she has in her life is validation. Hence, the reason why many women will stoop to lows in order to have a man. Many have lost the art of being a lady in waiting. Sadly, it has become the norm for women to have children without a man giving his life to her and her children; the proof is in the child support arrearages.

- **More than half of births to American women under 30 are outside of marriage.**
- **Four out of ten births are to unmarried women.**
- **The 1.7 million out-of-wedlock births, marks a 25 percent jump from five years before.**
- **As of 2011, 11.7 million families in the U.S. are headed by a single parent. (85.2% headed by a female, 45% have never married.)** [1]

Just look around, how many of your friends or family members have children by men they are not married to? Perhaps your own situation confirms this. The sad part is that this dysfunctional way of relating is perpetuated from generation-to-generation where we teach it to our children. Tamara is single mother with three children by three different fathers. At night, while she thinks her children are asleep, she allows the men that she is dating to come over and have sex with her, often allowing them to creep out the door before she thinks her children will awake. Children are not as naïve as we think they are; they hear the "awkward" noises in the middle of the night and the car in their drive-way start up just before they get out of bed for school. Tamara was only teaching her young children to repeat that same destructive sexual behavior; she trained her daughter to think that it's okay for a man to run in her house like it's a hotel and taught her son to be the kind of man that does not commit to a woman and that she is only good for casual sex. Tamara went on to have more abortions and two more children out of wedlock. How my heartbreaks when I go to speak at middle and high schools and hear the many stories that teenagers tell me about the live-in boyfriends and lovers their mom allows in their home.

- Half of single mother families have an annual income less than $25,000
- Median income for single mother families is $24,487, which is only 1/3 the median for married couple $77, 749.
- 1/3 of single mothers receive any child support; the average amount is only about $300 month.
- 2/5 of single mother families are poor, triple the poverty rate for the rest of the U.S. population. Nearly 5 times as likely to be poor than married-couple families.
- Research has consistently found that children born outside marriage face elevated risks of falling into poverty, failing in school or suffer emotional and behavioral problems.

"Johnny and Jennifer sitting in a tree, kay i ss i in gee! (k-i-s-s-i-n-g) First comes loves, then comes marriage, then comes a baby in a baby carriage!" I remember as a little girl learning this on the playground at school but somehow many of us have forgotten, so let me remind you: if he's not going to make you a wife, then don't let him make you a mother. Even birds know you're supposed to build a nest before you lay an egg.

> "So Boaz took Ruth and she became his wife. And he went in to her, and the Lord caused her to conceive, and she bore a son." Ruth 4:13 AMP

We need to restore dignity and value in our lives, where you will not allow someone to make you a statistic! Boaz married Ruth, then he had sex with her, and after that they had a child. The requirement from this point moving forward is if someone wants the privilege of being a part of your life, then there must be a commitment *before* they try to build a life with you; and I'm not talking about some elementary commitment: will you be my girlfriend, circle yes or no. You're no longer kids on the playground playing with toys; but even with a toy you have to assemble it first before you *play* with it. So if he wants to "play" with you then "assembly is required." I have a confession to make: I love country music! Yes, I do! And to make my point I want to share with some wisdom from one of my favorite country songs, Little White Church. The song's basic premise went a little something like this: like an old broken record, you've been singing that same old song too long, saying that you're gonna buy me a ring, but your empty promises don't mean a thing. So you might as well stop calling me baby because I ain't cooking you no more chicken, pot roast or gravy! And I especially ain't having your baby (add neck roll) until you take me down to the church and marry me!

Whewwww, I love that song! If you want sex you have to take me down to that little white chapel and marry me! It's gonna cost you to have all of that. No more riding the gravy train. No more chicken and gravy and biscuits or having your babies 'til you take me down the altar and marry me! In my Madea's voice, "no cooking, no clean-ting, no sex-ting!" We have to restore God's order in society where we come to the place that sex and wife privileges are reserved for marriage. I don't care what your background is, what your upbringing was, what you weren't taught, the disadvantages you had to face, and the disorder of relationships that you've been in: you do not have to be a statistic! You can reverse all the negative consequences, defy the odds, and rebel the stats! How do I know? I'm not just a living witness, but I'm a recipient of grace! I failed at doing relationships the right way, I come from a bloodline and a generation of fatherless households, uneducated, poverty-stricken upbringing, raised in a single-parent household, I had sex outside of marriage, out-of-wedlock pregnancy, absentee father with no child support…the odds were stacked against me…but GOD!

I got pregnant by a man that I wasn't married to, that I knew would not take care of his child, with no job and one late payment away from being put out of my home, facing the option of aborting a child that I knew I couldn't take care of, I instead chose to have my baby and I made a decision, from that point on, that I would do life and relationships God's way. I submitted my life *imperfectly* and completely to the Lord and made Him my baby's daddy! My daughter, Heaven, is now seventeen years old, honor roll student since kindergarten, traveling the world competing in ice-skating, running her own company and online brand, and a virgin who has committed to celibacy until marriage...and all of this without one child support payment and a single mother who didn't even have a quarter in the bank, but I had one priceless possession: a dedication to God! I came to the place where I was no longer willing to sacrifice who I am for a piece of a man, I was no longer going to be a victim of my past, and I made God's way and His word the final authority in my life and I would now only do sex and relationships God's way. I walked away from the comfort of short-lived, toxic relationships and sexual relationships and escapades with men and fell into the open arms of my God who loved me beyond my wildest imagination! I know many of you desire that and want that kind of life. You're tired of the destructive ways that you've been approaching relationships and its deadly consequences, but how tired are you?

I had a young lady that came to me crying, desperately wanting to put an end to the vicious cycle of poisonous relationships but yet she had one foot out the door of that kind of lifestyle but still had one hand on the man she was having sex with and the car, the shopping sprees, the rent money, the paid-for blow and go, relaxed hair-do's, and the comfort of the relationship. Every time I confronted her about leaving, she made excuses about how she was not going to be able to pay her car note and her rent every month and how it was difficult to give up the lifestyle this toxic relationship provided her. Her financial and emotional dependence on this man stood in the way of her completely committing to the Lord and achieving the kind of love life that she really, deep down inside, longed for. Without blinking or stuttering, I said, "Monica, you can hang on to this prostitute career camouflaged as a relationship or you can make a commitment to the God you say you love and pull your hair to the back in a ponytail, move back in your momma's basement and catch the bus to work if you really love God and want to live your life truly for Him. Do you love God more or that car you're driving? Is whatever this man giving you every month worth more or higher than the price that God paid to give you life?"

Are you going to choose cheap and temporal over priceless, immeasurable, and endless love? The choice is yours; the cycle can end with you. You can begin again and start to live according to God's plan and do love and relationships the way that He intended and live in the overflow of blessings as a result of doing it God's way! And what is God's way: sex and children come by way of a covenant, where a man sacrifices and lays down his life for his wife and his children. You are worth that and you certainly deserve it, because when you do it God's way and save yourself for marriage you put yourself in position to receive a king; a man that will treasure you like a queen and make you queen of the palace. But this can only begin when you stop casually dating God and playing the field and make a commitment to him and accept his proposal (first) to a covenant of true love. Until you enter a marriage of commitment with God and accept His ring, you can never really bear and wear another man's ring. You can only give and receive love at the level in which you receive it from God. When you accept God's hand in marriage, you open yourself up to receive genuine and lasting love on a natural level; but you first have to accept God's proposal:

> "For your Maker is your husband—the LORD Almighty is his name—the Holy One of Israel is your Redeemer; He is called the God of all the earth." Is. 54:5 NIV

I, _____, take You, Lord, to be my wedded husband, to have and to honor and to worship and to live faithfully unto Your Word from this day forward, for better or for worse, for richer or for poorer, in sickness and in health, to love and to cherish, and because You paid the price, death will not even part us, according to God's ordinance; and thereto I pledge thee my troth. I hereby give myself to you in this cause, with my sacred vow to You Lord, Amen.

You may now praise and worship your God!

What are the contributing factors as to why some men delay marriage? _____
_____
_____

Why do you believe you are still single? _____

Why is it important that single women collectively make a decision to refrain from sexual activity in relationships? _____

What are the effects of single parenting is your family or community? _____

Has some aspects of your upbringing contributed to how you approach relationships? _____

In what aspects has the shortage of available men affected the way women approach relationships?
_____

How can you make a difference in your family and community to aid in bringing awareness and fostering healthy relationship habits that align with God's plan for sex and relationships? _____
_____

What is a key attribute that causes a woman to increase her chances at finding real love and lasting relationships? _____

Read Song of Solomon 8:8-10. Reflect on or discuss with the group as to differences between a door and a wall. _____
_____
_____

Have you entered into a committed marriage with God? How has this affected your life or how do you see moving forward in a committed relationship with the Lord will affect your life. _____
_____
_____

1 National Center for Health Statistics
2 U.S Census Bureau 2011
3 SOS 8:8-10 NLT
4 KJV
5 Ruth 2:11-12
[6]Proverbs 30: 21, 23 AMP

* Single Ladies (Put A Ring On It) Beyonce Knowles/Columbia 2008
** Little White Church by Little Big Town/Capital Nashville 2010 See actual song for lyrical content

Chapter 3
Playing House

Play clothes are garments you put on when you're not going anywhere special, that you can play in and don't mind getting dirty. You know those jeans that have holes in 'em, the knees are worn, have ripped pockets, and shirts with ink marks in them or have grape Kool-aid stains on them. When I was little girl my mother would make me change my school clothes and put on play clothes. I was not allowed to play in my school clothes, nor clothes that I wore to church or dresses for special events. When my friends would come over knocking on the door for me to come out and play, my momma would holler downstairs, "You better get out of them good clothes and put on your play clothes before you go out and play!" She knew that by the time the streetlights came on, I was coming back in the house with dirt on me.

When my friends would come and knock on the door, they'd say, "You wanna come out and play house with us?" It was our favorite thing to do! I loved pretending to be the momma because I would make my friends be the kids and I could boss them around and tell them what to do. The little boy named Johnny who lived down the street was quite fond of me and I sure had a crush on him! Johnny loved playing the daddy because he knew that was prime time to 'smooch' on me. We would make a tent that looked like a lil' old shack, like it was barely gonna hold up but we would act as if it was our house and I would take one of my shirts that I used for play clothes, tie it up like an apron and would make mud pies and I would serve them to Johnny and he would act like he was eating them…LOL! I bet you played house too when you were little. The problem with that though is many single adults are still stuck in their childhood and never left it, because they are still playing house. Putting on play clothes, rolling around in the mud, playing *wifey*, making pies, moving in your little tent together, shacking up and letting *big* Johnny smooch on you without any sacrifice or commitment from him. Playing house is equivalent to taking monopoly money and trying to buy property and real estate; it's not real.

Shack, (n.) 1. a small, crudely built house usually a ramshackle building. 2. Shack up, to cohabit.

Shack up, (slang) to sleep together or live in sexual intimacy as husband and wife without being married.

     If you're living with a man that you are not married to, then the house that you're in is a shack. I don't care if it's a mansion with fifteen bedrooms, eight-and-half baths, marble staircase, an elevator that takes you to the master suite, marble-encrusted floors flown in from France, sitting on ten acres with a heated in-door, Olympic-size swimming pool in it; it's a shack! Yes, that was not a misprint; you read it correctly. You've justified it, vindicated his lack of commitment and here's your argument, "This is just temporary; we are going to eventually get married…It's better to try things out to ensure that the marriage will last…we need to save up money…he's not ready yet, but this will help him get ready…him moving in proves his commitment to me already…you don't need a piece of paper to prove your love to one another…" No matter how you justify it, the statistics prove that your house is a shack and will crumble before you can even build it.

- More than 65 percent of altar-bound men and women live together before getting married. –Bride's Magazine
- Couples who live together before marriage are unlikely to marry. A Columbia University study found that "only 26 percent of women surveyed and a scant 19 percent of men" married the person they were living with. Another study showed that even if they do marry, couples who begin their marriages through cohabitation are almost twice as likely to divorce within 10 years compared to all first marriages.
- The dissolution rate for couples who lived together before marriage is 80 percent higher than it is for couples that didn't.
- Couples who cohabit are three times more likely to divorce during the first two years of marriage than couples who do not live together.
- The Boston Herald sited that a study on cohabitation concluded that after five to seven years, only 21 percent of unmarried couples were still living together.

     It begins with going Dutch, then paying half on the dinner bill, and then half on the rent, pay half the utilities, split everything down the middle and move in together. I've seen women exhaust their 401k, put their boyfriend on their health benefits, and sign their name on the lease. Like Lisa, a thirty-two year old successful business woman who owns two lucrative day care centers, gross earnings in the ball park of 35,000 a month, met Jordan and within two weeks of meeting him took him on an all expense paid trip to Las Vegas and bought him clothes, gifts, a 64 GB- iPad with a Louis Vuitton carrying case and of course sex was included. Within two months he called her place, 'home.' Then there's Kim who met Mark and they hit it off really well and started going on frequent dates. After escalating to a committed relationship, they began discussing what would be the next move of their relationship. Surely, not marriage; at least not now but in the 'somewhere-near-future' is what Mark's bright idea was. He wants to treat the relationship just like he does the house they were moving in: *rent with an option to buy*; he wants optional commitment with the relationship also. He suggested they move in together to see if they're a "fit" for marriage and to prepare for it first. Though it wasn't the ring she wanted, for Kim that was good enough; it served as a sign that they're moving towards marriage and it was better than leaving him if he hadn't made that at least an option after she gave him the ultimatum.

Before you move forward with this kind of living arrangement, you need to understand how cohabiting can negatively affect your marital hopes. The future of your relationship has already been "prophesied" through statistics that relationship failure is in your forecast when you move in together because it's crudely built on fear, lack of trust and commitment; all of what the very fibers of a long, lasting successful relationship is built upon. But long before any research was done to gather the stats, our Relationship Manual foretold us what was to come.

"That will be the day when seven women will gang up on one man, saying, "We'll take care of ourselves, get our own food and clothes. Just give us a child. Make us pregnant so we'll have something to live for!" Isaiah 4:1 MSG

The Bible forewarned us that the time would come when there would be a shortage of marriageable men and women would become desperate and settle for sharing a man with other women, taking care of themselves, have sex with them and bear children that they don't have to take care of, just for the sake of having a man. Proof of that is in the overwhelming number of single women who find it acceptable to continue to have sex with men they are not married to, get pregnant, and then raise children as a single parent on their own. If you're a little more sophisticated girlfriend, then you opt to be a live-in girlfriend who acts as a wife, without getting the benefits of a wife. We've taken helpmeet, one of the greatest aspects of being a wife, and trivialized it down to a mere live-in girlfriend.

Vivian Ward, played by actress Julia Roberts in one of 1990's highest grossing films, *Pretty Woman,* was a prostitute hired by a wealthy businessman to escort him to several business and social functions for a week at the rate of $3,000 for her "services" and even access to his credit cards to buy evening dresses to wear to those events. Edward the businessman, played by Richard Gere, begins to see that Vivian has more to offer than sex privileges and starts to fall in love with her, offering to "take her off the streets" and put her up in an apartment so that she would be available for him and continue to see her when he wanted. Vivian responds with my favorite line in the movie, "When I was a little girl waiting for my prince charming to rescue me, I didn't dream he'd say, 'I'll put you up in a penthouse.'" Though in the beginning she was hired for sex, Vivian realized her worth and that she had more to offer than just her body and a trophy to be escorted on a man's arm; she turned and walked out of the hotel, making a bold statement, and basically said, 'The penthouse, the private jet, money, credit cards, jewelry, and the dresses are not enough for me to move in a penthouse-apartment and be your live-in girlfriend and available for dinner dates, nights out at the opera and accessible for sex whenever you want; your money can no longer buy me.'

Prostitute: 1. One who solicits and accepts payment for sex acts. 2. One who sells one's abilities, talent, or name for an unworthy purpose or use.

Vivian realized that prostitution and moving into a penthouse to be his girlfriend was the same thing. You may not be walking the streets for hire but you are certainly taking your wife assets and use it for an unworthy purpose by shacking up. As a helpmeet, God created within you one of the highest abilities that a man can ever encounter; someone to aid, support, and undergird the most important thing to him: his life! You're helping, aiding, and assisting him in his life, for free. You've heard of the statement before, "Why buy the cow, when the milk is free?" Well why would he buy the cow when he can have access to the whole farm for free?! If he's drinking the milk, eating the cheese and the beef then he has no reason to get married to you when you're living together and he has all the privileges of having a wife without making you one.

"And the LORD God said, It is not good that the man should be alone; I will make him an help meet for him." Gen. 2:18

His life is not good without you. God knows it, the man knows it ("At last!" the man exclaimed. "This one is bone from my bone, and flesh from my flesh! [1]), but apparently you don't because many women have allowed it to become acceptable to give their life without commitment. Our women's lib mentality has gotten a little out of control. Prior to the women's liberation movement approximately nine out of ten women got married without living with their dating partners in the 1950's. A 2000 Census survey found some 3.8 million unmarried men and women were sharing residences and the woman was listed as the householder in 44.5 percent of those homes. Now that we're "independent," head of the household, educated, and CEO of the company, the man as the provider has become insignificant and so has the helpmeet. We have marred and distorted God's plan for women to be a helpmeet by no longer making life-long commitment viable and necessary for intimate relationships to exist; and the church is following suit. The decline in marriage and the increase in unmarried couples living together is an indicator that even God's church is forsaking wedding bells and wedding vows at the altar. Though a great majority of Americans believe in God, a study released by the Pew Research Center in association with Time magazine in November 2010 revealed that 4 in 10 say marriage is becoming obsolete.

- U.S. Census data released in September 2010 that showed marriages hit an all-time low of 52 percent for adults 18 and over. In 1978, just 28 percent believed marriage was becoming obsolete.
- About 44 percent of people say they have lived with a partner without being married; for 30-to-49-year-olds, that share rose to 57 percent. -Pew Research Center, Time Magazine
- Nearly one in three American children is living with a parent who is divorced, separated or never-married.
- About half of all currently unmarried adults, 46 percent say they want to get married. Among those unmarried who are living with a partner, the share rises to 64 percent.

With some Americans accepting the idea that marriage is not needed to have a family, cohabitation is a rapidly growing trend were the Census Bureau is incorporating a broader definition of family to include unmarried couples. Some experts say the trend is an indicator that the American family and the institution of marriage is weakening. Many people are losing hope in the sacredness of a committed, life-long love relationship between a man and a woman and allowing societal views to change their perspective about marriage and opt for temporary, live-in companionship. What's sad is that people want the benefits of marriage, without the commitment of marriage. The majority want to marry and still believe in marriage while using cohabitation (playing married) as a step towards it. But as the statistics reveal, the more you try to redefine relationships, alter and tamper at the original design of it, the greater society will decay.

Many couples are attempting to delay, short-circuit or even bypass commitment so they can either experience the benefits of marriage without obligation or shack up in hopes to prepare them for it, but you are only creating an unending, defeated cycle of live-in relationships because cohabitation does not prepare you for marriage, *it's actually delaying and preventing your access into it.*

"Go and get your husband," Jesus told her.
"I don't have a husband," the woman replied.
Jesus said, "You're right! You don't have a husband—for you have had five husbands, and you aren't even married to the man you're living with now. You certainly spoke the truth!" John 4:16-18 NLT

I love this! Who would've ever thought you would find Jesus addressing cohabitation in the Bible? This single woman had developed a pattern where every time she entered a relationship she hijacked marriage by moving in with her boyfriend, playing wife and having sex with them. We will pick back up with this story in the another chapter but there are two things I need to point out: one, every relationship she got in she played house with them and two, her consistent "practice" at marriage didn't give her the ability to access it. Her repeated attempts at playing house no more prepared her for marriage than me playing with mud pies with lil' Johnny in our little homemade shack; it only created a revolving door for men to come in and out of her life.

When a woman moves in with her boyfriend they essentially give the relationship its death certificate. What often happens with cohabiting is it becomes comfortable and there isn't much incentive to get married; you no longer look forward to it because you're embezzling marriage. Because women tend to take on the same roles as wives, doing most of the cooking, cleaning and other household chores without the legal benefits of marriage, cohabitation kills love faster than marriage. And the excuse about waiting to get more money is ridiculous because you are already managing money while you're playing married. You share everything but have no economic or fiscal benefits or financial security for your future. Unmarried couples who live together are less stable than marriages overall and it doesn't improve a couple's chance of success in marriage. In fact, it has a higher breakup rate, a higher infidelity rate, higher violence rate and lower sexual satisfaction rate for women because women subconsciously disengage and don't enjoy sexual pleasure without commitment; they disconnect sexually without assurance, security and stability. Without her even being aware of it, she unintentionally and instinctively, emotionally withdraws from the relationship because she feels as if she's 'sleeping with the enemy' because this man is robbing her and taking away something of great worth without him sacrificing for it.

There are many single women who are either live-in girlfriends right now, have been one or contemplating becoming one. About half of all women in the U.S. have cohabited outside of marriage at least once by the age of 30, according to a comprehensive report on cohabitation, marriage, divorce, and remarriage released by the Center for Disease Control (CDC). This substantiates that women desire long-term committed relationships and will accept a relationship even if it's demoted to a lower level of significance or value. But why would you accept a downgrade? Many women will devote themselves to men for the sake of having a man and will accept the terms of a live-in girlfriend rather than maintaining her position that she is worthy of wife status. You will instead devote yourself to a man who will not commit himself to you? Playing house is for people who want to play, and your life is not a game. For some reason, many singles have allowed themselves to be tricked into believing that they have something special but they have nothing more than a hotel key with temporary sleeping arrangements until they finish the housekeeping and the sexual favors. You delay the need for marriage because it's convenient. It's convenient sex; sex that doesn't require commitment and sex without commitment is dangerous and destructive.

The try it before you buy it concept does not work because couples are trying to test the waters of marriage to determine relational fitness, domestic harmony, and sexual compatibility before they commit. They'll take the relationship through a series of test, sexual experimentation, and putting it through a laboratory of performance, positions, twist and turns and if I'm not satisfied, then I leave. The relationship is based on performance instead of commitment, sacrifice and working to bring the relationship to wholeness and meeting the needs of the other. I have an announcement to make: there are no auditions for marriage. You can't try on marriage to see if it will work, because marriage has to be "worked." Just like all the other couples that have made a commitment to working the marriage, you'll have to do the same. Shacking up is simply a comp out of the "work" that it requires in sustaining the marriage. Cohabiting doesn't have the substance to maintain and preserve marriage because it is developed with the mentality that, "I can always walk out on you rather than 'working' the relationship." You are avoiding the very fundamentals, the foundational key components of a successful relationship: COMMITMENT. And no amount of trying it out will ever prepare you for that because commitment is devoting to stay to make it work.

This is why shacking up is just a transitional relationship: until the next thing good comes along, until the flame dies down, but marriage, true covenant, is the opposite. It is committed to rekindling the flame should it die. Cohabiting is simply having the option of getting up and leaving whenever one chooses, should something else better come along, without having the obligation to seeing the relationship through the tough and hard times. But a covenant is a binding agreement not to leave you, 'til death do us part.' Most cohabiting relationships die because it doesn't have the nutritional substance to feed a life-long commitment. No matter how much people attempt to minimize the paper, it's worth more than what some would like to give it credit for. It's not just paper; it's a commitment, signifying that I love you, not with just lip service, but sacrificing my life to have you. And true love warrants commitment; you can't separate the two in half.

"Trying to experience marriage without a lifetime commitment is like going to a doughnut shop to buy your meals. You can fill your stomach, but eventually malnutrition." Dr. Roger Hillerstorm

My strong advice to those of you who are cohabiting: move out, now! Yes, get up, get your things and leave. Call your parents, tell them you're coming back home or text your best friend and tell her you need to sleep on their couch. Hey, I don't know where you're going, but you're going! You may be concerned or worried, perhaps even frightened about stepping out on faith while in the middle of an unstable economic climate and recession, with not knowing how you're going to take care of yourself since you've relied on a man to provide for you. Your decision to move out or not will reveal to us if the Lord is your God or if money is your god. When I had no job and only a thousand dollars to my name, as a single parent, I moved in my own apartment not knowing how I was going to pay for the rent or take care of my daughter. In the face of uncertainty, I turned down the offer of a man that wanted to shack and pay my bills, and instead, I fearfully trusted God to be my provider[2]. God will not fail you when you put your trust in Him and put Him first by doing life and relationships His way.

"No one can serve two masters. For you will hate one and love the other; you will be devoted to one and despise the other. You cannot serve both God and money. That is why I tell you not to worry about everyday life—whether you have enough food and drink, or enough clothes to wear. Look at the birds. They don't plant or harvest or store food in barns, for your heavenly Father feeds them. And aren't you far more valuable to him than they are? Can all your worries add a single moment to your life? And if God cares so wonderfully for wildflowers that are here today and thrown into the fire tomorrow, he will certainly care for you. Why do you have so little faith? So don't worry about these things, saying, 'What will we eat? What will we drink? What will we wear?' These things dominate the thoughts of unbelievers, but your heavenly Father already knows all your needs. Seek the Kingdom of God above all else, and live righteously, and he will give you everything you need."
Matt 6:24-27, 30-33

Your live-in boyfriend needs to know that your relationship and commitment with God is greater than your love for him and in fact, your love for God and the perfect plan for relationships that He has laid out for you are non-negotiable. Now if you believe that you have a solid relationship and it's worth fighting for, and if you truly believe, I said believe, not emotionalizing this relationship into existence, but if you believe that God's hand is on this relationship and you've just made a unwise, premature decision to move in together, then by all means, for the love of Jesus, do what's right! I do believe that a couple, though they have been cohabiting, can still survive…by doing the right thing. Just because you made a poor decision previously, doesn't mean that God can't restore the relationship so that you can receive His blessings. It's never too late to do what's right. Don't become a statistic. Get premarital counseling and move forward. Let your significant other know that you care too much about yourself and them, to allow cohabiting and premarital sex to undermine the future of your relationship. Your relationship can become even stronger and more meaningful when you make a decision beyond your own desire and make a commitment to God; it actually gives you the ability to make a deeper commitment to the relationship, one that you weren't able to make without your dedication to God. If you are still developing the relationship or relational skills, don't use cohabitation to be the training ground. God's Word is the training ground: the assurance for successful relationships. Give your relationship a chance to survive. Journey through this book with me and allow God's plan for relationships to shape and develop you with the capacity to preserve and experience love the way it was meant to be. ♥

Prayer: Heavenly Father, this may not be an easy decision for me but it is the right decision. I have been influenced to believe that cohabitation is the way to establish relationships but Your way is the only way and living together with a man I'm not married to is not an option. Lord, thank You for wanting the best for me that You won't allow me to settle for and be content with secondary relationships. I repent and tear down the concepts of society's way to establish relationships and I transform and renovate my mind with Your Word about how to establish it. I trust that Your way is the way and in submitting to that I allow

You to empower me to make the right decision and in turn place the future of the relationship in Your hands. I trust You for provision, not my relationship, and I allow You to be the provider and sustainer over my life. In Jesus name, I make this commitment, amen.

How does cohabiting negatively affect relationships? _____
_____

How has the passage in Isaiah 4:1 regarding the shortage of marriageable men affected society? How has it affected you personally? _____
_____

The character Vivian realized that prostitution and moving into a penthouse to be Edward's girlfriend were the same thing. Why do you think this is so? _____
_____

In what ways does a woman aid a man with helpmeet qualities? _____
_____

What lessons can be learned in John 4 when Jesus addressed cohabiting? _____
_____

Have you ever lived unmarried with someone you were in a relationship with? How did that experience affect you and the relationship? _____
_____

Are you currently living together with someone that you're in a relationship with? How important is it for you to make the right decision to leave so that you can please the Lord? _____
_____

How can you trust God with your decision to leave? Who can you call on for help or counseling? _____
_____

Is there someone you know that is in a cohabiting relationship? How can you minister to them and help?
_____
_____

[1]Gen. 2:23 NLT [2]Gen. 14:22-23, Philippians 4:19

The Dating Bible by Ty Adams

SEXUAL PURITY WILL NEVER GO OUT OF STYLE

Chapter 4
Fashion Statement

"What you say goes, GOD, and stays, as permanent as the heavens. Your truth never goes out of fashion." Ps. 119:89 MSG

Like a trending topic on Twitter, I've seen a lot of fashion trends come and go but one thing that will never go out of style is sexual purity! Purity is classic, chic, timeless fashion that never goes out of style! Keeping your clothes on is the greatest fashion statement you can ever make because when you put your clothes back on, you then set yourself up to find real love. That's right, ladies, button your blouse up, keep your skirt down and, gentleman, zip your pants up! Because taking off your clothes with someone you're not married to is so out of style!

"[Therefore beware] brethren, take care, lest there be in any one of you a wicked, unbelieving heart [which refuses to cleave to, trust in, and rely on Him], leading you to turn away and desert or stand aloof from the living God. But instead warn (admonish, urge, and encourage) one another every day, as long as it is called Today, that none of you may be hardened [into settled rebellion] by the deceitfulness of sin [by the fraudulence, the stratagem, the trickery which the delusive glamor of his sin may play on him]. Heb 3:12-13 AMP

There is a fascinating and alluring charm that accompanies the kind of sex that society has to offer. The unbridled, indulgence of sex with no consequences and the romantic persuasion in movies that portray single couples falling in love after having sex and "living happily ever after" is a web of enchantment and entrapment that even a pew-sitting Christian falls prey to. The glamour of sin leads many to believe that it is the best of what sex has to offer in contrast to what God has is an outdated design to relationships. Sin's glamour is enticing to many and those that give in to its sparkle and shine all too soon find that its pleasure and thrill is temporal, fleeting and deceptive because it doesn't provide the fine print on its label: deadly, short-lived pleasure with lasting consequences.

"It is obvious what kind of life develops out of trying to get your own way all the time: repetitive, loveless, cheap sex; a stinking accumulation of mental and emotional garbage; frenzied and joyless grabs for happiness; trinket gods; magic- show religion;

paranoid loneliness; cutthroat competition; all-consuming-yet- never-satisfied wants; a brutal temper; an impotence to love or be loved; divided homes and divided lives; small-minded and lopsided pursuits; the vicious habit of depersonalizing everyone into a rival; uncontrolled and uncontrollable addictions; ugly parodies of community. I could go on." Gal 5:19,20 MSG

I was very good at being a sinner and had loads of fun living in it. When I was living sexually active, I sinned in style, grand style! I would creatively pair the most stylish, shortest, sexiest dress with a four-inch stiletto, take all that time to dress in the latest fashions and then allow a man to take all of that hard work I put into fashion and undress it within minutes: the ultimate fashion faux pas! I dabbled in a smorgasbord of sinful pleasure and I've personally had the best of what sex had to offer; yet, it still was not enough. The temporal high left me empty and the consequences were not worth the three-second thrill! Eugene Patterson coined it precisely in the Message translation of the Bible: repetitive, loveless, cheap sex.

Like many of you, I continued in it despite the hole it left in my soul and the empty cavity in my heart. It was either that or get saved, become a nun, and get "none" anymore! I didn't want to get saved because too many Christians made it look dull, boring, depressing, chained and shackled to religion. Saved but still looking like hell and living like it and then no sex, on top of that? Foolishly I thought, 'I'll take the empty hotel bed that a man left me in.' But if I had known that it was going to be this good to live sexually pure, I would've made a fashion statement and put my clothes back on a lonnnng time ago! I played myself playing half-Christian like so many do, which caused me to be blinded by sexual sin and its grip. It wasn't until I truly and completely gave my heart to the Lord that I realized that what society and media offered with sex was just a knock-off, fake designer bag trying to come across as the real deal. All society did was take sexual pleasure, God's original design for sex, and made a counterfeit of it and tried to pass it off as genuine pleasure. You and I both know that when you get the imitation that it may look like the original but there are grave imperfections, it won't last long and in a short time will fall apart. That's why with counterfeit sex you get pleasure, but also pain.

"Try this new sex act-this will bring you pleasure-get more and you'll be satisfied..." Please; stop it! You're boring me! No matter what society and media comes up with or new ideas of sex they invent, it will never compare to, match, outdo or even come close to the original design of sex. God's design of sex will never go out of style! Many of you have tried to put on the latest fads & trends of sex and it caused sexual addictions, emotional scars and wounds, a distorted view of sex, and an unquenchable, distorted longing for love. You want to be fashionably pure, yet you try and cut corners and attempt to tailor the original design of sex by making some alterations to how you engage in sexual relationships. You limit or reduce the number of sexual partners, engage in other sexual favors other than sexual intercourse, or take pornography out of your sex diet but continue to masturbate. But you can't put purity on layaway with a lil' purity here and there, then making convenient, partial down payments to fully be pure at a later date.

> "And so I insist—and God backs me up on this—that there be no going along with the crowd, the empty-headed, mindless crowd. They've refused for so long to deal with God that they've lost touch not only with God but with reality itself. They can't think straight anymore. Feeling no pain, they let themselves go in sexual obsession, addicted to every sort of perversion. But that's no life for you. You learned Christ! My assumption is that you have paid careful attention to him, been well instructed in the truth precisely as we have it in Jesus. Since, then, we do not have the excuse of ignorance, everything—and I do mean everything—connected with that old way of life has to go. It's rotten through and through. Get rid of it! And then take on an entirely new way of life—**a God-fashioned life**, a life renewed from the inside and working itself into your conduct as God accurately reproduces his character in you. Eph. 4:17-24 MSG

Abstinence Medical Institute defines sexual abstinence: the calculated decision and deliberate action to refrain from sexual activity.

You must make a deliberate decision that you are going to fully and completely make a fashion statement and do relationships in style by engaging in relationships with your clothes on! From this point forward, you will live a God-fashioned life where your relationships will be designed based on the Word of God, working through the fibers of your dating decisions. Are you ready to make a fashion statement? Say this prayer with me:

Dear Father God, I confess that I have not used my body for the original design of sex in which You created it. I know that Your plan for sex and relationships is the only way and there are no options or alterations that can be made to it because it is perfect in its design. I submit my life to Your plan and will fashion my mind after this plan and make a fashion statement by dressing my life in that. I will no longer undress in society's concept of relationships and sex because I am now living a God-fashioned life. Teach me Your ways and I will embed it in the fabric of my life and the decisions that I make. I'm making a firm decision to make a fashion statement by committing to a life of sexual purity by keeping my clothes on until You call me to marriage. In my deception with the glamour of sin, You have forgiven me and redeemed me from the destruction I suffered and in return I am privileged to honor and glorify You with my body in Jesus name.

Chapter 5
We've Crossed The Line

My question deals with being saved and having a relationship with someone who is saved as well but not as saved and dedicated as I am in my Christian walk. Once that line has been crossed and you have repented and asked for forgiveness is it totally necessary to cut all ties with that person or is it possible to begin again into a \"dating\" type relationship and continue to see each other?
Alexis in Michigan

There are many of you that when you picked up this book you were already engaging in sexual activity or you started dating someone and you fell and messed up and began having sex with one another. I'm often asked, "What do we do now? Can our relationship survive after we have started having sex?" Let me share this story with you.

A young woman named Angela in her thirties was dating a prominent minister and they were heavily engaged in a sexual relationship. Angela was torn; she had to make a hard decision to stop having sex with her minister slash boyfriend because she was constantly vexed with conviction as she had to face her father and his congregation each week, killing her insides that she was serving God's people with a secret sexual life with a man she wasn't married to. One evening she cried all night long about how she was living a life that was not pleasing to the Lord and how it would break her dad's heart if he had found out about it, so the next morning Angela, with mixed feelings of boldness and apprehension, pushed the speed dial number two on her cell phone and said, "Terry, I couldn't sleep all night long…I cried all night."

In his comforting, concerned voice, he said, "What's wrong, baby?"

Her voice shaking, Angela cleared her throat and said, "We…I can't continue to go on like this. This is not right. We're both ministers and foremost, a child of God, and we've been having sex and fornicating like nothing is wrong with it. I can't do this anymore!"

Terry interrupts her, "Awww, come on Angie! We're not going there today, are we? Don't *be* like these other religious folk who don't know how to interpret the Bible! That's not what fornication means!"

Angela was appalled! That comment caused her apprehension to fly out the window and with indignation rising up in her, she shouted, "I know you're not going to try and twist Scripture to justify us sleeping together?! Instead of you being a man about it and just say 'it's a struggle and we will work on living sexually pure,' you have the audacity to distort God's Word! I can't believe this! I can't do this anymore!"

In disbelief Terry snapped, "You mean you're leaving me?! You mean you're gonna leave all of this?! You're gonna wake up and see me on worldwide TV preaching and wish you had never left me! You might wanna think about that and take two seconds to change your mind…!"

Jeopardy music plays and then dead silence…Angela hung up the phone and wiped the black stained mascara off her cheeks and never answered his calls after that! I know; you're flabbergasted! I don't make this stuff up! Then there's Jason. He meets this woman during a company conference and he began entertaining and succumbing to her flirtatious come on that was camouflaged as a nice girl just having conversation. Though she was a Christian, there was something that Jason couldn't put his finger on and couldn't give an answer even to himself as to why there was a silent alarm going off in his spirit about her, but she constantly came on to him. He finally gave in and began dating her. After a few entrees and iced-T dinner dates, she sexually threw herself on him and three sexual hook-ups later, Jason found himself preparing to marry this woman. She showed up at Jason's church broadcasting that she was his fiancé, joined the church that day and requested to meet his pastor so that they can get "this show on the road!" She began to operate in a series of erratic behavior and Jason realized that there were a few books missing out of her leather engraved Bible and some screws missing from her brain though she was a savvy businesswoman. I told you guys, I don't make this stuff up! That's when Jason called me, "Ty, I don't know how I got myself in this mess! I consider myself to be an intelligent, God-fearing man and to get caught up in this kind of mess and so quickly, is disturbing!"

I empathized with Jason and I emphatically told him, "You made a mistake, bad judgment on your part. You walked right into the persuasion of her seductive lure…and I know, *with a Christian woman;* you were caught off guard because you didn't think you had to have your guard up when someone is wearing that title but now you need to repent and close the door on this relationship. I want you to honestly ask yourself where you failed at, learn from the mistakes and the things that you saw, the flags you ignored or justified, because I can promise you, there were flags. You're not a man that casually dates. You haven't dated a lot of women but all the details you just told me on the phone, I know all the signs were there that this was a woman that you should have never been involved with. She is emotionally disheveled and has not allowed the Lord to heal her and she wants you to be a band-aid. Mark my words, she's gonna come back. She's going to try to persuade you to still consider making her your wife. She'll try to use other baits and traps to get to you, conjure up opportunities for you to meet and talk but I beseech you by the mercies of God, don't fall for it. Repent and move on!" And just as sure as I am a clone of my daddy, she came slithering back like a snake trying to get him to have sex with her again! This is what happens when Delilah gets saved but not delivered. Jason stuck to his decision and did not allow her back into his life.

Then there's Kim and Billy. They attended the same church; though a large church, they managed to bump into one another in passing after the 11 am service in the lobby and he introduced himself and the next thing you know, they ended up in a "five year dating and having sex relationship" where Kim had half of her wardrobe at his apartment and treated his house like her second home. I don't know who brought it up, but going into their sixth year of dating they ended up at the intersection of make a decision about where this relationship is going or turn left on "go our separate ways." So Billy proposed to Kim and they began planning for a wedding and started going to premarital counseling at their church. They didn't even get through an ounce of premarital counseling before the sessions revealed that they were no more compatible than Kermit and Miss Piggy. If only they had gone to premarital counseling before Kim had gone around their church showing off her shiny ring that she now had to take off and give back to Billy. I know; you want me to answer your question. Heck, I don't know what Billy did to the ring: sold it, pond it, or proposed to another woman! Oh, you're other question; does that mean your relationship won't survive? Hold on a hot second; I'm getting to that.

Now where was I going before you interrupted me? Oh, yeah; so as I was saying…I was sitting on the phone with David and Tamela Mann (Tyler Perry's Madea's Family Reunion, Meet The Browns) and they began to tell me about the early days of their relationship. They were young, very much in love, shacking up and having sex. One Sunday morning while sitting in church during a service, David turned to Tamela right while their pastor was preaching and said, "Let's get married; right now!" Tamela looked back at David like he was crazy but knew from the look on his face that he was more serious than a heart attack. Before their pastor could even seal the "Amen" on the benediction, David pulled Tamela right up to that altar and told their pastor that they wanted him to marry them, right now! An instant wedding! No invitations, no sizing up for a dress or tux, no wedding cake, no bridesmaids in blue chiffon dresses, and no flower girl; just an instant decision and a made-up-mind that they were no longer going to live in sin.

David said, "Ty, we were living the title of your book, "Single, Saved & Having Relations; I meant, having sex. Hahahahaha! Seriously though, we were Christians going to church, living in sin but expecting God to bless our relationship. That day in church, I said, 'enough is enough!' With no more excuses, I made a decision to do what was right and married Tamela, right then and there!" Now lean in and glue your eyes real tight because his next statement is my favorite part. David went on to say, "Now we had been having sex all this time and it was good but when we went up to that altar and got married, we went home that day and made love! The sex was soooooo good that afterwards it felt like I had rolled over and had a spiritual cigarette! Hahahahaha! It was intoxicating good! Because when you do right by God, He'll multiply the pleasure! We thought we were having sex while we were sinning, naw! Having sex the right way, God's way, is the real pleasure!" David had me crying laughing on that phone but that story blessed me real good. Though David and Tamela didn't start off right, they made a decision in the middle of wrong to do what was right and more than twenty-two years later, they are still happily married and have one of the most successful careers in media, music, movies and entertainment today!

Am I saying that you need to go and get married? No; but what I am saying is that if you are not prepared for marriage or have the capacity to sustain a marriage right now, you need to at least make a decision that you will no longer engage in sexual sin. You need to stop having sex, right now! If you continue to have sex you will ultimately destroy the relationship. You're expecting God to bless your relationship but you don't want to bless Him with an obedient life. If you want your relationship to have any hope for survival then you need to take your hands off each other and let God put His hands on the relationship. If you truly care and the love the person you're dating, if you want to honor God with your life and to have Him bless your relationship, then you need to stop having sex, right now! Put a complete end to it; no sexual favors, no foreplay, no sleepovers, no sex at all!

I know, it may not be an easy thing but it's the right thing. Once you begin introducing sex in the relationship it makes it hard on the relationship when you have to stop. You've opened Pandora's Box and it's hard to close it back and this can put a strain on the relationship when you now have to refrain. This is a delicate situation and like a garment that has special care instructions, you can't just throw it in the washing machine, you have to Dry Clean it ONLY. What does that mean? That means that the relationship is fragile and weakened and you're going to have to take special measures to repair it, strengthen and maintain it. Can the relationship be repaired? Absolutely; you may feel like it's too late, "why should I stop, what difference would it make, I've already messed up." Just because you initiated the relationship in sexual error does not mean that God cannot or will not restore the relationship. Just like David and Tamela, I've seen many sexually broken and ill-developed relationships turned around and now extravagantly flourishing. When you build the relationship on sex, you have nothing but that. But when you put sex on the back burner so that you can see what's really behind the smoke and the fire, you can determine if you have a real relationship, one that you can truly build on or if the sheets are actually covering up what you haven't been able to see. Once Angela took away the sex, she saw the true colors of Terry; he was only there for the sex. When Jason began having sex with that unhealed "Delilah," he couldn't see that she was spiritually unstable, emotionally toxic and needy. Once he stopped having sex with her he began to see who she really was; her behavior even amplified, revealing that the shout in the church aisle was an emotional facade. When Kim and Billy started going to premarital counseling, they saw that the only thing that they had in common was that they carried the same King James Bible, loved the same steak restaurant, and the glue from the sex was scarcely holding their artificial relationship together.

You need to detox and go on a sexual fast. I know that may feel like you're putting the relationship at a halt or stopping it, but you're actually moving it forward. The relationship is sustaining itself off the temporary, artificial chemical high of sex and lust. You have two problems on your hand: sex outside of marriage is not lovemaking; your relationship lacks love's true essence, so by default it is lust driven and lust won't stop until it destroys. (James 1:15) Essentially, you're relationship is silently dying. When you detox from sex, you untangle lust from you and you pull the relationship off "sex support." Similar to life support, sex is the only thing keeping the relationship alive, only it's a false heartbeat; it's not feeding the relationship life, it's feeding it death. But when you take it off *sex support*, the relationship can now breathe on its own and become wholesome because you can build a solid foundation by developing healthier ways in feeding the needs of the relationship than by sex. Because of the sex, you have not been able to fully develop key components of a relationship and true intimacy for a deeper and more meaningful connection. Making a decision to now refrain from sex will allow you to fully focus on building a new solid foundation, giving you an opportunity to discover new depths of the relationships that was obscured and covered up. You will come to trust one another knowing that sex is not what's keeping the relationship and that you have a greater commitment and love for one another outside of sex. You will then eliminate the guilt that's holding you and the relationship down and can begin allowing the relationship to please God so that He can ultimately bless it.

On the other hand, when you remove sex from the relationship you may find that the only thing that was holding or keeping you together was the sexual chemistry and you may not have much more in common or concrete to hold it together. Without sex, you're forced to see the relationship for what it is and that may be terrifying for some of you because you may be afraid of what you might discover. You now put pressure on the relationship to reveal itself, its strength and its true colors. You force what's concealed to expose itself because without sex and chemicals blinding you everything that was obscured gets a searchlight illuminating on it. Once the chemical high is taken away and you're sexually sober, you may wake up and realize, "what in the world was I doing with him/her?!" They may have fatal flaws or a crooked nose that you didn't notice. Well, leaving someone because they have a crooked nose is stupid and that can be repaired, but when the person you're in a relationship has fatal flaws then you can't put plastic surgery on it and think that the relationship will look or be good. Many times a relationship can't survive without sex because that's the only thing that was holding the relationship together, like Kim and William. That may be a hard pill for some of you to swallow, but the truth can medicate you if you simply swallow it. Will your relationship end after you make the decision to stop having sex? If it's the only thing holding it together it most probably will. And if that's the case, then it was in your best interest to stop having sex. And if the relationship proves itself to be strong without it, then it was to your advantage as well to stop having sex. It's a win-win, my friend.

One of my dearest friends, Jillian, began dating her tall, athletic, basketball playing boyfriend, Robert. They were having major sex like they had a license to drive it for two years straight, when all of sudden Robert gets saved and becomes a born again Christian and cuts all access; he roadblocks every entrance to sex in the relationship. Jill wasn't having it! She didn't want to stop but Robert was serious about his salvation. I love how Mike Murdock says it, "If you met God and nothing changed in your life, then you met an imposter!" Well, Robert met the Lord and did a 360! He made a separation between sin and anything that would come between him and God! Every time Jill would try to get him to have sex, as much as his body wanted it, he empathically told Jill, "NO!" Jill told me that she kept trying and trying and trying, but Robert wouldn't budge! He told Jill, "I have given my life and my body to the Lord. I'm not going to have sex with you again unless you're my wife. I love you, but I love God more!" Now that's sexy.com! I don't care what you or your cousin says, that is attractive! They went the next two years, NO SEX! I'm not kidding you! After rocking and rolling in the hay for two years, Robert puts a firm restriction on sex and they began focusing on building a sure, solid foundation for the next two years. Jill and Robert have been happily married now for fifteen years and counting! I will not pretend and lead you on to think that this will be an easy walk in the park. You will face some challenges, your decision will be tested but I know you can do this! Keep God at the center of your relationship and you could end up with a love story even greater than Jillian and Robert's or David and Tamela's, but more importantly in right standing with the Lord and pleasing your Father's heart.

If you are currently in a relationship and you are having sex, what now?

- First things first! You must stop having sex with your boyfriend/girlfriend and repent. Stopping and repenting are simultaneously and they are one in the same; do both quickly! Should you ever sin, you must be quick to repent and get in right-standing with God or you will be miserable and your spirit will be heavy until you do[1] and satan's ultimate goal is get you to prolong repentance in attempt to get you so far out there that you never return to the Lord. Oftentimes people will do just as Adam did and will run and play hide and seek. When Adam fell victim to satan's ploy of temptation, he ran from God and hid.

"At that moment, their eyes were opened, and they suddenly felt shame at their nakedness. So they strung fig leaves together around their hips to cover themselves. Toward evening they heard the Lord God walking about in the garden, so they hid themselves among the trees. The Lord God called to Adam, "Where are you?" He replied, "I heard you, so I hid. I was afraid because I was naked."[2]

Shame always accompanies sin and rebellion against God, and so does satan's condemnation. He will condemn you and cause you to think that God won't forgive you and that you've messed up too badly for His forgiveness, but there is nothing that you have done or ever will do that will keep God's love and grace from you so you must not allow it to keep you from receiving it. Ask God for forgiveness, receive it, and then make a clean break away from all and any sexual activity. No "half-sex," necking on the couch, nothing! There's no such thing on God's part to *half-forgive* you, so then there's no *half-repenting* on your part. Repentance means that you are turning completely away from sin and going in the opposite direction of absolute purity. Repent and receive God's forgiveness so that He can restore you. Ok, so let's do it, right now: "Lord God, I repent and renounce sexual sin in my life. I forsake and abandon every form of sexual immorality and I surrender my body back to you for healing, restoration and a pure and holy place for You to live in. I release shame and guilt and I accept Your unending love and forgiveness, in Jesus name, amen." And just like that! Forgiven and in right-standing with God!

- Now it's time to have the brave, grown up conversation with the person you're dating. You need to let them know how important this means to you and that you are making a decision to refrain from having sex to focus on building a true and meaningful relationship without hindering you both from making a clear, conscious and heartfelt decision about the direction and development of your relationship. And then you pause and wait for their response. If they leave, then celebrate; you don't want anyone that is going to stand in the way of you living right with God. If they negotiate with you and try to talk you out of celibate relationship, then you're forced to make a decision between

them and God; that is not even a hard decision because no one is even worthy. If they breathe out a huge sigh and say, "Whew, it's gonna be hard, but what do we need to do," then blow a kiss to your Heavenly Father and get ready to upgrade your relationship!
- Now let me warn you upfront, in the beginning you'll get withdrawal symptoms and may feel like you're going to die if you two don't have sex! I promise you, you won't die! The only thing dying is your flesh; you're killing it and your flesh is going to have a fit once you decide that you will not give in to it! But by the end of this book, you're going to be inviting me over for dinner for some southern fried chicken to thank me when you come to realize the freedom and the real pleasure you experience doing relationships God's way, without the sexual sin.
- Both of you will have to want to be pure. You both must be willing to change and make a firm decision that for the relationship to move forward both of you have to be committed to sexual purity in the relationship. You want to stop, but he/she doesn't? If your boyfriend or girlfriend does not want to stop or refuses, or does not have the same commitment or conviction as you, you will have a battle on your hands. In hindsight, there are some of you in a relationship that you would have never entered had you known the principles in this book and understood God's plan for relationships. Many of you right now are in relationships with someone that you know is not on the same path, not interested in going in the same direction and have no desire to live sexually pure: **leave now.** You must make the tough decision to end the relationship and walk away. Yes, you're going to have to make some difficult decisions that many often fail to make to achieve the kind of love you're looking for and to get to extreme levels in your relationship with God, but somebody has to live completely for God and it might as well be you and I!
- If your relationship was more than sex, you will know. If you really loved one another, then the absence of sex will confirm that all the more by both of your willingness to fight for the relationship. If you love one another, then that love will become stronger as a result of you both committing to doing the right thing to please the Lord so that He can bless your relationship.
- Seek counseling and began putting the microscope on the relationship. Analyze and examine the relationship's true foundation. Ask the hard questions, be honest with yourself and ensure that you're not holding on to something that feels good or you're simply together because of the sexual soul ties. If your relationship is going to survive it has to be built on something above sex. Seek to find the answers as to what really substantiates and authenticates the relationship and what is valuable about it.
- After reaffirming your commitment to sexual purity, structure a new plan to safeguard the relationship and reestablish boundaries that work. Implementing chapters like *Bodyguard* or *Better To Marry* can dramatically increase the chances of your relationship evolving into one that will last and bring honor to God. I also strongly

encourage you to get a copy of my other book, ***Single, Saved, and Having Sex: A 30-Day Guide To Celibacy*** where I show you, step-by-step, how to live in sexual purity within thirty days. With everything in me, I know that God can deliver you and empower you to live sexually pure. ♥

Prayer: Dear Daddy God, I pray for my brother or sister who may be facing a tough decision in their relationship. Enlighten their understanding of your plan for relationships and the power they access when they make the bold decision to live sexually pure. I ask that You give them the ability to push pass their flesh and comfort zone to do what is right and pleasing unto You. Give them the strength and the fortitude to tap into the power of Your Sprit to do Your will concerning them and their relationship, in Jesus name, Amen.

Did you take the big, bold leap and repented? What does this mean to you? _____

Have you ever been in a situation where you prolonged repentance? How did it affect you?
_____

What does half-repentance look like? How does it differ from full repentance? _____

What do you imagine a relationship would be like when a couple does not allow sexual lust to enter into it? _____

What fears do you face in making this decision? What would you like to say to God about those fears?
_____

How can you approach the conversation with someone you're dating about refraining from sex to build a stronger and wholesome foundation?
_____

How are you prepared to handle their response? _____

Who can you turn to for sound advice or to help you with the decision to live sexually pure in your relationship? _____
_____

[1]Ps 32:3-7 [2]Genesis 2:7-10

Chapter 6
Price Tag

Did anyone see the movie, "Taken?" Oh my goodness! That movie was so gooood! Ok, if you have not seen the movie then you need to "Netflix-it" or something. Actor Liam Neeson plays the father of a seventeen year-old daughter who is kidnapped along with her friend in Paris and the entire movie he is trying to find his daughter *before it's too late*. Wait, let me back up a little to tell you one of my favorite parts: he's actually on the phone with his daughter as the kidnapping is taking place and he tells the kidnapper, "I don't know who you are; I don't know what you want. If you're looking for a ransom, I can tell you I don't have money but what I do have are a very particular set of skills; skills I have acquired over a very long career. Skills that make me a nightmare for people like you. If you let my daughter go now, that'll be the end of it, but if you don't, I will look for you, I will find you and I will kill you!" Whew, I love it! Somebody's about to get a butt kickin'!

Okay, so the kidnappers snatch up the young girls to sell them off into sex slavery and now he is racing against time to save his daughter with only a small window of about ninety-six hours or less before never finding his daughter. With these special set of skills, Liam's character hunts down the location of the kidnappers but only to find his daughter's friend: drugged, raped and killed, with his daughter nowhere to be found! Ut oh...! Relentless, vowing to stop at nothing, he continues in his search and finally finds her alive, naked and in the dark room of an auction to be sold off to several men who were bidding to have her. As the bidding for her begins, the auctioneer proudly states, "As usual, we saved the best for last; speaks English, some French. Certified pure. The bidding will begin at one hundred thousand dollars." The bid escalates and she is sold to the tune of a half-million!

Why was her price tag so high? Why wasn't she drugged, raped and killed like her friend? Because the auctioneer indicated the "item" for sale was **certified pure!** She was sexually pure and still a virgin; unlike her friend who was no longer a virgin, sexually loose and had given up herself to other young men. As a result, her life was spared because she was sexually pure and *worth more*. Society and media may tell you to give yourself up sexually, but you're worth more when you're pure. The question I want to ask is, "How much are you worth? If you were placed in an auction, how much would your price be?" The problem with many of you is that you don't know your own value and worth, so you squander your body off as if you're cheap goods. Many of you need to simply do an appraisal to find out how much you're worth. I'll tell you how much:

"What's the price of a pet canary? Some loose change, right? And God cares what happens to it even more than you do. He pays even greater attention to you, down to the last detail—even numbering the hairs on your head! So don't be intimidated by all this bully talk. You're worth more than a million canaries." Matt 10:31 MSG

"For God bought you with a high price." 1 Cor. 6:20

Your Father, God, purchased you with something that exceeds the value of money: His precious blood. When Jesus died on the cross for you, He paid the ransom for all of your sins. He paid the price to save and redeem you with His own life. There's no money on earth that can match that; it was the highest price paid. He not only saved you from having to pay the penalty of your sins and gave you eternal life, but He delivered you and set you free, made you whole and cleansed you from all unrighteousness! That means every contamination, every sexual violation, and every impure act: cleansed and erased! There are no traces of sexual contamination anywhere in, or on you! When God purchased you, HE CERTIFIED YOU PURE! Do you hear me? That is why it is insanity for you to go back and lie down with anyone you're not married to and have sex with them because you have been certified and declared pure!

I've seen many women give their bodies up cheaply when a man takes them out for dinner, pay their bills, buy him clothes or jewelry and go back and lie in filth and get contaminated. There's no difference between a "woman of the night" getting money for sexual favors and a woman that allows her boyfriend to have sex with her in exchange for dinner, hair & nails, car note, light bill or rent being paid; *that's still a prostitute.* You cannot allow a man to treat you like trash when there's no amount of money that a man has that he can give you in order to have you. He can't buy you a car and not even a mansion on a hill; none of those suffice or meet the requirements! God says, "If a man wants you, he has to do what I did to get you: he has to **GIVE YOU HIS LIFE!**" And nothing short of that because that is how much you're worth: a life! God laid down His life to have you and when a man wants you, he has to do the same. When you look inside our Love Manual, you see that Adam understood that nothing short of his life was adequate enough to have Eve. And Eve even knew, "In order to experience me sexually, you have to give me your life and make me your wife!"

"This one is bone from my bone, and flesh from my flesh! She will be called 'woman,' because she was taken from 'man.'" This explains why a man leaves his father and mother and is joined to his wife, and the two are united into one. Now the man and his wife were both naked, but they felt no shame." Gen. 2:23-25 NLT

When someone gives you anything less than their life you reduce the value of sex and yourself; you then squander that which is precious for pennies. You're worth more than thirty minutes of a 'gymnastical,' acrobatic roll around in the hay. God invested too much in you to be cheapened to some temporary girlfriend or somebody's sex partner, riddling your body with sexual contamination. Yet, many people think that if they don't succumb to a one-night stand, sex should at least happen within or by the third date, *or you're not connecting or compatible with one another.* And if you want to be classy, sophisticated and a "trending" Christian, then you wait ninety days. You mean to tell me that is enough time for someone to give you to qualify to have sex with you? You're kidding me, right? Remember that Algebra class you had to take that you didn't think you were going to ever need in life? You need it right now because this is not adding up. Do you think all you have, all that God has invested in you, the sacrifice you paid to get to this place in your life, that someone can just come and get all of that in ninety days? All they have to do is give you ninety days of their life in exchange for yours?

Steve, I love you, man, but it takes more than ninety days to get a driver's license. It takes more than ninety days to grow a perm out my hair or get an associate's degree. Isn't my life, my body more valuable than these? Then why would I give my body to someone just because they took me out on a few dates, bought me a happy meal or took me to the movies? No, sir, I'm worth waaaaay more than that! And it's going to cost you more than a mere, measly ninety days! For more than a decade now, I have been advising women, based on the 90-day rule correlating to job benefits: to not give benefits until the relationship has proven itself at least ninety days; that has nothing to do with sex. Please, that's not even an option! Temporary employees do not get benefits and neither should temporary men. My advice is to not offer benefits like excessively pampering him, giving him extensive degrees of your time, intense emotional intimacy, 'relationship insurance' or commitment of your heart within the first ninety days. Do you see that sex was not even mentioned? Sex is not a benefit given until "life" insurance is given. If he doesn't give his life, then he does not get sex benefits. While it is great to know how a man thinks to improve the quality of your relationships, you must above anything, act like a lady, *and think like God.* And God has made His thoughts clear: a life in exchange for your body.

I love how Dr. Henry Cloud noted that many Christians have "un-integrated sexuality." They have yet to connect their sexuality with love, relationships and values. Many singles think that their sexuality is a separate component from their spiritual life and do not equate sex as a high commodity as their spirituality. There's so much wealth on sex that it should have an ATM card attached to it: **A**bstinent '**T**il **M**arriage; and you can only make deposits or withdrawals on it when a person commits their life to you in marriage! When a man wants to have sex with a woman, she needs to simply ask him, "How much would you value your life at? Like, if someone wanted to buy your life, how much would it be?" As he sits there, clueless, trying to find a number in his head, you respond before he can even answer, "Exactly! You can't even put a price on it. Well, that's what I cost: PRICELESS!"

You need to make a statement with your life that, "What I have doesn't come cheap. I have the ability to meet your needs and if you want me to meet them, it's gonna cost you.

God has invested a lot in me and I'm worth everything I'm asking!" A real man will value and respect you when you're pure, when you know your worth and refuse to give it to him without him paying the cost of his life for it. He will be willing to pay the cost to have you through commitment of his time, his substance and willing to invest his life in something that has been appraised at such a high price. You must esteem yourself this high because that is how God sees you! God values your body so much that He decided to live in it and if He thinks that much of you, then there's nothing or nowhere on this earth better than your life. And that means holding out and waiting for someone who has the ability to appraise and discern your worth; not being moved by the time in waiting, because God saves the best for last!

"You realize, don't you, that you are the temple of God, and God himself is present in you? No one will get by with vandalizing God's temple, you can be sure of that. God's temple is sacred—and you, remember, are the temple." 1 Cor. 3:16-17 MSG

How much are you worth? _____

What does it mean to be "Certified Pure?" _____

_____

What lessons can you learn from the movie, "Taken?" _____

_____

How much time does a person need to invest in your life before you have sex with them? Why?
_____
_____

In what way does your sexuality have just as much value as your spirituality? _____

_____

According to Matthew 10:31, what are you worth more than? _____

Make a list of other things that you are worth more than _____

_____

Prayer: Father God, thank You for rescuing me from the auction where men where bidding to buy me, but You paid the highest price to have me and now I can no longer be bought with gifts or material things. Thank You for giving me Your life, so that I could have life. I am priceless now that You have certified me Pure again. You have made me whole and I will no longer allow my body to be used for sexual contamination. Teach me to grow and develop in sexual purity as I continue to commit to You, honor and glorify You with my body in Jesus name.

10 Things I Wish I Had Know About Dating Before I Started Dating

1. Over dating will emotionally kill you. It will ill-prepare you for relationship
2. No one can give you the love you need apart from God. If you're not getting that filled from God, no man can give that to you
3. No amount of explosive, sky rocketing sex will keep a relationship
4. Even with great sex, you will regret having sex. True love is really waiting
5. If you have sex with your date you will impair and destroy the relationship
6. Do not waste your single life in passive or toxic relationships
7. Get your life together emotionally, spiritually and Emotional and spiritual well-being is a must.
8. Trust your spirit, not your heart.
9. Don't ignore the warning signs.
10. Any forms of sexual expression should be prohibited. Sexual intimacy does not belong in dating relationship. Instead build a foundation on

Did I say ten…I meant thirteen!

11. Passive, callous dating. Don't allow people to just drop in your life. qualify to be in it.
12. Time is my best friend, so Wait as long as you have to. there is really someone awesome that will love you, be faithful. Don't settle or compromise
13. Dating is not a filler space for my single life. pass-by time I can be happy single and I don't have to be in a relationship or use dating to be complete or happy. Throw myself completely in love relationship with the Lord and consume myself in my God-given purpose for fulfillment while I'm single. Being single is not a curse if you let God fill your life. He really wants me happy and in a loving relationship more than I do and if I just trust Him and allow Him to do it, I will really be okay.

Write yours here:

There's An App For That

- God's plan for your single life ---→ Jeremiah 29:11
- God's will for your life ---→ 1 Thessalonians 4:3
- God's plan for your love life ---→ Genesis 2
- How to know if the relationship you're in is real love -→ 1 Corinthians 13:4-8
- How to get the mate you desire ---→ Psalms 37:4
- When you feel incomplete ---→ Colossians 2:10
- When you feel alone ---→ Hebrews 13:5b
- When you feel lonely ---→ John 14, Psalms 68:6a
- How to live pure ---→ Psalms 119:9-11
- What to look for in a mate ---→ 1 Samuel 16:7
- The kind of person not to date or marry ---→ 1 Corinthians 5:11, 2 Corinthians 6:14-18
- What to do when you have relationship anxiety or worries about your single or dating life ---→ Philippians 4:6-7
- What to do if you want to do right but keep making mistakes ---→ Romans 7:
- What to do if you've fallen short of God's plan ---→ Psalms 32:1-6, 51:1-17
- What to do if you're heartbroken ---→ Psalms 147:3
- How to go from sexually active to sexually pure ---→ Romans 12:1-2
- How to be led to the right person ---→ Proverbs 3:5-6
- How to escape temptation ---→ 1 Corinthians 10
- How to keep your mind pure ---→ 2 Corinthians 10:3-5
- When you feel like you can't hold on -→ Isaiah 40:28-31
- Where to go when you get tired of waiting or holding out ---→ Galatians 6:9
- What to do when you face temptation ---→ James 4:7-8
- When you're tempted to settle or jump in a relationship ---→ Song of Songs 2:7
- What to do when you don't know what to do ---→ James 1:5
- What to do while you're waiting for marriage ---→ 1 Corinthians 7
- What to do when you face sexual pressure/temptation ---→ 1 Corinthians 6:18
- Where to go when you face temptation ---→ Hebrews 4:14-16
- When you feel like it's getting hard ---→ 1 John 5:3
- When you feel unwanted, dateless or in a single wilderness ---→ Deuteronomy 32:10
- Above anything else, do this ---→ Proverbs 4:7, 23

Chapter 7
Window Shopping

Just looking; not buying anything
Your eyes meet, there's a spark and it's like love at first sight! There are many times, with the best intentions, I have simply gone out to just look to see what new styles are out or perhaps to just get one blouse to match with that pencil skirt I need to wear for an event this weekend and with no fault of my own, I turn and look, our eyes meet and there's this perfectly-tailored cocktail dress starring me right in the eyes, screaming and yelling my name for me to get it and take it home with me! I don't know if you know it or not, but there's a conspiracy against us! Department stores put the best of the best in the window so that when you walk past it, you get hypnotized, fall madly in love and get all googely-eyed and it causes you to turn around and say, "Now, I *gotta* have that! You pretty little thing; you're coming home with me!" Do you see what I'm implying and where I'm going here?! Yes, don't just leave out the house without putting your best foot forward. Even if you're just dashing out to the store because you noticed there's one drop of milk left in the carton; make sure that you are presentable (or perhaps you may end up on the "people of Walmart" site). You never know when there's a divine opportunity being set up by God and you run into them in aisle seven and your eyes meet and bam! A match made in Heaven!

I'm not leaving this store without that dress!
It's the perfect shoe or handbag and you have to have it! When you want it, you'll go nothing short of forcing yourself on a fast so that you can use the money you would have used for food for that dress! (I know; *don't judge me.*) I don't understand how a fashionista can understand a hot-handbag-pursuit but don't know if a man is in pursuit of her...I have had many women who email me asking questions as to whether a man is interested in her. "I don't know if he likes me...he hasn't called yet; should I call him?" If he's interested, girlfriend, you'll know it! When a man wants you, it's obvious! It's like Steve Urkel and Laura, Pepe le pew and Penelope, Alfalfa and Darla, Clark Kent and Lois Lane, Chachi and Joanie and the way Popeye wanted olive oil!

Yes, Joanie loved Chachi and he chased after her, wooing her in song, standing outside her window at night calling her name. Urkel, from the hit show Family Matters, was over to the Winslow's house every day, bringing flowers and candy, constantly begging Laura for a date no matter how many times she declined! That little rascal, Alfalfa, would do whatever he had to do to get away from the boys to be with Darla! That stinkin' skunk, Pepe le pew, was always chasing Penelope down with his odorous cologne! And Clark Kent did whatever he had to do to become Lois Lane's superman! I recently read a report that says a man knows within eight seconds of sitting down in the restaurant on the first date if he likes her and if he'll ask her out for a second date. I don't know how accurate that eight seconds is, but I do know this: when a man likes a woman and is interested in her, he'll call her, he'll respond to her text, he doesn't want to get off the phone with her, he's bragging to his buddies about her, he'll give her flowers, ask her out on a date and then ask for a second, third and a fourth one and won't ask for you to pay half the bill or go dutch because when a man really likes you, his treasure will follow. When a man wants to be with a woman he'll spend and invest his time, money and talents. If not, then he's not interested and you need to be okay with that and move on. But if he's interested, he'll go nothing short of getting your attention to make it known that he wants to be with you.

> "Naomi said, 'Sit back and relax, my dear daughter, until we find out how things turn out; that man isn't going to fool around. Mark my words, he's going to get everything wrapped up today.'" Ruth 3:18 MSG

A woman that knows her value doesn't chase a man because she knows that she is worthy of being pursued. Naomi told Ruth, "don't you dare go after Boaz; sit back and relax, honey child!" Why? Because a real man will not play games with you, fool around with your feelings, or lead you on. Iif he's interested, if he wants you, and if he wants to spend time with you, he's going to make it known and do whatever he needs to do to be in your company. So sit back and relax, ladies!

In hot pursuit!

With that said, it is important to know that a woman should never, (I repeat, never), go after a man! Ladies, God will present you, and make you noticeable to him, just as he brought Eve to Adam. (Gen. 2:22) Men are achievers and wired to pursue; it's innate. That's why some men will even sit and play on his X-box, run up and down a basketball court to score a basket, or work hours detailing his car because they love a great challenge and achievement is a drive for them. A man loves a woman who *ain't* thinking about him! A woman needs to be unavailable; you need to be so busy in your God-given purpose that he has to come up with ways to win your heart! Notice in just about every action and heroin movie or love story, a man is attempting to rescue her or battle to get her because he wants to win her affections. Don't take that away from him by pursuing him; let him win your affections. A man doesn't value something that he didn't have to work to get. If he gets it without effort, he will not value it. If you make it too easy for him, he won't place a high value on it. Women have become too accessible, asking the man for his number and pursuing him and causing him to become lackadaisical in his quest for a relationship with her.

He is the pursuant; she is the responder. The woman attracts; the man pursues. A woman can show her interest without taking on his role as the pursuer. If you make eye contact, gaze longer than a second, then smile. Smile with your eyes and say hello. If he asks you how you're doing, say, "I'm fine; and, you?" Not, "I'm blessed and highly favored," with an attitude but learn how to have a normal conversation without speaking in tongues and quoting a scripture every other second. Ask yourself, "Am I approachable?" Your posture and body language will tell him if it's safe to introduce himself. Gentlemen, if you're interested in her, then make it known. Many times people will hide their interest, hoping the other person will catch on; we're too grown for that. Approach her like a gentleman without sizing her up with your eyes, minus the catchy, player lines, "I need to give you a parking ticket because you've got fine written all over you" or "Excuse me, I believe one of your ribs belongs to me." She's probably thinking in her mind, "Sir, have several seats." A lady likes a gentleman who is genuine and unrehearsed. Eye contact, a polite introduction and an invitation to a cup of coffee or lunch over a smoothie is quite sufficient, *minus the corny pickup lines.*

"So, last night I was reading in the book of Numbers and I realized I don't have yours."
"You're looking for a knight in shining armor? I just happen to be wearing the armor of God."
#CornyChristianPickupLines

If a woman is interested in you, gentleman, she will make herself available to you. A woman of dignity and class will not chase after you but will gracefully let you know that she reciprocates and welcomes your interest with a smile, glaring eyes, innocent flirting, and a, "yes, sure I would like to go out for coffee." She'll respond to your calls or text with cute emoticons and make herself available to you, but if she's not responding but suddenly or randomly accepts a date then unavailable again, then she's probably only interested in a free meal and you should save your money and reserve it for a lady who will respect and honor you for the man of God that you are.

Mannequin
Men, just like you want a lady, a woman wants a gentleman; a man that has self-control and sex-control, not throwing himself on her, one that opens door, walks her to the door at the end of the night without trying to force himself on the other side of it. Many men say they don't want an easy woman but you must understand that it's a man responsibility to not make her easy by attempting to get sexual favors at the end of the night. When you find a pure woman don't try to deflower her; leave her presence the way you found her. And again, ladies, if you want to be treated like a lady, then that means you must be one. When you're in the window, don't advertise what's not for sale. If the mannequin is half-dressed then he may assume that he can just take the rest of the clothes off. If you use your body parts to get his attention, he will think that he can just pay for dinner and get sex at the end of the night.

Make a clear statement with his first impression of you that he understands you're not for sale and that he just met one of God's best!

Price Tag

"May, I help you," the store clerk asks.

"No, thank you. I'm just looking."

Many times a man is simply window shopping, not interested in pursuing a relationship with a woman, but a woman's irresistible beauty and unique qualities will grab his attention and perhaps compel him to change his mind. His curiosity will peak his interest to at least check the price tag and if he can't afford it, then he should keep it moving and go to the back of the store and check out the clearance rack. Your very own persona should unapologetically echo that you have to pay the full price here because there are no markdowns! The best gets put on display in the window and he should recognize that he has just discovered rubies and it should cost him something to be in the presence of a queen! And I'm not talking about money, sweetie! It should be difficult to get you and not everyone that ask for your phone number gets it or should have easy to access into your life; *they have to qualify*. We sit across the table and have a Carmel Macchiato with anyone without 'qualifying the buyer' or determining if they're a serious shopper or just looking for a good time.

Does he/she have relationship debt and carrying balances or liabilities from previous relationships? Does he/she have good credit: credibility with God? I travel all around the world and there is not one airport that I can go into without going through security checkpoint and searched before I have access into the airport. If the country has increased its security measures, then shouldn't you? You must value who you are and Who's you are. Your high-profile Christian life is the residency of God, yet you allow anyone in it without being searched! There should be high level security over your life and access shouldn't be easy. Access should be limited to those who can only get pass God through a high-end inspection that determines if they qualify by measuring them through the filter of God's word. If the Holy Spirit is the security checkpoint of your life, then relationship terrorists shouldn't be able to get in; they should be denied legal access and should not be afforded that opportunity to have entry into your life unless God grants them access. Your life is not some hangout where people can just trespass through with casual acquaintance. Don't play hard to get, ***be*** hard to get. Women should act like a butterfly: pretty to see, but hard to catch! Don't accept dates for the sake of having one. God paid such a high price tag for you and you're worth every bit of what you're asking for in terms of the high qualifications you have in order for someone to have access into your life. Don't lower your standards; instead they should arise to it if they want access.

What are some of the things you can do to enhance and improve on a "Window Display" look and lifestyle? _____

How can a woman know if a man is interested in her or not? What are some examples of couples in TV or movies that are examples of where a man truly was interested in a woman? _____
_____

Why should a woman not pursue a man? _____
_____

What are some ways that a man can show his interest? How can a woman show that she is open and receptive to his interest? _____
_____

Why is it important to set the standard of purity at the beginning of a relationship interest? _____
_____

Why should you place a high value on the requirements for access into your life? What requirements or qualifications must a person have to get access into your life? _____
_____

I am Ready To Date

You are ready to date when you can answer with a resounding yes to the following:
- I am secure in who I am. My identity is solely founded in Christ.
- My relationship with God is the most important part of my life.
- I am clear about my values and what I believe. I am faithfully committed to God.
- The Word of God is the fabric of my life. I use the Word of God as the blueprint in which I live by and govern relationships.
- I have standards set by my Relationship Manual (Bible) and have boundaries that govern and protect my life.
- I love myself and I am happy with my life and the direction I am going in.
- I live in integrity and I am responsible in my personal life and affairs.
- I am emotionally healthy and available.
- I am well capable of pursuing and sustaining a relationship without sex.
- I have made a commitment to reserve lovemaking for marriage.
- My life is led by my spirit; not my body.
- I am legally single.
- God is my First Love and His love is the standard by which I gauge a true love relationship.
- My body belongs to the Lord.
- I have a strong support of family, mentors, and accountability.
- I have a full and healthy social life with healthy friendships.
- I do not squander my single life with reckless dating.
- I am ready to date because I don't need to.
- I have identified and overcome negative relationship habits and behavior that have contaminated and fostered my previous relationships.
- I will not pursue or entertain a relationship with someone that does not have a consistent, dedicated, and committed relationship with the Lord.
- I don't need to be in a relationship to feel whole or complete; I am complete in God.

I know I am ready to date because _____

I have this to offer in a healthy relationship _____

"When you regard dating as a matter of choice rather than necessity, you are ready." Dr. Myles Munroe

Chapter 8
Tailor-Made

Have you ever seen a woman with a dress on that was too big for her or a man wearing a suit that was hanging off of him or even too small where the hem of the pants was too high above the ankle? Look at your neighbor and say, "Not good!" There is nothing like a tailor-made suit; trimmed, cut, measured and custom-made to fit you perfectly! "Not too big, not too small; just right," said Goldilocks! That was God's original intent when He created relationships: for you to enter into a relationship with someone that would be suitable for you, fit you just right, and to complement your life.

"Now the Lord God said, It is not good (sufficient, satisfactory) that the man should be alone; I will make him a helper meet (suitable, adapted, complementary) for him." Gen. 2:18 AMP

"Then the LORD God said, "It is not good for the man to be alone. I will make a helper who is just right for him." NLT

It is not God's will for you to have people in your life that hang off of you; He would rather you be alone, than to be with someone that does not suit you. Yet, many single Christians will get in relationships and stay in them, even when they don't fit. The objective then for Christian dating is to determine if the suit fits. It is not for people to come and hang out vicariously in your life but to establish if they fit and form to your life, and as we established earlier, it is to also discover yourself inside your mate.

"Oh yes, you shaped me first inside, then out; you formed me in my mother's womb. I thank you, High God—you're breathtaking! Body and soul, I am marvelously made! I worship in adoration—what a creation! You know me inside and out, you know every bone in my body; You know exactly how I was made, bit by bit, how I was sculpted from nothing into something. Like an open book, you watched me grow from conception to birth; all the stages of my life were spread out before you, the days of my life all prepared before I'd even lived one day." Ps. 139:13-16 MSG

God chose you and set a plan in motion for your life before you were born, before your first cry, before your mother held you and laid eyes on you and yes, even before He created the world! (Ephesians 1:4) Imagine that! God chose you and purposed your life before He created the earth, the sun, the sky, the universe… Wow, God esteems you higher than that; you're amazing! God is concerned with every detail about you and every aspect of your life. Everything that God created for your life was on purpose, it was calculated and done intentionally so the people that you have in your life is very critical to God's purpose for your life. The people you allow in your life will either draw you towards God's purpose or away from it. This is why just any random person can't be in your life; they have to qualify and align with God's purpose.

This means that dating has to have a purpose to it, not simply just to hang out and have a good time; 'but do you further God's plan for my life or frustrate it? Are you pulling me towards my destiny or are you a destiny killer?' For this reason, it is fundamentally important that you know God's purpose and His will for your life because it will dictate and empower you to choose correctly who you will enter into a relationship with. Above commonality, compatibility or chemistry: do you fit and align with God's purpose and plan for my life? Purpose serves as a guide; like a GPS, it gives directions to where you need to go and it will help you formulate decisions. Knowing where God wants you to go eliminates and prevents wrong relationships.

> "Then the LORD God said, 'It is not good for the man to be alone. I will make a helper who is just right for him.' So the LORD God formed from the ground all the wild animals and all the birds of the sky. He brought them to the man to see what he would call them, and the man chose a name for each one. He gave names to all the livestock, all the birds of the sky, and all the wild animals. But still there was no helper just right for him." Gen. 2:18-20 NLT

When you know God's plan for your life, it makes it easy to pass up wild animals! Because God's purpose is definitive and governs your decisions, you can look at "bird-like people" who do not align with your life and say, "You're cute, fashionable and stylish like a flamingo; you're a handsome, exotic looking thing and kinda "fly," but not suitable" Or, "You're a wild, untamed beast, not governed by God, living a compromising lifestyle and you don't compliment or match the plan that God has for me." Adam passed through a few "wild animals" and determined that none of them were right for him. The problem is with many people is that they will go window shopping and see something cute, stylish and "fly," try the suit on, see that it doesn't fit, but will buy and settle for it in spite of, "It's not what I really wanted, it's a little too tight and doesn't fit on me that well, but it's cute; it'll do." The person is too small-minded in their living, but you try to force yourself in it. Your life is bulging out the sides of the suit, yet you try to force and squeeze in it. Look, fruitcake, it just doesn't fit! When you try to force or make a person fit in your life, you're just going to end up being hurt and in lots of pain!

You trivialize your life when you make meaningless relational decisions and the people you choose to spend your time with. Many of you treat your life like the Bachelor or Bachelorette Show: haphazardly trying on multiple dates. You put on and take off relationships like clothes, jumping from one relationship to the next, using trial and error as a measurement stick to determine if they fit, when you can simply look at them on the rack and see that they are not tailor-made for you! Good grief, how many relationships does it take? How many people will you allow to come in and out of your life before you find the right one? Let's add this up: Melissa was with Michael two years, with Tony six months, Ricky one-and-half months, Carl four years…like Melissa, many of you are your wasting time and your life, allowing "unsuitables" to pull you away from your purpose and even the person that God would have for you because if you're wasting time with the wrong one, the right one can't come.

You have to be willing to hold out from "cute" things, from discounted, significantly reduced, clearance-racked people and wait for the *suit* that fits. One size fits all doesn't apply when it comes to your life. It breaks God's heart when we live beneath what He has for us, settling for second and third best, when He designed your life to be abundantly blessed! (John 10:10) Settling is the best way to lose out on what God has for you. The key then is to be selective, saying no to mediocre or substandard relationships, holding out when you would rather have the company of a (wo)man and declining dates on Friday nights, instead of using your life as a holding pattern for substandard relationships until the right one comes.

> "So the LORD God caused the man to fall into a deep sleep. While the man slept, the LORD God took out one of the man's ribs and closed up the opening. Then the LORD God made a woman from the rib, and he brought her to the man. "At last!" the man exclaimed. "This one is bone from my bone, and flesh from my flesh!" Gen. 2:21-23 NLT

This is going to require that you rest and be consumed in the peace of God and trust His will for your life, while some of your friends are out hanging on a Saturday night in futile relationships that they have no business in. While others are living in vain, you're at peace, busy living out your God-given purpose, trusting that God is preparing and tailoring someone for you. God put Adam to sleep while He prepared Eve for him and when God tailor-made and custom fit Eve for him, He brought her to Adam and all the waiting and holding out, and passing up wild, beastly women paid off! "Finally, someone that matches me!" He was blessed with someone who was tailor-made, custom fit and suitable for his life. Wait now; pump your brakes! If you're looking for Mr. or Mrs. Perfect, close this book, give it to a friend and join a nunnery! If you think you're *gonna* find someone perfect then you need to go search on another planet because you won't find them here on earth because we're all being perfected in God's image; including you. Suitable does not mean perfect but an imperfect person who is allowing our perfect God to perfect them. Yes, I established earlier on what you should have and what you should also look for in a mate:

- Spiritually, emotionally, mentally sound, healthy and whole
- God sufficient
- Self-sufficient
- Singly content
- Healthy lifestyle

- Relationally competent
- Ability to communicate effectively
- Financially progressive or stable
- Purpose driven

But also add this to that list:
- IMPERFECTION!

Yes, get yourself and your single life in order, throw yourself into your God-given purpose, know and discern God's timing and season for you to date and seek out a relationship, keep your non-negotiables and your "top five must-haves" but allow a margin for imperfection. Let me take this side bar here, because I find that there are way too many people looking for perfection and the perfect timing and the perfect idea of what they think a relationship should be, holding up their life to begin a relationship because they're waiting for perfect, but I know plenty of people who married fresh out of college, ate pork-n-beans out of the pot and moved up the financial ladder together. And I know people who are like Mark who had this idea of the perfect woman that had to have everything he desired in a woman and it kept him single, jumping from one relationship to the next until he met Kristi, who was not his 'beautiful-model type' but found himself madly in love with her to the point of falling down on one knee and asking her to spend the rest of her life with him in marriage! Are you sitting at home on the couch waiting for your idea of the perfect mate while you're missing out on the perfect, imperfect person that God has for you? We must bring Godly balance to this, my friends! Don't confuse suitable with perfection. You (or your mate) do not have to be the "perfect Christian" and everything does not have to be in complete order or perfect in your life for God to bless us with love!

Some people subscribe to the idea of having the perfect soul mate because to them that implies or suggests that the relationship won't require any work or effort and it'll be a happily-ever-after-fairytale every day. While I'm parked right here in misconception lane, I think I need to clear up the idea of the one perfect, soul mate out there waiting to show up miraculously on your doorstep, out of all the seven billion people on earth that God Himself is going to pick for you! I love how my papa says it, "Just as salvation is a choice, so is the person you marry. God would never take your will and choose salvation for you, nor will He do that for a mate for you." (Dr. Myles Munroe) God will not pick your mate for you, but He will certainly supply you with a suitable choice. He will do the presenting, but you must do the choosing, just as Adam chose Eve when God presented her to him. That is why you need to be equipped with spiritual discernment, some common sense, wisdom, guidance from the Lord and daily downloads from our Romance and Love App (Bible). Hence, the reason why so many people end up with the wrong person and why relationships fails: because they started the wrong way and did not use God's design for relationships to guide their choices! Which leads me back to the focus of what I wanted to say in this chapter…(thanks for letting me take a side bar). Though many Christians profess Jesus as Lord, they fail to include Him in the decision-making as to whom they will allow in their lives. Far too many single Christians will accept dates and get into relationships without ever seeking God.

It is alarming to see the number of Christians who begin dating before getting the green light from God, whether the timing is fitting or if God would even approve of that person having access into their life. The look on a person's face tells it all when I ask the question, "Did you even pray before you decided to give him your number and go out on a date with him?" When I see a Christian couple dating, I will ask them, "Do you pray together? What is God saying about your relationship?" …Both looking as clueless as a McDonald's employee on the cash register on their first day of work! If you suppose for one New York minute that you can just jump in the relationship and wing it, thinking that it'll work because you two are Christians, then you're in for a rude awakening! Being a Christian alone is not an automatic endorsement that the relationship is suitable or right for you.

Many singles jump into relationships and attempt to make that God's will, instead of seeking God for His will. Most often many of you don't include God until the relationship faces trouble or well after your hearts are committed and emotions are too entangled to even hear God. Since God has established and knows the plan for your life, don't you think it would be critically important that you seek Him first? Safeguarding your life and your heart by getting God's approval before you date, including Him in the selection process, and allowing Him to steer and navigate your love life is the only way to custom design your relationship because:

- God knows exactly what you need, even better than you know. He is a better Matchmaker than anyone. "I will make a helper who is just right for him." Gen. 2:18 NLT
- God knows exactly how to prevent you from falling into destructive relationships and weed out people who are deceptive and reveal true motives. "All the ways of a man are pure in his own eyes, but the Lord weighs the spirits (the thoughts and intents of the heart). Prov. 16:2 AMP
- God's Word serves as a GPS to the right mate! Directions to the right mate is found in Psalms 119:105. Our Relationship Manual says that God's Word is a lamp that will guide your feet. If you end up with the wrong man/woman then that means you've abandoned your relationship with the Word. Make a firm, unwavering decision to maintain a relationship with God's Word and it will help lead you into the right relationship.
- God can be trusted. You can trust God with your heart because He knows exactly where to lead it. "Trust in the LORD with all your heart, and lean not on your own understanding; in all your ways acknowledge Him, and He shall direct your paths." Proverbs 3:5-6 NKJV
- You can trust Him to fulfill your desires. God wants to give you the desires of your heart without you having to compromise or settle. All you have to do is delight yourself in Him. "Delight

yourself also in the Lord, and He will give you the desires and secret petitions of your heart." Ps. 37:4 AMP

Wait! Did you read that? God just showed you how to get the love of your life! The man/woman of your dreams! The mate you desire! All you have to do is delight yourself in Him? And even the secret petitions of your heart, the desires that you have not even revealed, that are hidden in your heart…God will give that to you. So go ahead, make your requests known to God and ask Him for what you want (Phil. 4:6). There are reserved rights and privileges that come with having a relationship with the Lord. You can ask God for something and just because of your covenant relationship with Him, He can grant it.

- "But if you remain in me and my words remain in you, you may ask for anything you want, and it will be granted!" John 15:7 NLT
- "Seek the Kingdom of God above all else, and live righteously, and He will give you everything you need." Matt. 6:33 NLT

God doesn't operate according to statistics, ratios, or odds; He is not moved and does not give a doodly-squat about statistics! While others are fretting and jumping into relationships and settling because of the fear of being alone, biological clock is ticking, a lack of suitable and qualified mates, you can rest, knowing that God is not moved or worried about any of those things because He has everything under control when He's pre-planned your life and already tailor-made someone for you for your choosing. God is wise, with infinite ways and endless possibilities to bring someone in your life. Want me to prove it?

"Ruth *happened* to stop at the part of the field belonging to Boaz." (Amp)

Oh, she just happened to stop in the 'office' of the wealthiest single man in town, hunh? No, it wasn't happen stance; God led her to him. (Ruth 2:3) Adam woke up from a nap, and out of nowhere, there was Eve! He probably thought he was still dreaming! He wasn't dreaming; God brought Eve to him! (Genesis 2:21-22) Isaac took a stroll out in the park one evening, sat on a park bench and started praying. As he was coming out of prayer, he looked up and behold, there was Rebekah and her little Chihuahua coming…well, it was her and her camels, but you know what I'm saying! (Genesis 24:63) I'm telling you that you don't have to sit around trying to figure out how it's going to happen with the limitations of the human brain; with just one of God's thoughts, He can make it happen! Whatever God ordains you can be assured that it will come to pass! All I have to say is watch out, the camels are coming!

- Just as the heavens are higher than the earth, so my ways are higher than your ways, and my thoughts are higher than your thoughts. "Rain and snow fall from the sky and don't return until they have watered the ground. Then the ground causes the plants to sprout and grow, and they produce seeds for the farmer and food for people to eat. In the same way, my words leave my mouth, and they don't come back without results. My words make the things happen that I want to happen. They succeed in doing what I send them to do. Is. 55:9-11 ERV

While others are running around confused about the relationships they are in and not knowing how to determine if the person is right for them, asking, "How will I know if they are the one for me?" You're at rest and you will know if you're with the right person because your relationship with God provides peace as an indicator that you're in His will, wisdom, and an open-line of communication where there are no dropped calls, where God speaks to you and reveals His purpose and plan for your life.

- ❖ "Then you will experience God's peace, which exceeds anything we can understand. His peace will guard your hearts and minds as you live in Christ Jesus." Phil 4:7 NLT
- ❖ My sheep listen to my voice; I know them and they follow me." John 10:27 NLT

I love Psalms 32:8! God says, "I will instruct you and teach you in the way that you should go and I will guide you with my eye." You do not have to worry about finding the right person because God will lead you exactly to the person who fits, adapts and is custom-made for you with His eye. In order for God to lead you with His eye, then that means that you need to be looking directly at Him. Eye contact with God denotes that you must be face-to-face with Him. As you prepare to have someone special, tailor-made to come into your life, the most important thing you must do is maintain a daily, intimate relationship with the Lord and He will guide you to the right person.♥

Prayer: Dear Father God, my heart beats in adoration knowing that You thought of me and had a plan for my life even before I was in my mother's womb and long before the foundation of the world! I trust Your plan for my life and I surrender to it. I put my trust in You knowing that You have tailor-made and custom designed someone to fit my life that fits in that plan. I will not settle or get restless and settle for mediocre or substandard relationships or consume my life with temporary relationships while I await the one You have tailor-made for me. I will seek You before entering a relationship because You know the timeline of my life and the season for me to pursue a relationship. I will delight myself in You, maintaining a daily, intimate relationship with You, my Lord. I love You with all my heart and it is an honor and a privilege to have You write and design my love story.

What is your idea of a custom, tailor-made relationship? _____

Why is it important to have purpose dictating your relationship? _____

Have you ever tried to force or settle for a substandard relationship? What was the result? _____

If you are currently in a relationship, measure your relationship as if it were a garment. What size would it be? Too small, perfect fit, or too big? Explain. _____

How can using your time to maintain temporary relationships hinder or affect you and future relationships?
_____

Read Genesis 24:57-58. What does this text tell us about the ability to choose concerning relationships?
_____

Discuss with a group/friend your idea or misconceptions associated with the idea of one soul mate and God choosing your mate for you. Share your thoughts here:
_____

Why is it important to include God in the selection process of a mate? In what ways can you include Him?
_____

How can you delight yourself in the Lord? _____

Chapter 9
Seamstress

When I travel to speak, I often ask singles, "By show of hands, how many of you have an accountability partner?" Unfortunately, it's typical that only about twenty percent will raise their hands. Sadly, many people don't realize the importance of having an accountability partner. If you look at the word accountable as it relates to dating, it does sound a little uninviting and burdensome. When some people think of accountability, they picture Aunt Bunny chaperoning over them while they're on a date, hovering, watching over their every move. I promise you, having real accountability in your life is nothing like that. In fact, it actually is a great advantage and will prove to be a blessing to your life. Accountability is not having someone policing your life but more like someone helping you design and improve your life. I look at an accountability partner basically like a Seamstress; someone who will come alongside you and assist you in designing your single and dating relationships and to help you keep your clothes on while you're single.

All too often, many singles try to do life and relationships solo. They attempt to pursue relationships without the necessary help that will hold them accountable to God's Word, to sexual purity, in keeping safe boundaries in their relationships, helping them to determine suitable partners, and to grow and nurture healthy relationships. Accountability is fundamentally necessary and should help you with:

a) Guidance
b) Reality and Objectivity
c) Responsibility
d) Wise counsel
e) Challenge you
f) Encourage you

Where no wise guidance is, the people fall, but in the multitude of counselors there is safety.
Proverbs 11:14 NKJV

"Without good direction, people lose their way; the more wise counsel you follow, the better your chances. Proverbs 11:14 MSG

"Refuse good advice and watch your plans fail; take good counsel and watch them succeed."
Proverbs 15:22 MSG

> Fools think their own way is right, but the wise listen to others. Proverbs 12:15 NLT

One of the reasons why many singles fail in relationships and fall sexually is because they do not have wise guidance. Accountability, in essence, is protection and safety. Accountability is the best liability insurance you can have to protect you from you! When your emotions and your brain are on romantic vacation, you need someone to be there in your absence. You need someone to "see" reality while your eyes are clouded by "love." You need someone to decipher between your emotions and what's real. In the beginning stages, everything is wonderful and you overlook all of his flaws because you're in love, you're in love, you're in love! You need someone to be objective and rational because you're under the influence of your emotions. When you're under the influence, you make allowances for some things you would never sanction or authorize. Accountability is giving someone who you trust to sign off and approve your decisions "while you're away" from the mind of rational thinking.

> "He who willfully separates *and* estranges himself [from God and man] seeks his own desire *and* pretext to break out against all wise *and* sound judgment. Proverbs 18:1 AMP

When someone refuses to place accountability in their life or think that they don't need accountability, it sounds an alarm, signifying that the person is unteachable, unguarded and led by emotions alone, or they know deep within that the relationship is wrong and don't want others to know. If you have to hide the relationship, keep it a secret or private from others than the relationship is not healthy or right for you. If you are defiant, ignore or can't heed to the sound advice of others around you, then you are headed for destruction. "But you don't know him (her) like I do," is the echo of many singles who found themselves in severely broken relationships. If you are not submitted to authority in your life, then you will find it difficult to submit to one another in a relationship or even in marriage later. Submission is a key component of marriage and if you are not submitting to accountability and governed by the influence of authority while you're single, then it will be problematic in marriage. Both you and your dating partner should have accountability in your life that you are submitting to, allowing them to pour into your life, while they challenge you to become your best in Christ and in your relationships.

> And let us consider and give attentive, continuous care to watching over one another, studying how we may stir up (stimulate and incite) to love and helpful deeds and noble activities, Not forsaking or neglecting to assemble together [as believers], as is the habit of some people, but admonishing (warning, urging, and encouraging) one another, and all the more faithfully as you see the day approaching. Hebrews 10:24-25 (Amplified Bible)

Many singles are so accustomed to doing relationships alone, but we were never meant to do life alone. We need community and the support of family, friends, mentors, and sound counsel to help us throughout life. When you refuse wise counsel or fail to appoint a community of believers to assist you in designing relationships, you increase your chances at failing in those relationships. When you have a support of community, you have a greater opportunity at succeeding in a successful, healthy relationship. I have comprised eight ways on how you can choose accountability, in which you can begin building a great support of community to help you.

1. Choose someone you trust, where you can be open and honest about your relationship, even the flaws, mistakes, fears, disappointments, accomplishments, and the progression of the relationship. When you're feeling weak, vulnerable, tempted, confused, or need relational guidance, you need a Seamstress you can trust.
2. Choose someone who will tell you the truth. You need to be accountable to someone that can tell you actually like it is, who will be unbiased! You need someone that will not sugarcoat or pacify your feelings or your wrongdoings and tell you what you want to hear, but what you need to hear.
3. Your accountability partner should be someone who genuinely cares about you and will speak the truth in love, yet tell you the hard things that your heart and emotions don't want to hear.
4. Choose and call on the help of friends also. In addition to my male mentors, I also have friends and my sisters who I can trust to provide me with sound wisdom and advice and that will check you when you're wrong. You need friends that can help you with your challenges, one that you can call up and say, "I'm vulnerable at night. If I don't answer your call, do a drive-by. Come get me! Rescue me!" If you're going to date, you need to have accountability that will put you on the witness stand and question your motives, keep you responsible, and slap some sense in you when you need it! And you need to also be that to your friends; if your friend comes to you and tell you about a steamy night they had on a date, don't sit there engaged; slap them! They will thank you later.
5. Choose accountability of the same sex. To protect yourself and interpersonal relationships from temptation, you need to have someone that is the same gender. You pose a threat when you become vulnerable and open to the opposite sex when you attempt to make them your prayer or accountability partner. An exception to this rule can be applied if the mentor for example is older and mature and serves as a genuine brother or mentor to a woman. Let me explain. I find that another man (mentor, brother in the Lord, father, spiritual father) is often best at discerning another man's character and motives. I have my spiritual dad, Dr. Myles Munroe, and my brothers in the Lord to give me advice about relationships with men. In addition, I have them as accountability and counsel on stand-by to meet any man that wants to share in my life. My papa Myles says

in his Bahamian accent to me, "Daughter, if a man wants to marry you, bring him to me!" I'm particularly placing emphasis on women having Godly men/mentors in their life because they see what women don't often see, or should I say, too clouded by love to see. Men look with a different eye instead of looking through the lens of emotions like women so often do. So the exception can only be applied under those terms.

6. Choose someone who will actually keep you accountable. I know she is your best friend but if she's struggling and barely holding on to her clothes, how in the world can she help you? You need to be accountable to someone who is not sexually struggling and living a life of integrity. Also someone who has demonstrated healthy, committed relationships. Don't choose people who are struggling or do not have accountability themselves.

7. Choose someone with wisdom, sound judgment, people you respect, and Godly men or women with wisdom. If you don't have a father, find a role model or father figure that will hold you accountable to God and His word.

8. Choose someone who is available. You need to have someone who will listen to you, answer your calls when you desperately need them and to be there to lend support and guidance should the relationship end.

Why is it important to have accountability? _____
_____

Who in your life can you trust to hold you accountable? Does your dating partner have accountability?
_____

In what circumstances or issues might you call on your accountability partner for? _____
_____

The 10 Commandments Of **DATING**

---

1 Thou shalt have no other gods before Me. Do not make your companion a god or put them before God. God must be your First Love. Love the Lord your God with ALL your heart, mind, and soul, and keep Him number one.

2 Thou shalt not make your relationship an idol. Thou shalt not bow down or worship a relationship, a companion, nor idolize or have an inordinate desire to be married. If finding someone or your current relationship is more important than building or cultivating your relationship with God, then your relationship has become an idol. If your single life is not predominately focused on how you can serve and please the Lord, and it is consumed more with dating or using dating to fulfill you, then it has become an idol.

3 Thou shalt not take the Lord's name in vain and tell a person that God said you're my spouse and manipulate a person into a relationship with you or use God's name in vain by breaking up with someone and saying, "God told me to break up with you."

4 Keep the Sabbath day/Saturday holy. Don't use your weekends to squander your single life and to wile out. It is good to rest from your labor and have a social life but make sure your dating or social life is marked with holiness.

5 Honor thy Father and thy Mother. Honor your Father God in your relationship and also honor your father and mother by including family and spiritual leaders in your dating decisions.

6 Thou shalt not kill or murder relationships with constant dating, mating and breaking up.

7 Thou shalt not commit adultery by having sex with someone you're not married to. Having sex with your date is adultery because they do not belong to you. Be faithful to your future spouse before you ever meet them.

8 Thou shalt not steal a person's heart or body. Your body, nor does your date's body, belong to you; your body (and theirs) belongs to the Lord. To have sex with your date is stealing from the Lord. Transient/temporary dating, leading a person on or playing with a person's heart is also theft.

9 Thou shalt not bare false witness against your date, discredit them, run your date's name in the gutter, or talk about them negatively after a break up. Take responsibility in your part in the termination/dissolution or failure of a relationship and always respect a person even if the relationship doesn't last.

10 Thou shat not covet thy neighbor's relationship. Don't covet marriage so badly that you that you'll do anything or be with anyone to have it. Be content where the Lord has you while celebrating your neighbor's blessings. You can be happy for them when you trust God's plans for your life.

Chapter 10
How To Get The One

Years ago, before I entered into full-time ministry and began my speaking and writing career, I, surprisingly, yes, Ty Adams worked in real estate. I know, shocking, right?! I learned quite a bit during my tenure there and I carry a lot of memories from my experiences. One of things that stick out as I chronicle through my memory bank is the zealous and anxious clients who wanted to sale their home. I do a quiet laughter in my head when I think of how some homeowners would get eager to sell their home, forgo a realtor and an appraiser and do a "do-it-yourselfer". They think it's easy as 1-2-3, put a store-bought "for sale" sign on the front lawn and kahboom! The house will sell faster than the ink will dry on the purchase agreement! But after months of sitting on the market and no buyer in site, the homeowner gets frustrated at no bites, no showings, no calls, no nothing!

Because of their own personal value they hold with the house and their emotional attachment and sentiment to it, they feel that someone else will drive-by and feel the same way and buy it. But after doing my own drive-by and I get out and do a site survey, I don't have that same warm, gushy connection and I find that in comparison to the other homes in the neighborhood that are selling, theirs fall far below and pale in size and comparison. In my sincerest, kindest, most humblest tones, I would turn and say to the eager and frustrated seller, the same advice I want to offer those of you who are on the market for love, "Pull off the market, get an appraisal, take inventory, go under construction and then upgrade."

You're thinking, 'I'm nice-looking, I've got it going on," but so are the other *homes on the block*. I know, you're very attractive and cute, but curbside appeal along won't get it. You're self-biased, and like the homeowner, you think that someone else is going to drive by and feel the same way, but often times, we have not conducted a true assessment or appraisal of who we truly are and what we have to offer. (Don't feel bad; we've all, even I, have thought we're the cat's meow and have thought more highly of ourselves than we ought to.)* Many singles that come to me for counsel are like some of the homes I've entered. Once I get inside past the beautiful landscaping, the inside has a lot of wear and tear, needs work and a little fixing up. After I get past their cute faces, and they sit down on the couch, I see past the smile landscaped on their faces and I see inside the wear and tear on their heart, broken emotions and the damage on their spirit. I often see many singles who have not taken a deep look within and don't realize that there needs to be some cleaning up and reconstruction before they attempt to put themselves on the market for a relationship. They're frustrated, confused and often envious when they see their friends around the block are finding a mate or marriage, "but why haven't I found someone?"

Many people have this grand idea of the person they would like to be with but the bigger question is, are you what your future mate is looking for? Is what you're looking for, looking for you? Often times what people are looking for in a relationship, they themselves have not yet become; so they inadvertently end up attracting what they don't want. You want someone spiritually sound, but you lack spiritual maturity. You want someone who is emotionally available but your last three relationships you've been in looks like an emotional roller coaster. If you don't like what you're attracting, then you need to change what's in you because whatever is in you is what you will ultimately attract. Simply put, you are your relationships.

"GOD put the man into a deep sleep. As he slept he removed one of his ribs and replaced it with flesh. **GOD then used the rib that he had taken from the Man to make Woman and presented her to the Man.**" Genesis 2:21-22 MSG

God basically gave Adam what he was. He took from what was in Adam and made his wife *from that*. Eve was simply Adam. I'll let that sink in for a moment… If you ever want to get the "one," you must become the one. Many people are busy searching for the "one" instead of becoming what you want by metamorphosing into the best version of yourself; by this, you will virtually attract God's best like a magnet!

You're done with that old life. It's like a filthy set of ill-fitting clothes you've stripped off and put in the fire. Now you're dressed in a new wardrobe. Every item of your new way of life is custom-made by the Creator, with his label on it. All the old fashions are now obsolete. Colossians 3:9-10 MSG

Designed by God

Becoming the best version of yourself begins with a life designed by God. How will we do this? We will "pull off the market, get an appraisal, take inventory, go under construction, and then upgrade." I know, many people don't like the step but as I indicated before, it's a necessary process in getting a healthy, successful and lasting relationship because you can't market yourself and reconstruct at the same time. You must pull away from dating because if you're on the "market" and suitable "buyers" come, they will simply pass you up and keep going when they realize that cosmetically, the outside looks good, but the inside and the foundation are not. All too often, I've seen homeowners having to result in what many singles have had to succumb to: a short sale; getting far less than what they desired. Until you determine or do an appraised value of where you currently are, you will put yourself on the market for a relationship prematurely and you will "short" yourself in substandard relationships. If you forgo this process, you'll find it difficult to establish and sustain a healthy and long-lasting relationship. So you must pull off the market, reconstruct, renovate your life and become the best you through Christ, thereby increasing your value and positioning yourself for a high-quality pursuant. For some, this process may be a short time but for some it may be longer for others once you see how you fare and how much reconstruction is needed. But once you complete this process, you will look back at yourself and love what you have become. So take the "for sale" sign off the lawn and replace it with a "Pardon our dust, we're under construction, remodeling" sign.

We will move forward by taking inventory of who you are and from this we will begin to create the love relationship you desire, simply by becoming the best you! We then put the control in your hands as to who you enter into a relationship with by becoming what you want and what you are asking for. After you have completed this list compare your list of who you are to what you desire in a relationship to determine if they match. See these chapters as well to help you navigate this process: Single, Baggage, and Shopping List.

Inventory of You:

Define who you are in a few sentences. What is it like being you? Describe your personality. What you list here will be what you draw and attract in relationships, so be honest about who you are. Don't worry, if you are not happy with your current state, we can always change that and become a better you:

_____
_____
_____

What is most important in your life? _____

_____

What makes you unique and distinct from others? _____

_____

What do you like most about you? _____

_____

List your current state and consistent patterns in each of the following. Place a rating between 1 and 5 next to each area assessing the strength of these areas, with 5 being the highest rating.

Mentally _____

Emotionally _____

Spiritually _____

Physically _____

Economically _____

Socially _____

What areas do you feel you struggle with _____
_____
_____

Interview 10 associates, family, and friends that you trust to be honest and sincere. Then ask them what they believe to be your 5 areas of strength and then ask what do they believe are 3 areas you can grow in. There are always areas of growth in each of us and there may also be habits, character flaws, personality quirks or behavior that you may not be aware of that is getting in the way or hindering your personal and perhaps even your professional life from skyrocketing to new heights.

5 areas of strengths
_____, _____, _____, _____, _____

3 things they think you should change/improve or areas of weakness

_____, _____, _____

How did you develop theses weaknesses _____
_____

Were these areas that you've already recognized or does this come to a surprise to you about what they have assessed about you? _____

Describe your relationship with God. In what areas would you like to improve your spiritual life or your personal relationship with God?
_____
_____

What are some small, consistent steps you can make towards that? _____
_____
_____

What big steps can you make towards that? _____

What have I learned about myself that may be keeping me stuck or stunting my growth? _____

What are your greatest desires? What are you doing to fulfill that? _____

What do you think you have to bring or offer in a relationship? _____

In what ways are you becoming ready for a relationship? _____

What would you like to change from this inventory list? _____

Romans 12:3*

How To Prepare for A Relationship/Marriage
Without Dating

- Join a singles ministry at your church. If you don't have one at your church, find a singles ministry in your town and connect with it. Develop friendships with a host of other singles that are dedicated to the Lord.

- Actively serve in your local church or community and go on missions trips.

- Develop friendships with successful married couples that will serve as role models.

- Baby-sit for married couples or volunteer in the children's ministry at your church and the children's hospital.

- Find your God-given purpose and develop your career.

- Submit under leadership and mentors.

- Adopt/sponsor a family that is less fortunate than you.

- Take a cooking class and a communications course.

- Meet with a financial advisor or take a financial or budgeting course.

- Buy resources on building effective relationships and take workshops on marriage.

- Maintain a healthy diet and a regular workout regime.

- Work on a broken relationship with a family member or friend to learn conflict resolution.

- Establish a healthy social life with friends. Join a club or take on your favorite hobbies.

- Visit a counselor or therapist to work on any unresolved emotional wounds.

- Develop and maintain a fervent relationship with the Lord. Maintain a personal, daily devotional with God. Spend time daily in prayer and in the Word of God.

Chapter 10
Shopping List

It's a known fact that if you go into the store to shop without a list, you're prone to buy things that you don't need. You end up with a cart full of stuff that you don't even want. When you have your list of must-need items, there's no need to go down unnecessary aisle or wait in long lines; you're able to grab those items that you need and jump right in the 10 Items Or Less line and get on about your merry way! It's the same with dating, when you have your must-have needs already aligned before you start dating, you prevent random or junk-food relationships. You're able to forgo relationships early on that do not fit or meet your list. When you already know what you want, you can avoid unnecessary relationships or going down the aisle to the altar with someone that doesn't match your list. Having your list allows you to make calculated, predetermined choices when dating. Having your list, knowing what you want before you shop for a relationship helps to prevent impulse shopping or allowing your emotions to make the decision. With that said, you need to make a list of the things you desire in a mate. When you know what you want in a relationship, you forgo temporal, aimless relationships and avoid falling into relationships that allure you out of infatuation, mere physical attraction, loneliness, or boredom.

The important thing about your list is not simply having one, but knowing what you want and what's most important. It's not being meticulous with a list of 101 things that he/she must have, but ensuring that you have a focused outlook and a foundation for a potential mate. It protects you from settling but keeps you from spreading yourself thin by wasting time with someone who is not conducive to your life and where you're going.

Ok, let's create your shopping list! Clearly define and list the top 10 things you desire in a mate. If rich, tall and fine lands on the top of your list, then that probably explains why you're still single. Qualities like God-fearing, leadership, honesty, and caring should dominate your list. Let's begin:

1. 2.

3. 4.

5. 6.

7. 8.

9.   10.

After you have created your top 10, go back over the list and ask yourself why you choose to put those qualities on your list. Ensure that you go over your list adding details in your Dating Vision. It's not enough to simply put: I want a Christian. That comes in variable degrees and if you don't clearly define it, you'll simply end up with someone who is "just" a Christian.

I know that we can sometimes get carried away with our "list" so you need to also balance your list because your "Mr. or Miss Perfect" will not have everything on your list. With that said, you need to shape and balance your list by distinguishing it with these categories:

Must Haves	Wants & Desires	Non-Negotiable/deal breakers
_____	_____	_____
_____	_____	_____
_____	_____	_____
_____	_____	_____
_____	_____	_____

I can help you by starting off your non-negotiable list: an unbeliever, physical abuse, emotional abuse, spiritual abuse, disrespect, addiction, dishonesty, and rage; there are some things that are intolerable and these are some of them. While developing your shopping list, know that there are certain things that will be non-negotiable but be open to things that are not necessarily on your list; you could be passing up someone great simply because they don't match it. Leave some room in the middle, like your wants and desires and perhaps leave a line or two blank for God to finish filling in; He may add to your list with something you thought could never be possible. (Ephesians 3:20)♥

Chapter 11
Online Shopping

I have dived into online shopping plenty of times; pretty easy, right? But there have been quite a few times where I've clicked on "Add to Cart" and when it arrived to my house it looked nothing like what I saw on my computer screen! That's just how Internet dating can be. You notice on the "about" page of his Facebook profile that his religious belief indicates that he is a Christian. So you think it's pretty simple, right? You click the "Add Friend" button and his wall reveals a bootleg demon trying to hijack Christianity!

Shortly after the Internet dating craze took off, I was asked to write a column for an online dating site and at first I was reluctant so I was going to decline their request until I logged onto the site and saw the profiles of some of its members and almost took off my shoe and threw it at my screen! With some of the profiles I saw, I wanted to do an Internet arrest and prohibit some of these poptarts from ever being able to do online dating! I'm screaming in my head, "Ladies, don't you clearly see that these buffoons are not men of character and integrity?!" I know, you're probably thinking, "That's to be expected in some of these secular dating sites," but no, my sweet muffins, this was a Christian dating site! Am I saying that Internet dating is of the devil? Absolutely not!

Some people have a misconception that out of 7 billion people in the world, there's only one soul mate out there in the world for them and God's *gonna* send him to your door, ring the doorbell, get down on one knee and say, "Hi, I'm your husband; will you marry me?" Oftentimes people will "over-spiritualize" and think that the Scripture, "he that finds a wife," means that he'll show up out of the blue because God is going to do all the matchmaking work in finding a mate or that love can only be found sitting in the pew or the four walls of your church. God is much more creative than that! Look at earth's skyline and landscape; don't limit God and yourself when it comes to finding someone. If God has someone on the other side of the world for you, then He has a way of getting them to you. It could be on your company's group Internet conference call or a spark through a comment on your blog. Yet at the same time, don't run online today thinking you're going to find Mr. or Mrs. Right. What I'm saying is that love can be found online but if you think that it'll be easy to Shift key yourself into a relationship, then you may find yourself stuck in a "caps lock" situation!

Social networking in many aspects is good but has a great portion of society on social overload where we have more online friends than our own personal phone contacts! We're more social than ever but still don't understand how human relationships function properly and lack effective communication skills that online interaction has created. We've simply transferred our dysfunction with actual human contact to engaging in improper online relationships; we've hit the shift key and just relocated our poor dating habits to a dot com. We vomit every detail of our lives in a hundred and sixty characters, backspace into "complicated relationships," and scroll into Facebook promiscuity where you throw yourself emotionally on a profile wall and become Internet entangled with every stranger you meet on the other side of the screen.

Again, in and of itself, there is nothing wrong with social networking or online dating, but it has more to do with how we approach and engage in it. Here is my sincere thought about online dating: it's a thin line! I'm sorry, but it's already difficult and has its own share of challenges to even date someone that you can physically see; how much greater through a 17- inch monitor? I'm afraid that many people, not all, but many are resorting to online dating as escapism from either loneliness or lack of suitable mates, while many use it to deceive unsuspecting, innocent relationship seekers. Others opt for online dating because of the hardships of maintaining relationships in the physical so they take on relationships that have them fantasizing with romantic words. You cannot allow your frustration or desperation to run you to an empty e-mail love affair, you must have a healthy pursuit of relationships, whether online or offline. The Internet has provided the world with a great advantage of connecting and meeting people worldwide that would have not otherwise connected with or would have ever met. With that said, meaningful relationships can and have originated from it but we must use wisdom and precaution. A good ole Google search wouldn't be bad to start with.

Firewall
Just like a physical relationship, you must protect yourself from a virus with online relationships. I don't know if you've ever had a virus infect your computer but it attempts to destroy everything and block you from accessing your own system! If you are going to pursue or entertain any online relationship, you must prevent anyone from downloading a virus in your life! Many people exaggerate online; I'm sorry, let me use the correct word: they lie! Yes, there are many people who make deceptive profiles, upload misrepresented photos, post vague background info, one-fourth of people who do online dating are married, and even worse, there are many reports of online dating that turned fatal and sadly, people have been killed from online dating. You must have firewall protection: a system set in place to prevent unauthorized access in your life. I highly recommend first that you have the Holy Spirit as a firewall to block people who will contaminate your life and use some *common* sense and plain old intuition. This will allow you to have the ability to discern whether someone should be allowed to pursue you by revealing a person's intent, motives, integrity and character. You must also protect your personal information, such as social security number, credit card info, or and even your home address by not even allowing someone to send flowers or gifts until you've established enough credibility.

If your online date leads to an actual date, meet in public and let someone know where you're going and who you're meeting. If your online connection becomes serious, then your interest won't mind sending a copy of their current credit report, a background check for any criminal history, HIV test results, their mother's information, job history, an authentic current photo, verifiable marital status…you get what I'm saying? Total honesty and openness is the only way that it can work, and hint of ambiguity and dishonesty is unacceptable! But make sure that you are not divulging personal information too early to a stranger. Allow the relationship to develop before you begin divulging your personal information. There should be a slow progression as you relinquish information given time for their credibility and authenticity to prove itself.

Ctrl-Alt-Del
There are many times that I have seen couples continue in a relationship when there are clear signs that you should shut it down. Known as the three-finger salute, the Control-Alt-Delete is your computer's command to reboot or interrupt a malfunctioning program. Should your online date show any signs of malfunction, give the relationship the three-finger salute! Here are some online flags to look for:

- Your online date completely lied about the other relationship they've been in or failed to tell you they're separated or married.
- He/she only wants to keep the relationship online instead of calling you.
- He/she sent you naked pictures in your inbox.
- You found a completely different profile of him/her on another dating site.
- Every time you have dialogue, he/she wants to talk about sex.
- Their profile indicates that they are a Christian, but there's derogatory photos and language on their profile.
- He says he's found the perfect girl, he's in love and it's only been 8 days since you began your online connection.
- He/she asks you to send him money so that he can keep his Internet service on in order to keep this great online relationship you two have going.
- Everything seems to be secretive and you just can't put your finger on it, but something doesn't seem right.
- You feel as if your online date has stalker-like signs and you feel uncomfortable or threatened.

I had a young lady ask me to counsel her along her journey in an online relationship with a Christian man. As their relationship progressed from passive e-mails to a serious long-distance relationship, I recommended that she not only get proof of his personal information, but a recommendation from his pastor and his other close confidants. He flew in to her city to meet her family and he also had a private meeting with her pastor. Their online meeting culminated into a successful marriage, but before you get your hopes up too high, not all online romances end up that way. I also have far more horror stories from Christian women and men who dated other Christians and even pastors online that ended up being their worst nightmare! *Don't download a virus into your heart.* Be cautious, selective, wise and led by God and allow Him to be your 'firewall' of protection.

What are your thoughts about online dating? _____

What obstacles or challenges have you faced with online dating? _____

Are there some areas that you can adjust in how you operate online? _____

If you use social networking, does your profile exemplify Christian values/principles? _____

If you currently use social networking, what can you do or what changes can you make to ensure that how you engage in online friendships/relationships are appropriate and safe?

_____
_____

Chapter 12
Dressed To Kill

There are many strong, God-fearing men whose desire and intent is to live in integrity, uprightness, decency and to be sexually pure but are taken down, weakened and destroyed by Bible-carrying women. The weapon: their body. There are women who will show up to church or a dinner date in a tight-fitting skirt plastered on her, with the hem high above the knees and a see-through blouse exposing so much cleavage you can sit a dinner plate on it. Ladies, it may be your favorite lil' outfit but when you put your body parts on display like an open buffet, it serves as an unspoken invitation to a taste test. What may seem harmless to you could be, in great contrast, a sexual ploy, a mental battle or a snare for him. Men are naturally wired with a heightened sexual response than women because men have twenty times more testosterone swimming through their bodies, provoking sexual arousal even without his prompting. God made him different from a woman, supplying him with a heightened visual sense to incite him to action, "God then used the rib that he had taken from the man to make woman and presented her to the man. The man said, 'Finally...a woman!'"[1] His capacity for sexual arousal through his eyes can motivate him to action, causing his thoughts to send his imagination and hands where his heart didn't intend to go. Because his sexual language is driven by physical instinct and he responds strongly to visual stimuli, his eyes need to be protected and guarded. Yes, he has a personal responsibility to purity and to guard himself, but women also have a role in helping to protect him.

"I made a solemn pact with myself never to undress a girl with my eyes." Job 31:1 MSG

It is perpetuated in society that women need to use their body to capture a man's interest that it is subconsciously embedded in the minds of many women so much that it dictates their wardrobe choices. God did a perfect job in masterfully designing a woman's body uniquely and distinctively with curves and He does not need any 'extra' help with you buying clothes to over accentuate that design. You can be stylish and attractive without being provocative and you can get a man's interest without sexually seducing him through your clothing. What text message are you sending to his mind with your conversation, your conduct or the way you dress? Again, while he does have a personal obligation to self-control, you also have a responsibility, as a woman of God, to help him live in sexual integrity and one way that you can help is by not allowing your body to unnecessarily provoke a sexual distraction and temptation for him. You want to attract, not distract; don't divert his attention from the important thing: you! If you draw him sexually, you'll sidetrack his interest from getting to know the great woman that you are. If you want to keep his interest, leave him wondering. God brought you out of darkness[2] so it is beneath you to dress like a "woman of the night."

> @TyAdamsTV: Dear Single Woman, Cleavage doesn't make a man cleave, but get the goods, then leave. When you advertise your body parts you sale yourself cheap. If you want to attract a great man, button up! Leave him wondering; keep Victoria a secret!

No one who treasures their valuables will leave them lying around or on display. A true gentleman respects, appreciates, and is drawn to a woman that values herself so much so that she conceals her valuables. If you are a woman of God, if you say you are pure, then dress like it: dress what you confess! Take a look through your closet, does your clothes convey that you are a woman of God and you live sexually pure? Beyond the label or the brand of your clothes, it should say, "Jesus is my style!" Your style should reflect the very essence of who you are: your principles, values and beliefs. Your clothing should speak for you; as to the kind of woman you are without you saying a word. You want to know how to attract a man? I love God because He even placed in our *Relationship Manual* how a woman can attract a man: "For women who claim to be devoted to God should ***make themselves attractive by the good things they do***."[3] It is befitting for women that profess reverential fear and devotion to God, to not draw a man sexually by the seductive clothing they wear, but by good deeds like kindness, gracious behavior, and service. Your good deeds will radiate beauty from you and will attract the right man to you!

> "Also [I desire] that women should adorn themselves modestly and appropriately and sensibly in seemly apparel, not with [elaborate] hair arrangement or gold or pearls or expensive clothing, But by doing good deeds (deeds in themselves good and for the good and advantage of those contacted by them), as befits women who profess reverential fear for and devotion to God." 1 Tim. 2:10 AMP

Modest: showing regard for the decencies of behavior or dress; not showy or ostentatious (making an exaggerated outward show).

> "And I want women to be modest in their appearance. They should wear decent and appropriate clothing…" 1 Tim. 2:9 NLT

Modest is Hottest! Many women have it backwards: instead of dressing modest, they find the hottest dress they can buy! It is disheartening that many women, in desperation to get a man, feel they have to use their body parts to attract him by wearing clothing that will allure him. I used to be like that; if the dress wasn't short and tight and the blouse didn't expose cleavage, then I wouldn't wear it. When I would get the interest of a man I still didn't have his attention because he wouldn't make eye contact with me because he was face-to-face with my chest, having a conversation with *it* the whole time we're talking. But what was I to expect?! When you dress as if you're trying out to be a back up dancer in a raunchy music video or in the attire of a prostitute *then you get "johns" who camouflage themselves as boyfriends.* You may get his attention, but it'll be short-lived. Many women use their body to attract a man, then get upset when she realizes that's all he wants from her is sex; but if it's not for sale, then don't advertise it. If you dress like a *garden tool*, you'll only attract snakes.

There are many women that use seductive dressing to get a man's attention and to draw him to them are esteem-deficient and have a scarce supply of self-worth. Women who dress revealing their body parts are most often trying to compensate for something lacking on the inside and do not believe what she has is good enough to get a man without having to give up her body. But if you would work on developing the inside, cultivating modesty and making it become the make-up of who you are, you will become a magnet that attracts the kind of man that is faithful, genuine, upright, respectful and one that knows how to honor a woman of God. You need to have more than just a beautiful face; cultivate your relationship with God, working on inner qualities that will cause your outside to glow. Your inner beauty should always outshine your outward beauty. (1 Peter 3:3, 4)

Love the skin you're in! Cosmetic surgery, Botox, tummy tuck, breast enhancements…are you engrossed with altering your look in attempts to run from who you are? No matter how short or tall you are, the shape of your nose, the length of your hair or the shade of your skin, God made you perfect, even with your imperfections. While there is nothing wrong with enhancing your look, you must fall in love with who God made you. God does not make junk; in fact He made you in His image and so everything about you is already perfect! You just have to grow to love your uniqueness and the great qualities about you and know that you are loved just the way you are! Psalms 139

Beautiiiiful! There is nothing wrong with being beautiful! God Himself is even into beauty; I mean look at the landscape of the universe. And who makes streets out of gold? The very fact that God made us in His image let's you know that He's into beautiful things. Look at few of these attractive people noted in the Bible: cause
    a) Rachel had a lovely figure and was beautiful (Gen. 29:17)
    b) Joseph was well-built and handsome (Gen. 39:6)
    c) Esther had a lovely figure and was beautiful (Esther 2:7)
    d) Queen Vashti was beautiful and lovely to look at (Esther 1:11)

- e) Absalom was very handsome! In fact the Bible says that there was not a man so highly praised for his handsome appearance and from the top of his head, to the soles of his feet, there was no blemish in him! (2 Sam. 14:25 NIV, 1 Sam. 17:42)
- f) Bathsheba was so beautiful that it captivated the very handsome King David, so much so that he committed adultery and murder to have her! (2 Sam. 11)
- g) Abigail was both beautiful and intelligent (1 Sam. 25:3)

Okay, we get that; you're beautiful! But are you so caught up in your looks that you forget to develop inward beauty? Are you trying to attract and impress people with your looks more than your internal beauty? There is nothing wrong with being beautiful but if you are building relationships on outward beauty, the relationship will not last. Outward beauty fades, *assets* will someday sag, and beautiful skin will wrinkle and lose its elasticity but inward beauty never fades. (Proverbs 31:30) Your internal beauty should be more attractive than the external.

"Let not yours be the [merely] external adorning with [elaborate] interweaving and knotting of the hair, the wearing of jewelry, or changes of clothes; But let it be the inward adorning and beauty of the hidden person of the heart, with the incorruptible and unfading charm of a gentle and peaceful spirit, which [is not anxious or wrought up, but] is very precious in the sight of God." I Pet. 3:3-4 AMP

Dress to Impress! While placing too much emphasis on the outer beauty is vanity, acting as if it doesn't matter, is not cute either. You should take pride in your image: styling your hair, updating your wardrobe, and taking the time out to look good on a date should be essential to developing and maintaining a good image as well. When Naomi wanted to find Ruth a husband that would take good care of her, where she would be well provided for, she told her to go and prepare to meet Boaz, "Now do as I tell you—take a bath and put on perfume and dress in your nicest clothes." (Ruth 3:3 NLT) She wasn't going to find a good, prosperous man with her hair tied up in a scarf, wearing a jogging suit in the produce aisle, looking like Molly the Maid just ran out the house to get a few things. Naomi told her to go and put on the best dress she had in her closet!

Ruth not only looked good on the inside[4] but also on the outside because your outside should convey or give a snapshot of who you are on the inside. My sister, image guru, Toy Banks, says, "Image is a reflection of the inside and it tells how a person thinks of themselves and it sends a message to others about you." How you look on the outside is a mirror that reflects how you are on the inside and it should make a statement that you take pride and highly esteem who you are, and that you are a woman of value and excellence and as a result you will attract that. Here are a few tips:

- Dress your age, wear clothing that are your size and are current; you might want to get rid of anything in your closet that your grandmother or a teenager would be seen in. If you have not changed your look in the last 5 years, consider donating old clothing or have a garage sale and use the money to upgrade your wardrobe. Either hire a stylist or have one of your most stylish friends accompany you on a new shopping spree.
- If you choose to wear hair extensions/weave, make sure it blends with your hair, the same texture of your hair and is refreshed often. If you color your hair, ensure that it enhances and compliments your image. Do not choose colors that will cause people to mistake you for having a career in the circus.
- Many men like women who wear make-up but not a mask. If you choose to wear make-up, make sure that it enhances you, not alter you.
- Poor hygiene is unacceptable! Fresh body and fresh breath is the standard. Clean your nails or get a manicure.
- Don't overdo the perfume! Your fragrance should be worn light, not a walking environmental hazard.
- "Exercise profits little"[5] does not mean you are excused from having a regular workout regimen. You most certainly do not need to be a size 2, but you do need to be healthy, along with a healthy diet. Outside of health issues, excessive weight is often an indicator of an undisciplined life and can affect other areas of your life. Incorporate 30 minutes of exercise at least 3-4 times per week, and be a good steward of the temple that God lives in.
- Get an inexpensive tummy tuck with shapewear and control the "jiggle!" Invest in good underclothes! Shapewear like, Spanx, will help to control the curves, give you a firm look, enhance your body shape, provide support and will give you a more definitive, attractive look.
- Wear a smile; it's a facelift that will outdo Botox any day.
- Be a lady: allow a man to open the door, pull out your chair, and pay the bill. Chew with your mouth closed, be kind, courteous and considerate; cross your legs, and keep them closed. Being a lady will never go out of style. ♥

Do you dress provocatively or subconsciously use your body to attract a man? What are the results of using this approach? _____

Describe modest apparel: _____
Take inventory of the clothes in your closet. Do your clothes reflect your beliefs? What items do you need to take out of your wardrobe that does not reflect your relationship with God?

Look in the mirror. What areas of your body have you not come to love yet? Go through each of those areas and say, "I love my *"nose!"* God made it perfect! _____
Does your outward beauty match your inward beauty? What areas can you improve?
_____

In what areas/ways can you upgrade your image? _____
_____
Why do good deeds hold the attention of a man verses sexual attention? _____
_____
What good deeds can a woman do that will attract a man? _____
_____

[1] Gen. 2:22, 23 MSG emphasis added   [2] 1 Pet. 2:9   [3] 1 Tim. 2:10 NLT   [4] Ruth 3:10, 11   [5] 1 Timothy 4:8

Chapter 13
Dating With Kids

There are approximately 13.7 million single parents in the United States according to the Center For Disease Control (CDC). Only 52 percent of American households are married couples; the rest are single, single parent household or divorced and if that's the case, there's a great chance that you're a single parent or perhaps will date a single parent with children. It is then in your best interest to consider the following:

Does your date even like kids?
Don't simply go by what your date says; you must investigate. If he/she has children, find out how they have been a parent to them. If they don't have children, are they the favorite aunt/uncle in their family? How was he/she raised and disciplined? Have they demonstrated if they will have the capacity to parent should your relationship progress? Do they respond in anger to children or discipline them appropriately? Can you envision them parenting your children? As you know, parenting is a great responsibility and requires mature adults. Hence, it makes no sense to introduce your children to a "child." If the person you are dating is not grown up and matured for a relationship or parenting, then you should not introduce your children to them. In fact, you should UN-introduce yourself to him. It's irrational, meaningless, and absolutely absurd to introduce your children or remain in a relationship with someone that's not going to be a part of your future. Refuse to date anyone that has not demonstrated that they can improve the lives of your children or be a good influence on them.

Baby Mamma Drama
If you're single and have an interest in someone that has children, you can observe their parenting skills by looking at how well-behaved their children are. Are the children respectful and polite or rude and talking back to their parent or does it seems as if every time you call your date it sounds like there's a circus in the background? Does your date complain about how she had to go up to the school because Johnny is constantly fighting and getting kicked out of school or failing in grades? And how about relationship drama? If

your date has a combative, terrorist-like relationship with the other parent then you probably want to reconsider other dating options until their issues are resolved; *unless you want to be enlisted in the war.*

Is it time?
How committed is this relationship? If you've only gone out on two dates, this is not the time to introduce them to John-John or Lil'Nay Nay; you need time to observe your dating partner before you do that. Introducing them before you have determined that this will be a long-term relationship is, quite frankly, unfair to your children. Your children do not need to meet every person you date. Only consider introducing your children when you are in a serious, committed relationship. Not only should you shield yourself from serial dating, but also your children; you need to protect them from becoming emotionally attached to "temporary daddies" or mommies. They need to know that your door is not a revolving one. They also need to understand and establish a healthy mindset concerning the importance of relationships even in their early stages of development.

As you know, break-ups are not easy for adults, how much more for children? Please don't risk emotional damage to your children because of the temporal pleasure of a short-lived relationship. You want to be especially careful if your children have already experienced divorce because you don't want to induce any more pain upon them with your constant termination of relationships. Remember, they will be someone else's wife or husband one day and you don't want to distort or ruin someone else's future spouse. Lay a strong foundation for your children about relationships and avoid sending messages that people and relationships are erratic and interchangeable. You want to ensure you are laying a healthy foundation about relationships. Your very own relationship is ultimately a foretelling of your child's future relationships; it's a template of what their future relationships will look like because we often mimic how our parents faired in relationships, so date smart.

Are your children ready?
Dating is not just about you. Your children need to know and understand that you are not splitting your affections but adding to the betterment, growth, and happiness of your family. Reaffirm your commitment to your children so that they feel secure and that your relationships will not cause them to feel abandoned. Your top priority is the stability of your children's emotions and ensuring them of your unconditional love. If it's anything that children need, it's security, a stable environment and unconditional love.

Sugar Daddy
If you are a single man that's interested in a single mom, ensure that her family is economically and emotionally stable and that she is not simply dating you to meet the needs

of her children or using you to alleviate her financial burdens. Some people are only interested in being rescued. But if you see that there is value in the relationship and a mutual benefit and you want to be a blessing to her family, by all means, be a gentleman and do so, as you are led by God.

Hanky panky
Your children should not see gross levels of physical intimacy between you and your dating partner in the early stages of your relationship. They should see that you are "friends", establishing a relationship to determine if you two are a fit. I shouldn't have to say this to grown folk, but I do: **ladies, don't entertain Mr. Tony in your bedroom! Gentleman, don't let your children see you *devour* your girlfriend.** Your children should understand that sexual expression is exclusive for the institution of marriage only. Safeguard your child's mindset of sexual purity.

Do your children like your date?
If you have already introduced your dating partner to your children, getting their thoughts on how they feel about your current relationship is important. Children have a good feel for people, and if little Madison says, 'I don't like Mr. Johnny,' you might want to look into it and not shrug it off. Determine if it's not the source of rebellion but your child's inner security system protecting you from what you don't see.

Can you divide your time?
Though having a significant other is your desire, it does not necessarily warrant that now is the time that you should have one. Relationships require your time. It's not as if you get any extra hours in a day when you get into a relationship. You get the same 24 hours but now it has to be divided; you have to let something go or alter your schedule. Ask yourself, "Where will this time come from and what will I have to cut? Do I have time to balance parenting, career and entertain a relationship now?" Time has to be factored into deciding whether or not you should entertain a relationship or not, because something is going to have to be divided or sacrificed. Ask yourself, what will it be? Your children should not feel the blunt of that division or feel neglected now that you have a new interest in your life. A relationship should be an added benefit to your life. Key word: add; it should add to it, not divide it.

On the same page
Introducing your children to someone is not a light matter
and should be taken seriously. Discuss what this means with your significant other. Clarify that both of you are on the same page and in the same paragraph; ensuring that you both feel that this is the right time and that your relationship has matured and warrants an introduction

to your most precious commodity. What does this mean for us? How will introducing the children affect, alter, or improve our relationship? Your significant other should know that your children are most important to you and that meeting your children is not trivial or any light matter for you. And the purpose for even introducing your children is because you plan on having a future together and understanding that meeting the children is a part of accomplishing that goal.

Board meeting
I look at my family essentially like it's a multi-million dollar company and my daughter has a high stake in it. Before merging "companies" with anyone, you need to sit down with the board members. I asked my daughter, Heaven, what she would like to see in a father for her and a husband for me. Children are not the final say in the decision-making. As the 'president', I have the final say, but the board does have an inclusion. Children will be more accepting of your new relationship when they feel they have not been left out. It will eliminate shock value once you finally introduce someone new to your child(ren), because the future plans of the "company" have already been discussed. You reduce the chances of your merger going "belly up" or bankrupt when your children feel that they've been a part of a corporate decision for the advancement of your "company." In addition, I include my other board of directors, which are my close mentors and counselors. I strongly encourage couples to seek counsel or therapist to help you navigate, assess, and offer guidance in making wise choices in your relationship.

The introduction
Your initial introduction and the next few dates will be the key to establishing a healthy foundation for merging your intimate life with your parenting life. Both facets of your life are both important but require wisdom and skill in intermingling them. The first few dates should be low key and without any pressure. Attempting to railroad your children into liking your date can backfire on you. Start off with simple, fun dates. They should not feel like they are being introduced to their "new daddy" but 'Mr. Johnson' who has an interest and care for Mommy. Share your genuine enthusiasm for your date but don't be over zealous in having an immediate connection or bond between your children and your dating partner. A gradual process will allow your children and your mate time to develop a positive relationship. If you establish a proper foundation in the beginning you will eliminate and avoid unnecessary hardships later on.

Have Fun!
Your children should view relationships and love as fun, purpose-filled and healthy. They should see that this relationship has improved your life and your smile, and that God approves of it. My prayer is that you would make wise and sound choices that will be a blessing for both you and your children.

50 Things You Need To Know About The Person You're Dating

1. How long have they been a Christian?
2. Are they in a solid/committed relationship with God?
3. What is their foundational/core belief system?
4. Are their decisions in life governed by God's leading?
5. Where do they worship at/attend church? How often?
6. What are their beliefs about pre-marital sex?
7. What are their overall views about sex? What are their beliefs on celibacy? Are they celibate and how long?
8. What is their sexual history?
9. What are their core beliefs about relationships? Have them explain what makes a relationship successful/work.
10. How important is their prayer life and how much time do they spend in prayer?
11. How much time do they spend in the Word of God weekly?
12. What is their life's purpose, vision and mission?
13. What are their personal goals in life: 5, 10, 20-year goals?
14. Job/career history
15. What are their personal habits: appearance, clothing, cleanliness, teeth, weight management, and eating habits?
16. What is their lifestyle like and is it agreeable with yours?
17. What is their social life like? Music? Movies? Hobbies? What are their Internet/online habits?
18. Have they ever engaged in any homosexual activity/relationships?
19. Any issues with pornography, masturbation, pedophilic activity, incestuous activity, adultery, sexual struggles? Past or current?
20. Sexual health? STD's? Have you personally seen the test result?
21. Who are their closest friends? How much time do they spend with them? Who are their confidants and/or accountable to?
22. Political views
23. Education history
24. Relationship history? Their last 3-5 relationships? We're those relationships sexual or abusive? How did they begin and end? How did they personally contribute to the

failure of those relationships? Are they (legally) single? Ever married? Legally Divorced? What are their beliefs on divorce?
25. Children from those relationships? What is their relationship like with the other parent? Child support? How do they contribute to those children: emotionally, psychologically, and financially?
26. Current living conditions. Own or rent? Cleanliness? Maintenance and upkeep?
27. Criminal background check
28. What is their relationship with money like? Debt? Gambling? Spending habits?
29. Health. Physical, emotional, mental health. Any medications currently?
30. History of drug or alcohol use?
31. Have they ever been abusive or violent in any relationships?
32. What is their definition of romance?
33. How do they define love? How did they learn about love? How do they express love and affection in your relationship?
34. How do they define intimacy?
35. How do they define fidelity?
36. What is their relationship with their parents and sibling(s)?
37. How were they raised? What was their upbringing/childhood like?
38. How do they handle stress or anger?
39. How effectively do they communicate/listen? How do they resolve disagreements? What conflicts or issues are prevalent and consistent in the relationship? How are you both resolving them?
40. What are their thoughts about marriage? Do they ever want to get married?
41. How do they help you to grow and develop? How do they support you?
42. What are their expectations of the relationship? What is their "must-have list" and what is on their "non-negotiable" list? Do you fit that list? Do they fit your must-have list?
43. How do they feel about you? How do they view your relationship? Its status? Its direction?
44. Are you spiritually compatible?
45. Are you emotionally compatible?
46. Physically compatible?
47. Mentally compatible?
48. Is there chemistry in the relationship?
49. What are their strengths? Areas of weakness?
50. Does any of the above conflict with your beliefs, your lifestyle, or the direction in life that you are going in? If any of the above never changes, will I be happy with this person? With all that I know about this person, is it safe for me to move forward in a relationship with them?

Chapter 14
Shoplifting

Shoplifting, n. 1. Known as the five-finger discount or theft of goods.

Taking an item from a store is blatant shoplifting; though it's not as obvious, purchasing a dress, wearing the dress while leaving the tag on it, then bring it back to the store for a refund is just as much shoplifting as running out of the store with it without purchasing it. I liken shoplifting to most Christian dating. Many Christians jump into relationships with no intent to develop it into a long-term one or for marriage or to nurture Christian values in relationships. It's not blatant and maybe the average eye can't see it but it's definitely the five-finger discount! Many SINGLES use dating as a means to meet their intimate and sexual needs until marriage or until the next best thing comes along. They hop into the relationship with no intention of developing it but to simply get their five fingers on someone else's body to fulfill their sexual desire. They wear the other person by putting them on their body, have sex with them, and then return it; leaving the "single tag" on the person, without having to pay the price of marriage and commitment to be with them. This, my friend, is more than shoplifting; it's theft: grand theft!

Grand theft is the crime of taking someone else's property with the intent of permanently depriving them of the property.

"For this is the will of God, your sanctification: that you should abstain from sexual immorality; that each of you should know how to possess his own vessel in sanctification and honor, not in passion of lust, like the Gentiles who do not know God; that no one should take advantage of **and defraud his brother in this matter**, because the Lord *is* the avenger of all such, as we also forewarned you and testified. For God did not call us to uncleanness, but in holiness. Therefore he who rejects *this* does not reject man, but God, who has also given us His Holy Spirit." I Thess 4:3-8 NKJV

Our relationship app says to not defraud your brother/sister in what matter? Sexual immorality. Defraud means to deprive of something by deception and fraud or to swindle or cheat someone out of their property. That means that it doesn't belong to you, but you use it anyway; taking something that is not rightfully yours and that you're not entitled to. We take a taxi cab ride into a person's life, leave the meter running because we're only going in for a moment to take advantage of them sexually, use the relationships as a pass-by time, a transitional relationship to temporally park in to satisfy your sexual or relational needs for now.

Defraud comes from the Greek (pleonekteo), meaning: to take advantage of another, to overreach, manipulate or stimulate sexual desire that can't be righteously fulfilled.

As you encounter relationships, you are not to defraud, swindle, or sexually cheat someone out of something that doesn't belong to you. You can't righteously fulfill it if it doesn't belong to you and the only way for it to belong to you is to make a commitment, a covenant in marriage. As we established early on, our bodies never belong to us. So essentially, they're trespassing on God's property.

"God's will is for you to be holy, so stay away from all sexual sin. Then each of you will **control his own body** and live in holiness and honor—not in lustful passion like the pagans who do not know God and his ways. Never harm or cheat a Christian brother in this matter **by violating his wife**." 1 Thess 4:3-6 NLT

In the New Living Translation here it says not to cheat your Christian brother by violating his wife; but your Christian brother or sister is not yet married, how could this be? Because your future husband/wife has rights to the property long before he or she even meet you. In our limited thinking, we think possession happens on the wedding day, but your body belongs to your future spouse now; they're just awaiting legal possession of it. I understand that my body does not belong to me, it belongs to God and when my future husband arrives, the Lord will turn over possession to him. So I am faithful to my husband now, long before I meet him because I am a wife now and I'm dedicated to him long before he gets here so that when I get married and my husband runs into one of my ex's I will not feel embarrassed or ashamed with my ex standing there with a cocky attitude, like "yeah man, I had her, too."

We should've learned to respect other's people's property in kindergarten so now that we are adults this should be a clear understanding and embedded within the fiber of our character: don't take property that does not belong to you. So we then need to value and respect them and their bodies because they do not belong to you. That is why the Word says that we must each learn to control our own bodies and that control is only learned and developed, not through hoping and wishing that we won't have sex in dating relationships, but through this key word: sanctification.

Sanctification, to be set apart; separation from contamination.
It means that we need to put a wall between God and anything that would separate us from Him by making a clear distinction between those that are holy and those that not holy. It is the process of becoming and growing in holiness and that should be woven in the fabric of who we are so that when we meet someone or begin dating that does not change. That means that our dating relationships must be set apart and holy. When you are becoming

acquainted with another Christian you must protect and honor that which belongs to God. It must be established in the beginning that the relationship is set apart to honor God. Our relationship app says to not defraud your brother; you call him your boyfriend, but he's your brother. When we get into relationships, we think that person belongs to us but they are first and foremost God's property. If the man you're dating right now is not your husband, then he's your brother. Therefore, what I'm about to say may shock your ears but it's the truth: if the person you're in a relationship is not your husband, then he's your brother and you're in an incestuous relationship. If she's not your wife, then she's your sister. I'm going to walk away from typing to allow you to let that sink in for a moment…

"Treat young women with all purity as you would your sister." 1 Timothy 5:2 NLT

Many Christians vicariously jump into relationships because they don't place a high value on the person they are seeing as another fellow brother or sister. Though Solomon pursued a relationship with his future wife, he called her his sister because first and foremost, before she is his, she is his sister in the Lord.

"You have ravished my heart and given me courage, my sister, my [promised] bride; you have ravished my heart and given me courage with one look from your eyes, with one jewel of your necklace." SOS 4:9 AMP

That person that you're in a relationship is God's son or daughter, not simply someone for you to hang out in their life to minimize the burden or longings in your single life. So it is a disgrace and a dishonor when we have Christians getting involved in relationships without the best interest of the other person, taking advantage of them sexually, breaking hearts, dumping them and then leaving them after we've gotten our needs fulfilled by them. And that is the sad scenario of many Christian dating relationships: we have an attraction to a person and then we just jump into a relationship with them. I have an announcement to make: NOT EVERYONE WE LIKE OR ARE ATTRACTED TO JUSTIFIES GETTING INTO A RELATIONSHIP WITH THEM. You then have a great responsibility to find out why that person is in your life and what are both your roles and purpose in one another's life.

Some people come into our life for a season, for a direct purpose for us to impart something into their lives, and they in ours; not for us to jump into a romantic relationship with them. There are some men that I've met and we were only meant to be friends but I <u>made</u> them into dating relationships. I wish somebody would just let me tell the truth! I knew some of these men where only coming into my life for a season, but I took advantage of that and used that short season to fulfill my longing for a man, when I knew they were not called to be in an intimate relationship with me or called to be my husband. We will sit, spend hours on the phone in conversation, becoming intimate with people that we're only supposed to remain in friendship status with, we make ourselves emotionally available in casual friendships, and even as Christians, take on and establish "friends with benefits." We have not learned how to have intimate friendships without sexual expression. Jesus exemplifies the greatest friend ever, yet many Christians have yet to learn to be a real friend.

"No one has greater love [no one has shown stronger affection] than to lay down (give up) his own life for his friends." John 15:13 AMP

A true friend lays down his life for his friends, not lay them down and have sex with them! Wow! Did you hear that church? Our love manual says that we must love our neighbors as we do ourselves (Matt 22:39). That tells you that many people don't love themselves because if you love them as you do yourself then you wouldn't violate your friendship. But many relationships skip the friendship stage and jump right to boyfriend-girlfriend status or lover's lane, never establishing the most fundamental aspect of a relationship and is the foundation needed in any committed, lasting relationship, especially marriage. Ask anyone who's married, they'll tell you that friendship is necessary in marriage. When you don't feel like being lovers (and yes, I know you want to have sex bad but there will be many times in marriage when you will not want to); there will be times that you will not feel like being married; that's when friendship kicks in. Friendship should be the foundation of any relationship because it will outlast any couple that skipped to lover's lane. When you do not develop a relationship out of friendship, you forfeit the chance of having a long, lasting relationship. The success of every marriage is a product of its friendship because you can lean on it even when intimacy, personality, and chemistry fail you. That is why successful dating requires that you have the mind of Christ because true love develops out of the pure motives of friendship.

"Don't just pretend to love others. Really love them. Hate what is wrong. Hold tightly to what is good. Love each other with genuine affection, and take delight in honoring each other." Romans 12:10 NLT

Many of us have messed up friendships, relationships with your brother/sister in the Lord, have even damaged potential marriages; hindering and contaminating both their ability and our own to have successful relationships in the future. There are many of you who could have been married eons ago! Yet you continue to get entangled in relationships that offer you a pass-by time until your husband or wife comes along, but you'll prolong a happy marriage as long as you allow someone to occupy their spot. We allow people to come and take up space in a spot reserved for someone else and by default miss out on the opportunity for the person who is really intended to be in our lives; all because you allow it to become acceptable to get in transitional relationships. If you know that the relationship only has the capacity for a friendship only, then why even get involved in an intimate, emotionally engaged relationship? Many times we know from the beginning that the relationship is going to be short-lived but get involved anyhow because we want the temporal satisfaction that it'll give us. There are few relationships that I knew from "hello, what's your name," that it would only last as long as the battery life on my cell phone but I signed up for the short thrill anyway. But there came a time in my life that I began to suffer from malnutrition because of junk-food relationships and the consequences of those relationships began to catch up with me. I made an unconventional move: I began to desperately run after God and allowed that relationship to fill me where I no longer needed dating relationships to be a pass-by time to amuse and entertain me until my husband would come alone. I made a decision that I would give up shoplifting and no longer selfishly rob my brother in the Lord of emotional *and sexual* intimacies in a disposable relationship that I knew, like paper goods, would throw it away after I used it. I put an end to the vicious cycle of getting into boyfriend-girlfriend relationships, break-up, then wash, rinse, repeat! It took me several stupid, unnecessary, bad relationships to realize that I no longer need temporary boyfriends to get me by until my husband comes along.

  I have a brother (in the Lord) that became a dear and close friend who developed an interest in me that intensified into deep feelings for me to the point that he believed that I would be his wife. He made it very clear that he was not interested in playing any dating games; he was ready to get married and wanted to pursue a relationship in that direction. He wanted a wife; I wanted a husband. Though I found him to be attractive, was highly impressed with his relationship with the Lord, and had fun with him every time I was in his presence, I didn't feel the same; I <u>knew</u> he was not my husband. I felt bad and was hesitant in telling him that my feelings didn't mirror his because he was a dear friend and I didn't want to hurt his feelings, and to be honest, wanted to enjoy having the company of his time and be the recipient of his affections but my conviction and commitment to God and myself to no longer allow my life to be satisfied and comfortable with temporal relationships screamed louder because I made a permanent commitment that didn't include a compromise clause with it. It would have been very easy to hibernate and lie dormant in a boyfriend-girlfriend relationship with him because he is a good, sound, mature Christian, established, respectful, charming, lives a noise-free life and he adores me; he was perfect! He just lacked what I needed in a husband. I know, you're like, "what?!" I'll explain more in the chapter "Blind Date," but in short, he would be a great boyfriend, *but not a great husband for me.* Did you hear that? I knew that our relationship didn't have the capacity for marriage and was limited to the shelf life of a boyfriend-girlfriend relationship. Therefore, this relationship could not be authorized to escalate beyond friendship.

  Sure, I could take advantage of the fact that I had his heart in the palm of my hands but what would that get me? A few nights on the town, gifts, hair and nails done, rent paid? If you're not interested in him but only want a free meal or for the purpose of not having to spend your Friday night alone, then you're shoplifting and setting yourself up to become intimately involved with your brother. When we allow friendships to illegitimately access a level of intimacy suited for committed relationships, then we set ourselves up for unnecessary heartache and emotional entanglements causing us to "fall" into sexual relationships with our brother or sister in the Lord. It's not a fall though; it appears to be a "fall" but we are the ones that put ourselves in a position to 'defraud one another in this matter' because we should have never moved beyond a friendship with that particular person in the first place. Many singles find themselves in sexual sin because they get in relationships that they had no business getting in; *it is how many good Christians unintentionally fall.* I would not allow the romantic pressures of his pursuit to sway my decision, so I had a very candid and necessary conversation with him to protect our friendship and to also guard his heart from moving any further or beyond the borders of friendship because he began to get frustrated when I wouldn't reciprocate his affections. I "braved it out" and said to him, "I don't want our friendship to become a temporal dating relationship where we enjoy a romantic season for a fleeting moment, then "break-up." I have no doubt that we would have an enjoyable time together, but is it worth risking our friendship to enjoy a short season of bliss? I know we have a powerful friendship, we would be great in dating, and could be great lovers, but I'm not convinced that we would be great at marriage together. It would be selfish and wrong on my part to enjoy this for a season and have a temporary dating relationship or even a temporary marriage with you and then get a divorce and loose what we have now, when I can have a permanent, lifetime friendship with you. I will not take advantage of or violate and abuse the gift of friendship that God has given to us."

Several years later, I can say to you that this gentleman is still one of my closet friends and it pleases God's heart that I operated in integrity towards this man. That is why it is important that you determine the purpose as to which a person comes in your life. Not every person that comes into your life is intended to be an intimate or dating companion. You have a responsibility to yourself, to God and your friend (brother/sister in the Lord) to discern the purpose of the relationship and respond accordingly, not to simply use people selfishly for our own advantage. When anyone comes into your life, they should be a better person as a result of that. When you meet someone, whether that relationship is a friendship or progresses to an intimate relationship, your goal and intent should always be to remain consistent in your beliefs and that you help to make them become a better, stronger Christian; that they develop or become closer to God as a result of having been in your life, whether the relationship is seasonal or for a lifetime.

Relationship progression level:
Strangers, acquaintances, associates, casual friendship, close friendship, exclusive dating, pre-engagement, engagement, marriage. If you allow the relationship to take its rightful course by starting and developing in friendship lane, then the drive to love will be a breathtaking journey.

- Be upfront and honest about the relationship; do not lead people on. It's like shopping: if you like what you see, try it on; if you like it, then you go buy it. It's that simple. We're not kids in elementary passing notes, having Johnny to have Stephanie pass Michael a letter to Erica for you that says, "Do you like me? Circle yes or no." If you have a relationship that is in friendship status and it progresses, say something; don't just allow the relationship to wander aimlessly. Make your motives and intentions clear; if you're interested, simply make that known, "I don't know where the friendship/relationship is going but I do know this, I enjoy how our friendship is growing and I will respect you, honor you, and honor God as we further this relationship."

- Christian dating is out of control! There should be a distinction, an undeniable difference in how we approach relationships since we have one with God. Some of this tomfoolery we're doing in relationships is unacceptable! There are many single Christians who lack **dating integrity.** The things that go on with many Christians while dating is repulsive! Swindling sex out of people, dating multiple people at once, lying, cheating, deception, leading a person's heart astray…these types of behavior shouldn't even be named among Christians! Are you leading him/her on? Don't send mixed, confusing messages; if you don't want a relationship and nothing more than friends, then stay friends. Don't mess up the relationship by becoming intimate friends or moving into a relationship because you need a pass-by time until someone else comes along. Don't lead people on, entangling their heart with no intentions of keeping it; you have a responsibility in guarding their heart. If you're seriously just friends and there's no romantic pursuit or interest, then fine; but don't horse around with people's feelings, sending them the wrong message by engaging in what couples do in exclusive dating while you're still in the casual friendship status.

Have you been in relationships where you didn't operate in dating integrity? It's never too late to ask for forgiveness and to do what is right. If you've been dishonest, betrayed a friendship/relationship or left a relationship with unresolved wounds, list the person(s) that you need to ask for forgiveness from and then make amends, even if the relationship doesn't have any future. If you were the person betrayed or hurt from a relationship, ask the Lord to open your heart to forgive them and to heal you of those past hurts. Even if they haven't asked for forgiveness or even deserve it, the forgiveness that you give to those who hurt you will open you up your wounded heart to receive healing, giving you the ability to embrace and welcome new and genuine relationships.

- There are so many singles who are accustomed to giving out and exchanging sexual favors during friendship and dating, that it is expected. If you're "so-called" friends then why are you kissing and necking on the couch? Don't kid yourself; holding hands, kissing, and "smooching" are not expressions of friendship. Many times people will say, "We're just friends," when actually you're in a relationship and someone has not been responsible in terms of committing to the relationship because they want benefits without commitment. Do not allow relationships to develop inappropriate levels of expression that do not match the progression stage. That means you can't expect dating benefits in casual friendship status or think that it's acceptable to give marriage benefits while you're in the exclusive dating or engagement stage. That is why it is important to establish guidelines and boundaries, and then define the relationship so that both of you are on the same page so you'll know what degree and level of exchange and expression is appropriate in the relationship. If you're dating and haven't done that yet, I think it's time to have *the talk*.

- Though your relationships may begin in the friendship stage, there are some of you who will have an immediate attraction or romantic interest, but friendship should still be the foundation. Even with a romantic interest, you should have brotherly love (phileos) and respect for your date/boyfriend or girlfriend. It may evolve into a romantic relationship, but if you maintain a level of respect and honor, you will not violate or defraud your brother or sister in Christ. When Christians pursue relationships, we need to have dating integrity. We need to be honest, honorable, and holy. Throughout dating you want to maintain a high standard while you engage in relationships without taking what doesn't belong to you. Shoplifting carries a high penalty and is a serious offense to our God and we want to ensure that we please Him in every area of our lives.

In what instances is shoplifting synonymous with how some Christians approach dating? _____
_____

What does it mean to defraud someone in a relationship? _____
_____

How can dating with the mindset that you are faithful to your future spouse help you with dating?
_____

What does sanctification mean? _____. How can you demonstrate this in your life? _____

Why is it important to face each relationship you encounter with the mindset that he/she is God's son or daughter? _____
_____

How should you establish relationships in the beginning? Why? _____
_____

In what ways or how can using relationships as a pass-by time be unhealthy or hinder you? _____
_____

Define what integrity in dating means to you? _____
_____

Go through each stage of the relationship levels, beginning with stranger all the way through marriage, and list the appropriate emotional and physical expression in relation to the relationship level: _____
_____
_____

What will you commit to do to ensure that respect, honor and integrity is maintained in your relationships? _____
_____

Do you have unhealthy friendships that you need to confront ungodly or inappropriate behavior? Explain_____
_____

Is there a relationship that you are currently in that you have moved beyond the appropriate level? Is there a friendship that you are in now that you have developed feelings/emotions for and have not made your intentions known and have not had the necessary conversation about it? How can you handle this with integrity? _____
_____

Is there a friendship/relationship that you are currently in (or have been in) that you may be leading the other person on or have not stated your intentions? You know they have interest or feelings for you but you only want to keep that relationship at friendship level? Let that person know, what can you say to them? _____
_____

Are there relationships in the past that you entered in knowing from the beginning that it would only be short-lived? What was that experience like? What regrets do you have? Did it ruin the friendship? Explain
_____
_____

Why is it more important to tell someone that you don't want a relationship beyond friendship, rather than lead them on? _____
_____

In what ways can a woman be responsible in her friendships with the opposite sex? In what ways can a man be responsible in his friendships with the opposite sex? _____
_____

What commitment will you make concerning friendships and ensuring that you do not defraud your brother or sister? _____
_____

Chapter 15
Counterfeits

There is an original, it is common that there will be someone that will come along and make a counterfeit of it and attempt to pass it off as the real thing. I don't know if you've ever seen the counterfeit of a designer handbag but it looks just like the original. There are some counterfeit goods, also known as fakes, replicas, or knockoffs, that are such good imitations that even some pros have a little trouble telling the difference but if you look a little closer you'll see that it's an impersonation. The Bible warns us that they'll be people just like that; they'll try to pass themselves off as a Christian: have a form of godliness but strangers to the power of it. The Bible uses the expression "form of godliness," but you're probably more familiar with the term: hypocrite.

> Hypocrite: a person pretending to have beliefs, opinions, virtues, ideals, thoughts, feelings, qualities, or standards that one does not actually have. A person who acts in contradiction to his or her stated beliefs or feelings.

"But know this, that in the last days perilous times will come: For men will be lovers of themselves, lovers of money, boasters, proud, blasphemers, disobedient to parents, unthankful, unholy, unloving, unforgiving, slanderers, without self-control, brutal, despisers of good, traitors, headstrong, haughty, lovers of pleasure rather than lovers of God, having a form of godliness but denying its power. And from such people turn away! For of this sort are those who creep into households and make captives of gullible women loaded down with sins, led away by various lusts, always learning and never able to come to the knowledge of the truth." 2 Tim. 3:1-7 NKJV

A hypocrite or having a form of godliness is the appearance or the pretense of living a righteous life but living like hell when no one is looking. The word hypocrite, deriving from the Greek, means "play-acting" or lacking the ability to sift or decide. It's what you see when a Christian straddles the fence: in God one day, then hops the fence and hang out with satan the next day. They have a form or the outward appearance of a Christian but if you look at a spiritual X-ray of their insides, you will clearly see dead men's bones full of sin. But if you watch them closely, you will see that what they profess totally contradicts their actions and the way they live.

"Woe to you, scribes and Pharisees, pretenders (hypocrites)! For you are like tombs that have been whitewashed, which look beautiful on the outside but inside are full of dead men's bones and everything impure. Just so, you also outwardly seem to people to be just *and* upright but inside you are full of pretense and lawlessness *and* iniquity." Matthew 23:27-28 AMP

This is why you can see someone who attends church, quote scriptures, use church jargon, sing in the choir, and preach in the pulpit but live a total different life when they're not at church, because they have denied and rejected Him and are complete strangers to the power of God. What is the power of God? The power to live right, the power to talk right, the power to walk right! It's a manifestation of God's Word in your life, thoughts and actions. There are many Christians who have not allowed the power of God to transform their lives, penetrating their nature and character to produce a godly lifestyle. There are many people that attend church who play-act as if they're going to win an Academy Award for "Fake Christian Of The Year." But no matter how many times you see them at church, quote a scripture, sing a good hymn, profess Christianity, or "do" what Christians do, it doesn't mean a thing if they deny the power of God, deny the presence of God, and deny Him access into his/her life to transform and revolutionize it.

"When once the Master of the house gets up and closes the door, and you begin to stand outside and to knock at the door [again and again], saying, Lord, open to us! He will answer you, I do not know where [what household—certainly not Mine] you come from. Then you will begin to say, We ate and drank in Your presence, and You taught in our streets. But He will say, I tell you, I do not know where [what household—certainly not Mine] you come from; depart from Me, all you wrongdoers! Luke 13:25-27 AMP

Wow, that's scary! All that church attendance, praying over your food in Jesus name, and listening to good sermons about Him but finally meet Him face-to-face and He says He doesn't recognize you…That, my friends, is the most detrimental thing ever! This validates that church attendance alone does not prove that are person is right with God. For many, Christianity is an activity, not a lifestyle. There are people who are religious, attend church and do religious activities but do not have a relationship with the Lord. That is the reason that many Christians are workers of iniquity: they don't know Him and knowing only happens as a result of a relationship. It's difficult to be in a relationship with God and work iniquity at the same time. There is a culture of Christianity where people are associated by name only. They wear the title Christian but they are not followers of Christ. It's a frightening trend of unbelieving Christians. No, they are not atheist, they believe *in* God but *they don't believe Him*. They believe He is God but they don't believe His Word and don't live it. It's the I-believe-God-but Christian:

- I believe in God but if it goes against what I believe…

- I believe God with the exception that it doesn't require me to change my life or give up anything.
- I believe in God but the world and society is changing and we need to alter and modify a few biblical ideas to adjust to the changing society.
- I know the Bible says that but, but, but!

"Are there still some among you who hold that "only believing" is enough? Believing in one God? Well, remember that the demons believe this too—so strongly that they tremble in terror! Fool! When will you ever learn that "believing" is useless without *doing* what God wants you to? Faith that does not result in good deeds is not real faith. James 2:19-20 TLB

I had a woman call my office requesting a copy of a DVD that I had recently recorded, entitled the same name as my first book, "Single, Saved & Having Sex LIVE." She indicated that a friend of hers attended the live taping and she wished that she had been given the opportunity to be at the taping. You should have seen the look on my face after I said, "Oh, you should've come; I would have loved having you as my guest." She explained that this friend said it was a private taping by invitation only. After I told her that it was not a private taping, she immediately started crying; realizing that he lied to her and simply did not want her to accompany him. As she was crying, she began to reveal to me that her calls to him had gone unnoticed, unreturned, and she had not spoken to him *since he persuaded her to have sex with him.*

That opened up a can of worms and led into a conversation where Cynthia revealed to me that she met Eric at the church they both attended, where she was accustomed to seeing him in the lobby ushering the congregants to their seats. As they began dating, ushering Cynthia to her seat changed to Eric ushering her to his house for dinner dates and Friday-night-at-the-movies on his living room couch. Sexual invitations, camouflaged as romantic interest, became frequent and escalated each time they would get together at Eric's house for "dates." Though sexual pressure always accompanied their dates, Cynthia would always decline his invitations through pacification of "romance" on the couch: the lights turned down low, while allowing your hands to roam and foreplay the body as you tell one another how much you enjoy one another's company.

One night while Cynthia was lying in Eric's arms during his attempt to have sex with her, he decided to pull out his heavy "artillery" since his romantic persuasion wasn't getting the results, "God has been showing me the plans for my life. I know my life has a future and I want you in it. I love you and I can't help but to want to show you how much by making love to you." He used the ole "I love you" trick and it worked; Cynthia gave in and began having sex with Eric and after a few times of him "expressing his love" to her he stopped calling her and hit the ignore button every time she called him. I could've told you that was going to happen; you can look back early on and prophesy what was going to happen without even being a prophet! "When wickedness arrives, shame's not far behind." Prov. 18:3 MSG

Eric was nowhere to be found for several weeks; it was as if he moved to Alaska and became an Eskimo, but he was right in Detroit, ushering at the church the following Sunday morning after my taping, where he looked her right in her face, but treated her as if she were invisible and didn't speak or acknowledge her...the nerve! That was the purpose of Cynthia's call: to get a copy of my DVD so she could get over Eric and begin her journey for sexual healing. What was ironic is that Eric came to the taping of "Single, Saved and Having Sex." Eric does Christian things, attend church, but does not live it because for some people Christianity is just an *activity*. Some people do it out of routine and others do it because it's a reputation or image builder; it has perks and it gives you entry into closed doors so when you walk up, you just point in the direction where God is and say, "I'm with the Big Guy." As is the case with many men who would never have VIP access into a church girl's life without walking up to the entrance of her heart and saying, "Oh, you're Christian? So am I! I'm with God, too."

I was invited to speak to a group of women where a woman in her forties who was in attendance raised her hand and said, "I want you to know that your book, *Single, Saved & Having Sex,"* saved my life. I was celibate for thirteen years and lost it!" I was thinking to myself, "Where is the testimony?" With tears welling up in her eyes and her voice box shaking her words like an earthquake, she began to share her story to a room full of women whose attention was completely occupied by every word that she could barely speak. Celibate for thirteen years, Valerie began dating a nice gentleman in her church. You can imagine how smitten she was with having the attention and pursuit of a Christian man; after stomaching through a long drought of good men, it was refreshing to have a man pursue her who was not an ex-convict or on the down low, had a job, wasn't living with his mother, not fluent in Ebonics, opened the door for her, and yes, even attended church. Valerie wanted him to know up front and to make it clear, "I've made a vow to not have sex again with another man I'm not married to." Much to her surprise and excitement, Robert responded, "Glad to know we're on the same page; that means we can move to the next chapter."

They began to spend a lot of quality time together going out on dates and Robert would even pick her up to go to Bible study with her, then Val's Facebook relationship status went from single to "in a relationship." Giving in to the romantic persuasion, she began to let her guard down, feeling free to let go and allowing Robert to caress her, kiss her lips and neck passionately as if he was going to devour her in ecstasy but then back out just short of the height of desire saying, "You make *waiting* hard for me." Robert had a different approach; instead of trying to get a "yes" out of her by asking Val for sex, he would simply break her down by weakening her "no." After several times of building sexual tension, Val felt safe; assured that they wouldn't go any farther because Robert was going to "protect" both of their vows but this time Robert didn't stop. Looking in her eyes as he seduced her, he passionately whispered, "You said you wouldn't have sex with another man you weren't married to. Well, we're not breaking that vow; *we're fulfilling it*…*b*ecause I'll be the man that will marry you. I'm dedicating myself to you right now, here in this moment…I want to be <u>one with you,</u> baby." He borrowed a Scripture he heard about Adam and Eve becoming one while attending church and used marriage as the bait. He pretended to be sexually pure long enough to get what he wanted. Robert knew exactly the kind of man to pretend to be for Val. People can tell you what you want to hear because you divulge to them what they need to say to make you think they are what you want. Instead of telling Robert the kind of man she was looking for, she should have just watched to see the man he would reveal he was. Little did Val know, Robert never had a vow to sexual purity; he just hijacked hers temporarily because he knew that would be his key to unlocking her treasure. It was a great Ponzi scheme: a woman investing her body for the return or so-called guarantee of marriage in the future. That is how many single women get swindled into having sex because they're promised marriage in the never-arriving-future. Many of you give sex on credit, "I promise I'm going to marry you; give me the goods now and I'll pay the price/cost later." Don't let someone treat your life like a credit card where they swipe on intention or a promise, then leave you with the debt to pay for it.

After he had enough of her treasure, Robert stopped calling her just after a couple times of them becoming "one;" he stopped showing up at church, and stopped answering her calls. Hoodwinked, used, and heartbroken, Valerie showed up at his house looking for him for two weeks but there was no car and no answer at the door each time she drove by. In desperation to confront him, she began showing up frequently in hopes to catch him. One night at one o'clock in the morning, Valerie drove to his house and finally found his car in the driveway with another car parked directly behind his…ut oh! Val got out of the car and just before she was going to pound on the door, she looked in the window and a glimpse of his figure appeared through the silhouette of the sheer curtains that she had picked out during one of their cute shopping trips together. Looking closer into his one-leveled, ranch styled home to get a clearer view, Val became hotter than a hissing tea kettle when she realized that not only was it him, but he was walking down his hallway butt-naked! He was fully unclothed in his birthday suit! Just before her mind could catch up with disbelief, a woman came walking behind Robert; you guessed it: in her birthday suit, revealing clearly they had just finished up "business" before she arrived on the sex scene. Robert and his new temporary *wifey* were headed to the bathroom to shower their sin down the drain.

Val began banging on the window, shouting his name, "Bobby, open this door!" Banging even harder on the window, she shouted again, "Robert, open the door! Open this door, you no-good-for-nothing-low-life, piece of &%#@!" Robert walked closer to the window, shouting back at her "Girl, you're crazy! You betta get your butt off my porch!"

With steam coming out of both of her ears, Valerie shouted back at him, "How you gonna play me like this?! You weren't saying that when we were *layin'* up in your bed two weeks ago! You messed with the wrong one; Vera Jean didn't raise no punk! Open this doe!" (For those of you who don't know what that is, it's short for door, but she was Burger King flamed-broiling mad to even use proper language.)

In an uproar, Robert said, "Get away from my house before I call the police on your crazy blank, blank, blank!"

As a God-fearing, Christian woman I can't even repeat what Robert called her; let's just say that Val's response will interpret it: she grabbed two of the biggest bricks she could find and reached all the way back to Mississippi and threw one through his perfect pictured-glass window and the other in the windshield of his car! The police pulled up and took her to jail and -with embarrassment and shame- had to call her pastor to come bail her out. Still looking for the testimony, I stood there, shocked with my eyes bucked open like a deer caught in headlights. You know how you can barely talk or get the words out of your mouth and your throat starts to lodge up because you're crying? Well, with tears now flooding her eyes, Valerie struggled to get the rest of her words out, "I was suicidal, ashamed, and heartbroken…I was mad at myself for betraying God for this man who didn't deserve me. I had gone thirteen years without allowing a man to touch me and then to have sex with a man I was only seeing for just a couple of months…I felt worthless! During one of the most painful times of my life, I stumbled upon your book, "Single, Saved and Having Sex," and I want you to know that it changed my life! It helped me heal from a broken place, restore my relationship with God and helped me forgive myself!" There was not a dry eye in the room! Why? Because there are many women that have fallen for men who are counterfeit Christians, play-acting long enough to get what they want and then leave.

> "For evil people can't sleep unless they have caused someone to stumble." Prov. 4:16 NLT

Don't think that all counterfeits wear a mustache and pants; they wear lipstick and skirts, too. I had a friend named, Mel, who had given his life to the Lord and made a decision that he was going to not just treat church like he was a member of the country club, but actually live his life completely for the Lord. Mel said, "Ty, I've made a decision that I'm not going to sleep around and fornicate any more. My biggest challenge though is that it's easy to get sex in church. Many women throw *it* at me and when I turn it down, they're both shocked and intimidated! The more I reject them, the more they try to throw it on me. I've seen easy in the streets but an easy Christian woman has spiritual strategies to manipulate you!" Every man reading this book need to lean in and listen closely to what I have to say: **it may come easy, but it will come with a price you can't afford.**

"A whore is a bottomless pit; a loose (promiscuous) woman can get you in deep trouble fast. She'll take you for all you've got; she's worse than a pack of thieves." Prov. 23:27-28 MSG
"For by means of a whorish woman a man is brought to a piece of bread." Prov. 6:26 KJV

And this is not just talking about your money; ask Samson.[3] Delilah ruined him! She performed sexual favors on him, wiped her mouth, grabbed the sack of money like nothing happened and kept it moving! The Bible says that's just how an a adulteress or a promiscuous woman will do, "she'll satisfy her sexual appetite, shrug her shoulders, and then say, 'what's wrong with that?'"[4] Sadly, there are many saved "Delilah's" in church; women who lived whorish, promiscuous-driven lifestyles, who gave their life to the Lord, but didn't get delivered from their past, so they are still sexually promiscuous. Then there are some church-going, Bible toting women who are sexually promiscuous that have no intentions of committing to a relationship with a good man but will use him to fulfill her unmet emotional needs or give sexual favors in order to get a man to be her "sugar daddy" and provide for her; if that's the price she has to pay, then so be it. Samson had no business getting into a relationship with Delilah from the beginning because a person like her, who is not living for God, is not thinking about living sexually pure; she only played the role to get what she wanted. Samson paid a high price for counterfeit love. Delilah took his strength and power, opened the door for his enemies to overtake him, his vision was snatched out of him, the purpose that God had for his life was destroyed and it ultimately cost him his life! You tell me if a thirty-second roll around in the hay is worth it?

How to tell the imitation from the real:
"Lovers of self and [utterly] self-centered, lovers of money and aroused by an inordinate [greedy] desire for wealth, proud and arrogant...abusive (blasphemous, scoffing), disobedient to parents, ungrateful, unholy and profane...without natural [human] affection (callous and inhuman)...intemperate and loose in morals and conduct, uncontrolled and fierce, haters of good...treacherous [betrayers], rash, [and] inflated with self-conceit...lovers of sensual pleasures and vain amusements more than and rather than lovers of God." AMP

"They will consider nothing sacred. They will be unloving and unforgiving...and have no self-control. They will be cruel and hate what is good. They will betray their friends, be reckless, be puffed up with pride, and love pleasure rather than God." NLT

"Self-absorbed, money-hungry, self-promoting, stuck-up, profane, contemptuous of parents, crude, coarse, dog-eat-dog, unbending, slanderers, impulsively wild, savage, cynical, treacherous, ruthless, bloated windbags, addicted to lust, and allergic to God. MSG

Imagine that: allergic to God; they sneeze, twitch and go into convulsion, totally uncomfortable every time they get into the presence of God. These are the signs of a person that has not allowed God's power to work through the fiber of their character or degenerate nature. Go ahead, highlight, circle and underline each of those characteristics of a counterfeit listed above because if you don't want to become a victim then you need to identify what a counterfeit looks like so that you can escape victimization. When identifying if someone has the above character, consider this:

- Do they shout at church but get to your house and act like a heathen? Actions and behavior are proof if they are real, not what they say. If you want to determine if they are authentic, then watch what they do. Their conduct validates the genuineness of their Christianity, not what they proclaim. If they have rejected God then "they deny and reject and are strangers to the power of it [their conduct belies the genuineness of their profession]"[1]

- They will make excuses about their ungodly lifestyle and when confronted they'll say you're judging them. They will constantly make excuses, compromise, and then become combative and say, "You're not suppose to judge me; only God can judge me."

- They will not acknowledge it as sin but instead will twist scripture or say it's not that bad or say other Christians are too deep.

- Watch their conversation and then watch the actions that follow. People who do not have a relationship with God will be vague or barely discuss their spiritual life. Prayer will be absent from their lifestyle and they will not incorporate the Word or God in decision-making. If their ungodly language won't spill from their mouth like water from a faucet, their actions will! You don't ever have to wonder if (s)he is a counterfeit or not; simply let their character speak for them. If you find holes or disorder in their character, RUN! "For [although] they hold a form of piety (true religion), they deny and reject and are strangers to the power of it [their conduct belies the genuineness of their profession]. Avoid [all] such people [turn away from them]."[1] Did you hear what the Word said? It said stay away from them because "they have depraved and distorted minds, and are reprobate and counterfeit and to be rejected as far as the faith is concerned."[2]

- How much does it cost? One of the major differences between the authentic and a counterfeit is the price. Something fake always comes cheap; whether it's a handbag or a relationship. If the relationship doesn't cost them something, if there's no sacrifice, then it's not authentic. If the person you are dating does not give their time, commitment, their substance, affection, and attention, then check the authenticity of their relationship with God and with you; you'll find that their pursuit is not genuine.

- The number one way to authenticate their Christianity is found in Matthew 7:20, "You will know them by their fruit." This requires more than just a bullet-point so we will dive into this deeper in the chapter Jeans. But plain and simple, is there any God-evidence in their life? I love how Dr. Mike Murdock says it best, "If someone says they met God and their life hasn't changed, then they didn't meet God." If God is truly in their life, you will see a life change as a result.

How to avoid counterfeit relationships:

"Post a guard at my mouth, GOD, set a watch at the door of my lips. Don't let me so much as dream of evil or thoughtlessly fall into bad company. And these people who only do wrong—don't let them lure me with their sweet talk!" Ps. 141:3-7 MSG

"Say to wisdom you are my sister and call understanding your intimate friend; that they may keep you from an adulteress, from the foreigner who flatters with words." Proverbs 7:5 NASB

- Counterfeits get access to spiritually weak or spiritually dwarfed women. They smooth talk or worm their way into the homes of Christian women who are either spiritually malnourished, weighed down with sin and swayed by their emotions and desires (2 Timothy 3:1-8). The same is true for men; if you want to avoid counterfeit relationships then a relationship with Wisdom, the Word of God, is fundamentally necessary. You have to be connected to Wisdom to weed out frauds. (Matthew 10:16) I don't care how smooth they are; they can't get past a Word-filled believer! When you have a relationship with the Word, you are not led or governed by your emotions; YOU ARE LED BY GOD'S SPIRIT.

- The key then is to have your spiritual life so intact that they can't get pass God to get to you. Your relationship with God is a firewall of protection, preventing counterfeits access. Keep God as your first Love, strengthen and maintain the fervor in your relationship with Him, and God will lead you to love that is authentic!

If you could give advice to a friend in Cynthia, Valerie or Mel's situation, what would you say? _____

What compromises have you made in relationships? What were the results? _____

Have you ever been in a relationship with a counterfeit Christian? Describe the relationship? What signs where evident in the beginning of the relationship that you overlooked? _____

Do you have friendships/relationships in your life that are hindering your Christian walk? What friends can you connect with that can help you in your Christian journey and challenge you to become more like Christ? _____

[1] 2 Tim. 3: 5 AMP   [3] Judges 16
[2] 2 Tim. 3:8 AMP   [4] Proverbs 30:20 NLT

Chapter 15
Unequally Yoked

Go ahead, slap yourself, make Kool-aid with the mop water, take your iPhone and sit it in the middle of rush hour traffic, let Joan Rivers' plastic surgeon give you a nose job, put pepper spray in your own eyes, take the water hose and fill up your gas tank with it, give Flavor Flave a kiss, drink toilet water, and let the late, great Michael Jackson's former doctor give you a prescription for a sleepless night, because these are all equivalent to you dating someone who is not in a relationship with God. You might as well leave your clothes on a hanger and don't even bother putting them on if you date someone who doesn't believe in or live for your God.

"When wickedness arrives, shame's not far behind." Proverbs 18:3 MSG

An unbeliever is his own god, leads and governs his own life and is not interested in your faith or fairytale, antiquated, out-dated belief system on sexual purity, holiness, and giving God prominence over their lives. Your commitment to sexual purity doesn't align or make sense with his "as long as you 'love' a person you should be able to express it sexually" mentality or his "as long as you put a condom on it you'll be safe" attitude. He/she doesn't believe that you have to be married in order to have sex, which is totally contrary to the original blueprint of love, sex and relationships. Your relationship manual says that if you date someone who is allergic to your God, then shame is not far behind because shame is the result of getting naked without commitment (Gen. 2:25). I know you don't want to face the fact that your boyfriend is wicked but if he doesn't have a relationship with God, then he is. And if God is not his father, then the devil is. Ouch, that truth hurts!

"You are of your father, the devil, and it is your will to practice the lusts and gratify the desires [which are characteristic] of your father." John 8:44 AMP

Because (s)he has not been regenerated through Christ, his nature and habit is prone to indulge and satisfy his sexual desires, so the thought of sexual abstinence is utterly ridiculous! So every time you get together he is trying to get you out of your clothes in the name of "I love you." Your beliefs will constantly be in battle with his and you'll always argue about why you two can't have sex and I bet with every ounce of Welch's Black Cherry Grape Juice in my kitchen cabinet that the ultimatum of "put out or I'm leaving" will come up or your competition with some other woman -who will have sex with him if you won't- will be a threat to your relationship. So go ahead, leave your clothes on a hanger and walk around naked because having sex with your unbelieving boyfriend is inevitable. You'll never get to wear purity or make a fashion statement with that wardrobe of yours because you will end up on your backside with your clothes off if you date an unbeliever. Such was the case with Angela.

"My name is Angela and I am 23 years old. I was wondering if your book is available to buy over here in the UK? I have been looking for a book that I can relate to due to the difficulties that I am having recently. I'm currently in a relationship with a man called Andre for over 2 years now. My problem is that recently I have been feeling very far from Christ and I have never felt like this before. I feel very empty. I am thinking that it has something to do with me being a Christian but not keeping up to the duties that I am suppose to follow and I am having sexual relations with this man outside marriage. I love him so much. I have never felt this way about another man before. He recently proposed but I am not sure if he is genuine or if he is only doing this due to the fact that he is scared of losing me. I asked him to accompany me to church but he says that he don't think that he is ready and he is going to come along when he thinks he is ready. In return, I told him that it's not when you are ready because when Gods calls you, you have to go. I don't know what to do. I try praying about it but it seems like I can't even do that as well; it's like I forgot how to pray; it's like my prayers are not strong enough for God to hear me. I need help!!!"

There are many Christians that get into relationships thinking they can change a person. They engage in "evangelistic dating" where they attempt to convert them while they date them. If God isn't first in his life, then you won't be first in his life. If God can't save him, what makes you think you can? He doesn't want to hear about your Jesus; he wants to get under your dress. No matter how you put it, evangelistic dating ends up converting you to his life of hell; as you attempt to salvage him, he pulls you back to where he is. He doesn't want to live holy, so all while you're "evangelizing" him he'll appease you long enough just to get you to think that he's listening as he's "foreplaying" you right out of your clothes. He'll pretend to like your God and may even go to church to pacify you. Your plan to evangelize someone into loving God so that you could have them for yourself will backfire on you because <u>missionary dating will put you in the missionary position!</u> You'll be singing in the choir, while anxiously looking at the clock, because you can't wait for your pastor to do the benediction so you can run out of church to meet him at the hotel to have "communion" with him as he uses your body as the "sacrifice." You were never to date this person in the first place. Your job is to pray for them; not lay with them!

Tweets: "It's a terrifying thing for a woman to trust a sinful man." @pastormark

I like how William Risk puts it: "How can someone who speaks the name of Jesus with love and reverence be bound for a lifetime to someone who uses His name only as a curse?" You'll end up compromising your standards in the process of trying to cure his allergies to

God. As you begin to constantly adjust your standards, you'll make allowances for his character flaws, minimize the impact of his sinful lifestyle, and justify his excuses as to why he won't live his life for God. You'll rationalize what was once unacceptable, you'll negotiate your standards, and the Word that you hear on Sunday mornings will now become watered down like an alcoholic whose fifth drink now taste like water because he's addicted and has to have more because one sip is not enough. You'll have sex with him for the first time, cry your eyes out in disgust at the thought of how you even allowed yourself to do it, then your sexual encounters will become so normal that you'll have your favorite room you book at the hotel on the west side of town and no longer even look at fornication as sin. That's because sin will numb you. It will sear your conscience and kill it like a hot iron was sat on it and fried it; burning all sense of right and wrong.[2] You'll sit right in church, no longer with conviction and sneer at the Word and it'll fall on deaf ears because it will no longer be enough and no longer satisfying because your sin will water it down. What once was the unthinkable, the forbidden, will now be pleasurable and you'll be ruled by sin itself and become a slave to it, even when you don't want to do it.

"But sin, finding opportunity in the commandment [to express itself], got a hold on me and aroused and stimulated all kinds of forbidden desires (lust, covetousness)." Rom. 7:8 AMP

"Jesus answered them, I assure you, most solemnly I tell you, Whoever commits and practices sin is the slave of sin." John 8:34 AMP

Now that your beliefs are negotiable, you'll begin to question your own salvation, God and His Word. It's interesting how many Christians, like Angela, are praying about something that God has already established and made final in His Word. No matter how hard you pray about it, God will not change His mind. You're "praying," trying to get God to fix the relationship so that you can stay in it because you know you're not suppose to be apart of. To all the Angela's: this is not a prayer issue; it's an obedience issue. "Do not be unequally yoked together with unbelievers." (2 Cor. 6:14) Though God has made it clear, you have disobeyed Him for more than two years in this relationship where you're having sex with someone who doesn't even want your God; yet you're with him though he has made it clear that he doesn't want to be with Him. And the most tragic part is that he has stolen your affections from God and now you're empty as a result of your "break-up with God" to be with this man. It's no mystery; you know exactly why you feel so far away from the Lord. You have chosen and decided to be with this man over God; and it would be a spit in God's face if you leave your marriage with Him, to marry this man.

The mind-boggling part about this is that you're trying to get your boyfriend to do what you won't do. You don't realize that both of you are in the same state. God is calling you and you won't answer; you won't respond or heed to His call to end this relationship with someone who does not want Him to be their God. You don't know what to do? I'll throw your words back at you, "When Gods calls you, *you have to go.*" God is calling you to come back to Him and you need to pick up one foot and start stepping. *You realize that I'm no longer talking to Angela, right?* God already made it clear a long time ago and your repetitious prayer to get Him to allow you stay in the relationship has gone unheard. That is why you don't hear anything but silence; you keep asking God the same thing, hoping for a different answer but God has already spoken and His answer is <u>final</u>. Imagine if someone keeps asking you the same question that you've already answered; you would go mute on them, and turn a deaf ear because they're not listening!

"God has no use for the prayers of the people who won't listen to Him." Pro. 28:9 MSG

"BEHOLD, THE Lord's hand is not shortened at all, that it cannot save, nor His ear dull with deafness, that it cannot hear. But your iniquities have made a separation between you and your God, and your sins have hidden His face from you, so that He will not hear." Is. 59:1-2 AMP

This relationship has already taken your prayer life away, your relationship with God, and the worse thing that could happen is that it pulls you so far away that you can't find your way back. There is no man worth that; none! I don't care how fine or how much money, there's no relationship worth violating or destroying your relationship with God. I don't care how he makes you feel and "how no man has ever loved you like this," because I can guarantee that his love could never be stronger, more intense, unconditional and unending like God's love for you; it doesn't even come close! You need to trust God by surrendering to His will and His Word, and end the relationship.

You need to make a firm declaration to your boyfriend, that nothing and no one is worth your relationship with God. You put your boyfriend before God, so God is "beneath him." He doesn't see you putting God first in your life and as long as he sees that you will put him above God, he'll never come to realize that God is worth him abandoning everything in his own life for Him. Isn't that what you ultimately want anyway, for him to come to know the Lord for Himself? Even if you can't have him, doesn't it mean the world to you for God to at least have him; that is if you really love this man? Listen, I don't know what will be the outcome or what will happen as result of you obeying God and frankly, I don't need to know that. I do know that whatever we do in obedience to God is worth it and are blessed beyond measure as a result of that.

Let me ask you this, "Do you think that your love is more powerful than God's that you can get a man to bow down?" God is the only One that can lead and draw people to Himself (John 6:44). I'm not saying that God doesn't use us to lead people to Christ; I'm not talking about that. I'm talking about how we think that we are so brilliant, so lovely and terrific that we can outdo God at His own job or attempt to become someone's god, thinking that we will change him or her. God has a way of drawing and bringing people to Him and His love is more powerful and potent than ours and when we attempt to use missionary relationships to convert people we end up doing more damage than helping. No matter how beautiful you are or how shapely your body is, you cannot change him; *ask Halle Berry*. Cute will not change him and neither will having sex with him will transform him into a good Christian boy because his relationship with sex is out of order and he has essentially made it his god and women continue to perpetuate and exasperate this dysfunctional relationship he has with sex by using their bodies to keep men in bondage. Sex is his god and he'll do what he has to do to worship it. Even if he has to pretend and hang out with your God or impersonate salvation to please you. Such was the case with Joann.

Just as Joann stood at pump number nine filling her car up, a white Range Rover with twenty-two inch, chrome rims pulls into the gas station and a "gentleman" gets out and immediately notices Joann's long, beautiful hair, pretty smile and the most gorgeous face he had ever seen! Taking "no" for an answer, Morris persuaded Joann to give her phone number to him and accept his offer to take her out on a date. As he drives away, Joann gets in her car that is filled with the sound of crying. She turns around with concern and says, "What's wrong? Why are you crying?" Crying like she was put in time-out for eternity, her eight-year old daughter sitting in the back seat responds, "Why did you give him your number, Mommy; he's a sinner. Waaaaaaaahhhhh!"

Despite the wisdom bellowing preeminent danger from the backseat, Joann proceeded to let Morris entertain her because she knew she had no intentions on sleeping with him. Joann was a PK, a preacher's kid, who had vowed to celibacy until marriage and was determined to keep her "second virginity." So Joann began dating Morris, making it clear that sex was not an option. Out to win her heart and her virginity, Morris began "wining and dining" Joann, medium-well steaks with garden salad drizzled with Ranch dressing, getting up going to Wendy's at 2 a.m. just to get her favorite number four (supersized with a Frosty), started attending church to impress her, impersonating praises to the left of him and moved from the back row to sitting right on the front row of the pew, looking as awkward as a toe nail with a bunion on it! *Wait, that may be normal for some of you.* As ill fitting as it is, there are many Christians like Joann who are persuaded and allured by charming, "good" men that are no good for you who are not "that bad" because they at least have *some* moral conscience.

I love how Ben young and Dr. Samuel Adams adequately describes it in *10 Commandments Of Dating*, "Men will do anything (yes, anything!) to impress a woman. If a guy needs to walk an aisle, get baptized, speak in tongues, bark, or even lick the lint out of Buddha's belly button, he'll do it, just to keep the girl." I love the image in my head of him licking the lint out of Buddha's belly button! LOL! Though humorous, there's so much truth in that. Morris became a magician, pulling all the tricks out of his baseball cap, though he eventually grew tired; tired of wining and dining her with no exchange because she wouldn't "put out." The relationship lasted about two, fondling-dry humping years before he drained his pockets, time and energy and before he realized that Joann was adamant about not having sex (at least not "all the way") until marriage.

I know some of you are thinking, "whew, Joann is safe; she didn't have sex with him." But many of you are playing Russian roulette with sexual purity, playing a game of 'A Chance Of Losing *It,*' by entertaining relationships that defy your beliefs and sexual integrity. You're thinking Joann is safe but she wasted two years of her life with a man that didn't serve and love her God, all while marring and contaminating her purity, and only escaped sex by the fraction of a second! Even if you're not going "all the way," you're still tainting and polluting the very essence of who you are. If I take a glass of water and give it to you with half of it laced with poison, would you drink it? Absolutely not! Because the poison affected the entire glass of water and it's no longer pure.

Essentially what many of you are doing is contaminating yourself with sexual impurity all during your single years and get to your wedding day with a white, beautiful dress on but it has red blood stains on it. Blood, toxins, and the stains of sexual covenants you've made with different dating partners throughout your years as a single. You allow people to come vicariously through your life, imitate what they've seen on screen or through soft porn, pounce on top of you, go inside your treasure vault and take your most precious treasures, but throw back scraps when they're done with you.

> "Do not give what is holy to the dogs; nor cast your pearls before swine, lest they trample them under their feet, and turn and tear you in pieces." Matthew 7:6 NKJV

Our relationship manual just gave us a very, critical warning about getting into a relationship with someone who is not holy, someone who does not have a relationship with God, using the metaphor of what was considered to be the most unclean animal: **a pig,** and then contrasting it with **a pearl:** rare, valuable, precious, and priceless. The New Living Translation says, "Don't waste what is holy on people who are unholy." Someone who is not living a holy and righteous life will only trample over your body and your purity and tear it into pieces. A dog will not honor, preserve and uphold the value of a treasure and neither will a pig. Do you realize what will happen if you give a pig something as precious as a pearl?

Pigs live in mud and will only get the pearl and put it in the mud with them because a pig doesn't have the ability nor the capacity to appreciate a pearl. A pig will lie around all day in the mud and will only jump up when it's time to eat or have sex. A pig will lie on his side all day, waddle in slop, and will consume and eat anything you throw at it. You've heard the statement, "Eat like a pig"? A pig will slobber, get food all over them, and gulp it down without swallowing. After "pigging out," he'll mount himself on the back of the female pig. He then screws himself into the cervix of the female pig (heifer); it's where we get the slang, "screw." This sex act will take around fifteen minutes and then the pig dismounts and it is his custom to then go and find a mud hole and lie in it.

    This is exactly how an unclean, unholy man will do you: he'll lie around in a dirty, filthy, muddy, lust-filled life where he'll devour and consume any woman he can get his mouth and hands on; he'll only call you when he wants to screw or have sex, put you in the "doggy" position, mount up on the back of you like a heifer and thirty minutes later he's putting you out of his house or leaving you lying in the hotel bed with his mud all over you; he only sees and treats the sex act and your pearl like dirt and of no value. This is what happens when a pure woman gives her pearl to a pig. All too often, I see many women get in relationships knowing that he's a pig or a dog from the beginning. You're giving what's precious to someone who will not even value your worth, doesn't understand why you're committing to sexual purity and frankly does not even care.

"Do not be unequally yoked with unbelievers [do not make mismated alliances with them or come under a different yoke with them, inconsistent with your faith]. For what partnership have right living and right standing with God with iniquity and lawlessness? Or how can light have fellowship with darkness? What harmony can there be between Christ and Belial [the devil]? Or what has a believer in common with an unbeliever? 2 Cor. 6:14-18 AMP

    How can light and darkness even be found in the same place? There is a separation between light and dark; light automatically cancels out darkness. When you come into a dark room and turn on a light switch, darkness instantly leaves. There should be something about the light, the Christ, in you that blinds dark's eyesight. What harmony can there be between Christ and the devil? None; you would never see Christ sitting across the table at Starbucks with the devil having a cup of coffee because they have NOTHING in common! There is no agreement, commonality or harmony in thought, mind or spirit. When dating a non-Christian, you need to understand that the relationship is already hell-bound. It's definitive of whatever hell has to offer: shame, pain and unending torture!

"Don't become partners with those who reject God. How can you make a partnership out of right and wrong? That's not partnership; that's war. Is light best friends with dark? Does Christ go strolling with the Devil? Do trust and mistrust hold hands? MSG

    I have often had many women say, "he has everything I wanted in a man, except he's not saved." Well, if he has "everything" but God, then he has absolutely NOTHING! No matter how great his personality is, what great career he has, or how much money he has in his bank account, if he has rejected God, then everything in his life is for naught. "And what do you benefit if you gain the whole world but lose your own soul?" (Mark 8:36) You can't make a partnership out of right and wrong, no matter how good you *think* you two will be together. I love how the Message translation says it, "That's not partnership; that's war!" You might as well put on your combat boots, grab your artillery, and instead of your Cover Girl lipstick, put war paint on your face because you're going into battle when you become partners with someone who rejects God. You will have a battle with peace and anguish in your mind and in your spirit. "How can two walk together unless they agree?" (Amos 3:3) There's no way that you can be together without spiritual agreement; that is the foundation that's necessary to uphold and sustain any relationship.

> "Do not be unequally yoked with unbelievers [do not make mismated alliances with them or come under a different yoke with them, inconsistent with your faith].

To plow a field, many farmers utilize an ox and they yoke or bind a pair of oxen, of equal strengths, in order to get them to work together, in the same direction and to pull the plow equally. The yoke is a heavy, U-shaped bar that fits around the neck of the oxen, which forces the animals to work together and carry the same load. Now, imagine a U-shaped bar around your neck, tying you together with an unbeliever; it will choke the life out of you! That's because you and this unbeliever are pulling in two different directions. Couples often ask me how they can know if they are equally yoked. One main way to know if you're unequally yoked is that your life feels like it's being choked to death! You're trying to force something that doesn't work; you're unequally yoked. You're going towards God; (s)he is pulling away from Him. It's kind of what happens when the alignment of your truck is off; the wheels are going in opposite directions making your Escalade truck wobble and steer off the road. When you're in a relationship with an unbeliever, you're being pulled in the opposite direction of your destiny and detouring off the path that God wants you to take. God has an established, pre-determined plan for your life, and dating an unbeliever would thwart that plan, "For I know the thoughts and plans that I have for you, says the Lord, thoughts and plans for welfare and peace and not for evil, to give you hope in your final outcome." Jer. 29:11 AMP

"Thou shalt not plow with an ox and an ass together." Deut. 22:10 KJV

"You shall not plow with an ox [a clean animal] and a donkey [unclean] together." AMP

An ox is a servant, with a sacrificial nature that is tolerant and submits to commands; while on the other hand an ass is rebellious, defiant, stubborn, and often called a fool. Whenever you see a donkey or an ass notated in Scripture, it is synonymous with an unbeliever or a fool: one who rejects or is without the nature of God. An unbeliever is a fool, like an ass, because he lives an unrighteous life and he is rebellious against God and lacks or is without the wisdom of God; he is unclean because he has not allowed Christ to cleanse his life of sin and unrighteousness. Our relationship manual says that we must not allow a servant, a child of God, one who sacrifices their life to Him, submitting and surrendering it to the commandments of the Lord, to yoke together with a foolish, rebellious, God-defiant, unclean person who refuses to submit their life to God...in which some of you are in a relationship with right now and need to let that *donkey* go!

"Do not make mismated alliances with them or come under a different yoke with them, inconsistent with your faith."
"These people draw near to Me with their mouth, And honor Me with their lips, But their heart is far from Me." Matt 15:8 NKJV

One of the most dangerous things a Christian can have is lip service but not action or relationship behind it. That is why God makes it clear to not enter a relationship with them; it's like having a pulse but no heartbeat. I have an announcement to make: unbelievers attend church, unbelievers carry Bibles, and they know a few Scriptures, too. Many people think that being unequally yoked only applies to unbelievers but you can very well be unequally yoked with a believer. The question is, "what do they believe?" There are some "unbelieving Christians" that don't believe or live what the Bible says. There are some Christians that don't believe you have to attend church, live holy or wait until marriage to have sex. What about their commitment to prayer, their pursuit and passion for God and their relationship with Him? Is their life filled with worship and the presence of God? Is God leading them and is God's Word the final authority in their life?

I've seen men attempt to take a Christian girl, new and young in her faith, and try to mold her into being what he wants in a godly woman. It only frustrated him and the relationship because you can't force anyone to change or be the kind of Christian you want them to be; only the Lord can do that. [1] I've also seen a church full of women try and throw themselves on the "new convert" in church; though a man, he's a baby Christian that's on baby formula and Similac milk and he does not need you to breast feed him. You wouldn't date a nine-month old baby would you? That's ridiculous! A baby:

- Does not speak and understand the same language
- The only language they know or the way they communicate right now is to wine and cry
- They're underdeveloped and irresponsible, so they're helpless and need you to come to their aid all the time.
- You have to clean up their mess
- They have to be looked after
- They don't know right from wrong
- They can't just eat on their own just yet; they have to be fed
- They want to be comforted, rocked and held all the time

- All they do is poop, sleep and eat!

It's the same with dating a baby in Christ. You don't speak the same language yet: you want to wait until marriage to have sex and they want you to hold them and rock their flesh, and see how far they can go with you physically. There will be communication barriers and a breakdown in the relationship, with lots of disagreements, arguments filled with crying because you two will be at odds with one another because you're not cohesive or in agreement on key spiritual issues. They'll wine about how much spiritual pressure and demands you put on them and expect you to pacify their childish play with sin. They will expect you to feed them spiritually instead of depending on God, so you will be burdened down with the responsibility of developing them. When God is getting the poop out of them, purging them of their old lifestyle, you'll have to change the dirty diaper, getting the residue of feces of their former sins on you. Do you get what I'm saying? In the infancy of their faith, a baby Christian needs the nurturing care of their Father to raise them up, building a strong foundation of faith in Christ because if that stage is not set right, when they begin to walk they are subject to *fall*. Their walk with Christ must begin on a firm foundation. He/she needs to nurture and cultivate their own personal relationship organically with the Lord, to mature and grow in his/her faith solely and exclusively with God because they have yet to develop their allegiance to the Lord and have yet to find their rightful place in worship, and if you date them during this process you'll get a premature Christian. Dating them during this stage is interrupting the process in which God needs their undivided devotion to Him so that they can become complete in Him or they will be incomplete with you. They need to "date" God solely before they try to date or be with anyone else. You hear me, women of god? Let the Lord make a godly man out of him before you try to make a boyfriend or husband out of him! Someone who is not spiritually mature most often do not have the same commitment to prayer, similar faith level, integrity, or character as someone who has developed a passionate relationship with the Lord, and therefore, is unequally yoked and "inconsistent with your faith." Are you better than them? Absolutely not! What I am saying is that your spiritual altitude should mirror one another. Lifestyle, life direction, spiritual maturity and compatible beliefs are critical factors in determining if you should date someone. Use the following as a guide to determine if you are equally yoked:

Equally Yoked	Unequally Yoked
Equality in Spiritual maturity	Infantile with Spirituality
Spiritual harmony	Spiritual discord
Shared degrees of holiness	Apathy for righteousness
Same level of drive/ambition	Unequal commitment to purpose
Like-mindedness	Difference in mindsets
Similar life paths and goals	Opposite direction and goals
Shared passion of worship	Unequal levels of devotion
Compatible Character Development	Different degrees of Godliness

Alignment of values	Divergence in morals & standards
Comparable in relating/communicating	Unequal relational skills
Shared views on family	Conflicting vision on family
Commonality with lifestyle	Divergence in daily habits/living

"I assume I'm addressing believers now who are mature... I don't want you to become part of something that reduces you to less than yourself. And you can't have it both ways, banqueting with the Master one day and slumming with demons the next. Besides, the Master won't put up with it. He wants us—all or nothing. Do you think you can get off with anything less?" 1 Cor. 10:15; 20-22 MSG

Whether they're allergic to God, an unbelieving donkey, straddling the fence, faith-deficient, a newborn Christian, or waning in spiritual apathy, it is fundamentally important that you do not yoke up with someone who is inconsistent with your faith. I don't give a rat's turd about how much you two click, how compatible you are, how well you two get alone, or how much money he makes, or how attractive she is, if they don't have a relationship with Christ, you're setting yourself up for devastation and unnecessary heartache when you date someone who is not after God. You put your own personal relationship with God in hostage and in critical condition; *or is it already?* For you to even consider such a thing, I have to wonder about the condition of your relationship with God. If an unbeliever feels comfortable with dating you, then you need to check the temperature gauge of your relationship and see if you are lukewarm, hot or cold for Him. Check your relationship with God, your fervency for Him, your commitment to Him and His Word, because a HOT Christian should never have the desire to be with someone who is COLD for God. Why would I give myself to someone who won't give himself to God?

"How can someone who speaks the name of Jesus with love and reverence be bound for a lifetime to someone who uses His name only as a curse?" William Risk

'The LORD had clearly instructed the people of Israel, 'You must not marry them, because they will turn your hearts to their gods.' Yet Solomon insisted on loving them anyway...And in fact, they did turn his heart away from the LORD. In Solomon's old age, they turned his heart to worship other gods instead of being completely faithful to the LORD his God. 1 Kings 11:2-4 NLT

Wow, wow, and wow! That's deep! There is no one, and I mean no one, worth you leaving God! Why does God instruct us not to date unbelievers? It's the very tenants of our faith, everything we stand for, the foundation of our life, so to date someone who doesn't believe or live for God is spiritual suicide. It seeks to kill everything that God sacrificially died for: to have an unending, eternal relationship with us. When God gives us an instruction, it's protecting us, it's protecting our freedom, and it's protecting His relationship with us. God says I don't want you getting into a relationship with anyone that doesn't have a relationship with Me because they will take you away from Me! I know many of you are so used to short-lived relationships, break-ups, and temporary people passing through your life but when God came after you, it was for keeps. He didn't get in this relationship for it to be short-term, ***but for eternity.*** He's invested a whole lot to get you and He's not going to sit back, lackadaisical about it and allow you to be taken from Him; He's going to protect it at all cost, separating anything that will take you away from Him. Look at this again: He told Solomon, 'let me make this clear to you, if you get in a relationship with someone that does not love Me, they're going to be the cause of you leaving Me and turning your heart and your affections away from Me." And you must do the same; you **must** close the door on any relationships that will pull your heart away from the Lord's. I can't stress this enough: don't enter into a relationship with someone who is faith deficient and allergic to God; it's contagious and infectious and you don't want to catch what they have because **it will spiritually kill you!** (I Kings 11, Proverbs 18:1 AMP, 1 Corinthians 6:18)

Question: "How do you move past that person who is everything on your list but saved? Particularly when most of the brothers who are saved have nothing else that is on your list?" D. Robinson

How do you move past that person? You keep on passing him/her by! "Christian" should be at the top of your list and if that person is not one, then your nickname need to be K.I.M and you need to KEEP IT MOVING! You should be petrified to be in a relationship with someone who is not in one with God! Knowing that a person does not have God in their life should cause you to run like Forest Gump in the opposite direction! Dating someone who is not a Christian or doesn't have a relationship with God is like trying to force yourself in a pair of jeans three sizes smaller: it's painful and no matter how much you try to force it, it won't fit; *epic fashion fai!* If you meet someone that has everything on your list but God, then everything on the list amounts to nothing; it should not even be up for consideration! When you date an unbeliever, essentially what you're saying is that your relationship with God is optional. You need to make this a firm, essential requirement for you to even consider a relationship because without God, you have nothing! My dating motto is this: I LIKE MEN HOW I LIKE MY WORD DOCUMENTS: SAVED! No exceptions!

If you still have a desire for the forbidden, then you need to allow God to change your taste buds. You shouldn't want the same things you as you did before coming to Christ. When I was younger I could eat all kinds of junk food and sweet candy. Now that I'm older, my taste buds have changed and I no longer have a desire for it and it's a turn-off to even eat it. Dating someone who is not in a relationship with God should be a turn-off to you. When I was a "young" Christian, I had the same appetite for the kind of men that I dated in my B.C days (before Christ). I was dating this guy named Vic who I thought was the epitome of everything I wanted in a man; he could do no wrong...he was perfect! And the most attractive thing to walk planet Earth, I might add. Even though our relationship ended I still longed for him and hoped that one day we would rekindle the relationship. Time past, my relationship began to mature tremendously with the Lord and then I ran into Vic one day and nothing in me leaped! The appetite I had for him turned sour because though he was still attractive, had moral decency, and all the qualities I wanted in a man, he had not given his life to the Lord and there was nothing in me that wanted him.

If you have an appetite for the same kind of men/women that you were with prior to your relationship with the Lord then you need to allow God to purify your desires and change your taste buds for things that are pure. You must develop and commit to your relationship with the Lord in such a way that nothing or no (wo)man should come between it. God is looking for unwavering commitment from us because that is what He gives to us. Your relationship with God is the most important aspect of your life and if you are not committed to your first Love, then any other attempts at love will prove to be an epic fail! In making a dedication to your relationship with God, you put yourself in a position to find committed, unwavering love in other relationships in your life. You must remain 100% committed to God, with your heart and your affections firmly, permanently fixated on Him! ♥

Prayer: insert personal prayer here_____
_____
_____

Why does God instruct us not to date unbelievers? _____
_____

What does it mean to be unequally yoked? _____
_____

Explain the illustration of the ox and the donkey and how that is compares to a Christian dating a non-Christian _____
_____

In what way will dating a non-Christian take away your freedom? _____
_____

Have you (or someone you know) ever dated someone who was a passive/wavering Christian that did not have the same beliefs as you? What was the result of that? What kind of problems did this cause?
_____
_____

Take a look at the history of people you have been in a relationship with. Is there a difference between the type of people you were attracted or have dated before you gave your life to the Lord versus now? Explain _____
_____

Why is it not good enough for a person to have everything on your list but God? _____
_____

What happened to Solomon when he entered into a relationship with women who did not believe in his God? _____

If you are currently in a relationship now, are you in spiritual agreement? Has (s)he made Jesus Lord over their lives? Explain. _____
_____

In what ways can you effectively minister to an unbeliever without engaging in an intimate relationship with them? _____
_____

Why does it benefit you to date someone that is a Christian? _____
_____

If you are currently in a relationship now, are you in spiritual alignment or on the same faith level? Are your goals and aspirations in alignment? Are you plowing in the same direction? Explain.
_____

[1]Proverbs 19:14, [2]1 Timothy 4:2

I'd Rather Be Single, than Sorry If...

My relationship with God is being affected
I've become emotionally ruined and unstable
My relationship is more physical than emotional
My relationship is more physical than spiritual
We are spiritually incompatible
My boyfriend/girlfriend won't commit/emotionally unavailable
He/she is constantly violating my boundaries
I am not respected or valued
My boyfriend/girlfriend is dishonest and unfaithful
I don't feel safe
He/she has my non-negotiables
The relationship is not growing/producing and is at a stand still
My boyfriend/girlfriend is not led by God or has fallen off/backslidden
I have a gut feeling that something's just not right
I'm not happy
I'm losing myself
Ever since I got in this relationship, I've been alienated from my family/friends
My self-esteem has taken a nosedive down
My boyfriend/girlfriend is not passionate about God
My boyfriend/girlfriend twists and manipulates scripture to justify their lifestyle
My boyfriend/girlfriend uses me for sex or money
We're constantly in conflict/fighting or disagreeing
We're always breaking up, then making up
It feels like I'm trying to force the relationship to gel
This relationship causes me to compromise
There's no passion in the relationship; I'm not excited about us being together
I know I'm settling and can do better than this
My boyfriend/girlfriend has fatal flaws
I'm hurting more than I'm happy
My boyfriend/girlfriend has controlling/obsessive behavior
I'm distracted from my purpose
I've stopped praying and going to church
God is no longer number one; they're becoming more of a 'god' than God
Our relationship is sexual
The only thing I do is this relationship; it consumes my life
My boyfriend/girlfriend has violent/abusive behavior
I don't have peace

Chapter 16
Breaking up

Have you ever purchased something from a store or offline, and when you got home you pulled it out of the bag and realized that the item did not live up to your expectations? Oh, how I remember that day so vividly! I had major plans for that dress but when I tried it on and looked in the mirror, what stared back at me looked grossly different from what the mannequin looked like in the store! I immediately scrambled to the bottom of the bag looking for the receipt, and then I ran for my purse, feeling my way to the bottom, only grabbing what appeared to be a tube of lip-gloss. The worse thing that could happen is losing the receipt and having to resort to a store credit or not being able to return it at all is a shopaholic's nightmare! I opened the inside zipper of my purse and a white, shiny sparkle of hope stuck out at me! I feel the entire universe is on my side, so I grabbed the corners of hope and out jumps the receipt to my 'not-what-I-expected-dress' and I grab the receipt and kiss it! Pulling the receipt from my lips, I look at the bottom of it and my face dropped, 'No refunds, exchanges ONLY! Exchange within 30 days!' Imagine that, stuck with something of no use to me. If you're going to ever invest in anything, you need to know the refund and return policy. Since dating often has a high return rate on it, I have created a dating return policy that will help you navigate through the ups and downs and uncertainty of relationships.

Buy At Your Own Risk

Whenever you make a purchase a receipt (acknowledgment that you paid and received goods) will accompany it and should the product not live up to your standards, you can get a refund. It's like relationships, you start dating someone and what they told you about themselves in the beginning of the relationship, they are not living up to those expectations and you think to yourself, "This is not what I signed up for; I want a refund!" If only it were that easy to refund a relationship. Remember that dating is a temporary, in-between state and either your relationship will lead to marriage or you will remain single…unless you intend on allowing someone to be a squatter and reside in your life for free. Since all of your attempts at dating will not result in marriage, you will have to stand in a long line like the rest of many singles and undergo the dreaded refund process to get your heart back, known as the "break-up." Yep, it's just what it sounds like: breaking, ripping, tearing, shattering, and rupturing the heart.

As we have already laid in the foundation of this book, God never intended for us to have our hearts dismembered and then have the pieces of it divided among multiple lovers. Breaking up is like that dreaded tooth extraction that you hate you have to have, but many singles can minimize break-ups by not allowing the cavity of broken relationships to become a custom in their lives and simply choose wisely and make smart dating choices in the beginning. As we discussed before in *Relationship Status*, all dating relationships have the risk factor but the more you are sure about yourself, your needs, and what you want out of relationships, and more importantly, maintaining a strong relationship with the Lord where He navigates your relationships, then you will greatly increase your chances of forgoing the refund line where so many other singles stand trying to gather the pieces of their heart and life back if you take calculated risk instead of just jumping into relationships.

Money Back Guarantee

Unlike some garments, the theory "one size fits all" does not apply to dating. You will meet many prospects that you may be attracted to, but not "equally yoked" or compatible with, where you two just "don't fit" and that is okay. I know that there are no guarantees with dating and just because you date someone does not mean that you're going to get married to that person, but forgive me, I just think there should be some guarantee policy, something quite different and distinctive when two Christians are dating. I'm not talking about a guarantee of marriage; I'm talking about a guarantee or an assurance of integrity, honesty, and respect when you see the "Christian seal." Even if the relationship does not lead to marriage, I should know, with *that seal,* that there is an unspoken warranty that: we will not lead one another on, this relationship will not be another sex partner added to my belt, and if the relationship does not lead to marriage, we should leave the relationship knowing a greater part of ourselves and have discovered more about God and have grown closer to Him, because I saw Him in you. Is that too much to ask? Or am I expecting too much from a Christian? Absolutely not! If you're a Christian, then dating should be earmarked with integrity, truth, honor, decency, respect, and the highest regard for others.

- If you are not interested in someone, do no lead them on, letting them think there's a chance when there's not. Don't send mixed messages and flirt with them outside of church but then act as if you don't see them on Sunday morning during praise and worship by closing your eyes to make them invisible. If you went on a date and you find that friendship is the only level you're interested in, then say that. Speak the truth in love; the truth will set you free, *from the relationship*. Be kind and respectful and extend the same graciousness that you would want.
- If you've hit a fork in the road, don't stop calling them, ignore their text messages or leave the relationship in limbo. Telling someone, "I think we should take a break" is like going on a vacation from your job and never coming back when you should have

put your resignation in. When someone uses the old "let's take a break," they know the relationship has ended but don't want to face the uncomfortable breakup. Saying you need time apart but in actuality you know you need to break it off completely is irresponsible. Instead of just cutting off communication or sending a text message that says, "It's over; satan, get thee behind me," you need to have a "grown-up" conversation and bring closure. Don't be vague or give the impression that there's still a chance, be respectful and honest and speak your feelings about the ending of the relationship in truth and with clarity. Leave the relationship with grace and dignity, for yourself and the other person.

- These common Christian break-up lines, "I need to focus more on my relationship with God; He told me to end the relationship; God revealed to me that you're not the one," are mere excuses for deferring responsibility instead of taking personal ownership. If God told you to end the relationship, then why didn't He tell you not to get in the relationship in the first place? The relationship is not God's will now but it was His will for you to get in the relationship? Instead of embezzling your faith and using God as an escape-goat or the "fall guy," focus on the broken infrastructure or the breakdown of the relationship, "We're incompatible in key areas" or "although there were some good times getting to know you, that alone will not sustain a relationship and the issues we have far outweigh the good times and are irreparable" as opposed to telling someone, "God said you're not good enough for me." Don't you dare even give people that impression of God and that He handles relationships that way, because He doesn't.

"What this adds up to, then, is this: no more lies, no more pretense. Tell your neighbor the truth. In Christ's body we're all connected to each other, after all. When you lie to others, you end up lying to yourself." Eph 4:25 MSG

Refund Policy
Issues that are eligible for a return include (but are not limited to): spiritual incompatibility, anger, dishonesty, disrespect, drugs, gambling, emotionally toxic, emotionally unavailable, sexual pressure even after you've established boundaries and they continue to cross them, infidelity, deception, verbally/emotionally/physically abusive, all your friends say you've changed for the worse, your mentors disapprove, and the relationship is unhealthy/not bearing fruit/unproductive.

*(Physical, verbal or emotional abuse should never be tolerated. If you experience any type of abuse you must get out of the relationship immediately and seek help.)

Hold on to your receipt, and assess the product for 90 days. If the product is not up to the highest quality and standards, then get a refund. If the relationship does not further you spiritually, mentally, or emotionally, if it doesn't further your life's purpose, if it doesn't' protect or honor your beliefs or improve your life, then please proceed to the customer service department and return it for a refund.

Any product with the "Christian" brand where the seal has been broken or is defective should be returned with or without a receipt to the Manufacturer for repairs or restoration immediately. This means that if the person you're dating names or associate themselves as a Christian and you fail to see working evidence of that, then this product is defective and should be returned to the Manufacturer immediately for Him to fix. Don't attempt to fix it yourself, that's the Manufacturers job. We cannot change or fix anyone. We must leave that up to God to change them.

Other than futile reasons for breaking up with someone, like you hate how they chew with their mouth open, I have comprised a list of more crucial grounds for terminating a relationship. To determine if the relationship should be *returned*, use the list in "I'd Rather Be Single Than Sorry" as a guideline, as well as this list:

- The person you're dating is a Christian but does not follow Christ.
- He/she is missing any of your top five must-haves.
- He has one or more of your non-negotiables.
- What (s)he does is not consistent with what he says OR his actions are different from his belief system.
- He/she has chronic issues or fatal flaws, such as anger, rage, consistently dishonest/deceitful, or unfaithful.
- The person you're dating is physically or verbally abusive.
- The person you're dating is a jealous person and attempts to isolate you from family and friends.
- Your children absolutely hate your date!
- The person you're dating has criminal, gambling, or drug problems/addictions.
- He/she encourages or pressures you to do things contrary to your beliefs.
- The person you're dating has these ongoing sexual issues: fornication, masturbation, pornography, pedophilia, or homosexuality.
- The person you're dating only wants to spend time with you when they want to be intimate with you.
- The person you're dating manipulates scriptures to control you, change your belief system, or in attempts to excuse irresponsibility or wrong/sinful behavior.

- The person you're dating is self-centered, selfish, does not respond to your needs, criticizes you, and does not keep his/her promises.
- The person you're dating does not have the same pursuit and attention to the relationship.
- Your date does not want to commit to the relationship but wants to spend a lot of time with you.
- The person I'm dating does not ever want to get married.
- The person I'm dating is emotionally unstable.
- My life goals and the direction that I'm going, is completely different from the person I'm dating.
- You are often unhappy or hurting in this relationship. Pain lets you know an intruder is there.
  You feel yourself drifting away from God. The relationship is a distraction from your relationship with God or your purpose.
- I can't put my hand on it, but something just doesn't feel right.

"God is not the author of confusion but of peace." 1 Corinthians 14:33

Remember I said that one of the greatest proofs that you're in the right relationship is God's peace? Well, a lack of peace is the greatest proof that you're *not in the right relationship* or it's not God's will. Your spirit will be unsettled and troubled if you're with someone that He doesn't approve of. That unrest will also happen if the relationship is a distraction and pulling you away from the Lord, or God knows something well into the future that is undetected or hidden from you. Trust Him and take heed. When you don't have peace, listen to your spirit and God's leading through that. If you lack peace, then that relationship is null and void, and it is no longer an option. Don't hold on to something that God is breaking or releasing you from.

Buyer's   Remorse
Are you an impulse shopper where buy something on the whim without consideration but get home and say, "Now why did I buy that?" Some of you are "impulse daters" where you jump in and out of relationship without careful consideration and you exchange relationships like you change your clothes. Just as you should give thorough consideration when entering a relationship, you should also do the same when determining if you should exit one.
- When there is a string of break-ups trailing behind you it's usually a sign that you are led and driven by your flesh and emotions. People are not disposable and are not to be used for selfish gain or pleasure; if you leave relationships because of boredom or only stay as long as there is a chemical high, then you need to take a hiatus from dating until you get your flesh and desires under God's control.

- During stages of your relationship, you should constantly take inventory of the relationship, it's progress, growth/decline, and its direction to determine if it is aligning with your expectations and your life plans. With each season or stage, there should be some contribution to your life where you're advancing and growing. Who would be crazy enough to remain in a company where there is no *profit margin* or where there is a consistent decline? At the end of the day, it boils down to basic arithmetic: people will either add or subtract from your life. If they're not adding, then you need to subtract them.
- Sit down and take inventory of your relationship and list what issues are prevalent. Ask yourself this question: "If I could change this about him/her, it would be _____." If it is one of your must-haves or your non-negotiables, then you're in trouble! But if you will be okay if "that" never changes, then it's safe to move forward in the relationship and begin working on managing your differences.
- The work of relationships are more about managing your differences than your similarities so conflict and disagreements does not necessarily mean that you're in a bad relationship; it could be that God is pressing against your flesh through your dating partner to drive out character defects or teaching you how to handle the ebb and flow of relationships. You need to learn the difference between drama and reality. Ensure that you are not leaving the relationship because it's time to put "work" into the relationship and develop it; but if your relationship has more issues than a magazine, I suggest you cancel your subscription. If your relationship looks like a "reality" TV episode, then grab the remote control and change it!
- If your shirt is simply missing a button, then you can easily grab needle and thread and fix that. If there are minor alterations, then the relationship may be worth keeping but if there are things like trust issues then you have a major problem. "Trust is like a car without gas; you can stay in it all you want, but it won't go anywhere." (Unknown) If the garment of your relationship is severely stained or torn, and there are negative or destructive patterns that your dating partner persists in, or they have fatal flaws and defects in their character, then there's no amount of patching together you can do to fix the relationship. You need to return them back to the Manufacturer for repairs, for God to fix them.
- When your dating partner does not live up to your expectations or to the standards in which they claimed in the beginning of the relationship or they persist in inappropriate behavior even after you've had "the talk," then it would be nothing short of insanity to remain in the relationship. In the words of Pastor Mark Driscoll, "It doesn't matter if he apologizes, does he repent?" Repentance means to turn away from the negative/destructive behavior. If he/she continues to say, "I'm sorry"

without changing their behavior, then I'm sorry, it's time to let the relationship go.

"SOMEWHERE…someone is out of place because their place is next to you." Mike Murdock

The Fine Print
Whenever you consider a relationship you want to make sure that you read the fine print. People don't always tell you what you really need to know about the relationship or the more important things that you need to know about a person are not as visibly seen. You want to make sure that you put on your spiritual discernment glasses and look at the relationship with your ears and not your eyes to determine if you are going in the same direction and if this person qualifies to be in your life. Don't simply buy the relationship based on the hype of what their advertising; you must read the fine print to know exactly what you're getting in to.

- I'm a grown woman! If you're looking for a fling then you can go down the street somewhere. I don't date like I did when I was sixteen years old. I do not date casually or allow people to use my life as a hang out or a playground. If I don't believe the relationship has the capacity for marriage in the future then I will not allow myself to be a temporary girlfriend or idle in a transitional relationship while I "wait" for my husband. Eliminating someone that is NOT my husband is just as important as being found by the man that will be my husband. The same goes for you, my brothers; if you don't see long-term potential or you perceive that she is not wife material then don't hang out in the relationship. One of the top reasons why singles stay single longer than they have to is because are in dormant or casual relationships, missing the opportunity for the person they are called to marry. Sitting in a transitional relationship is not an option because it will cause you to miss that special someone because someone else is trespassing in their spot. I'm not asking for marriage entering into the relationship or even asking for a commitment on the first date or the first few dates for that matter, but I do want to only consider relationships that have the potential or capacity for long-term commitment. Are you available for short-term relationships? Then why get involved with short-term people? Don't damage your life or risk finding a great relationship because of reckless, casual dating.
- Are you trying to find out where the relationship is going? Let me offer you some relationship GPS: look to the right of you, if that person is not moving you forward, then take the next exit on the left. Do not stay in a relationship that is going nowhere or hindering your growth. Exiting a relationship that is not aligning with your expectations or going in the direction of your goals, essentially will take you off God's path. One thing about time is that you can't get it back; so why waste it? If the woman you're dating makes excuses about taking the relationship to the next step

and wants to stay in the friend zone while she continues to enjoy your time and free dinner dates, then you're wasting your time and your money, my brother. If you've been in a relationship for quite some time and he never discusses the future, it's probably because you don't have one, girlfriend. If he only wants to *lease you with an option to buy*, while he shops around to see if he wants to be with another woman, then you want to stop making the relationship a priority when he's making you an option. Don't stay in a relationship where someone treats you like an alternative. Go where you're adored, not ignored. If you're in a one-way relationship, where it's one-sided, then go in one direction ---> out of the relationship. Do not stay in a relationship if the person you're dating is not "all in".

- It's not exactly what you wanted but you'll take it because you don't want to end up alone. If you feel that way then you need to dive head first in this text message from God: "Every good and perfect gift comes from the Lord."[1] Am I saying the relationship has to be perfect? Absolutely not! What I am saying is that God has designed His best for you and to settle for a substandard, mediocre, passive, half-hearted relationship is not His will for your life. Settling is the best way to lose out on what God has for you; I'm just saying.

Expiration Date

If you've ever seen milk past its expiration date then you know it's disgusting! There's nothing worse than expired milk or an expired relationship; consuming it is not good for no one! When the expiration date on a failed relationship arrives and the people in it are not responsible by leaving, then staying past the unauthorized time causes heartache, emotional ruin, compromise, soul ties, and sexual calamity. It's like a houseguest who has stayed past their welcome and now they have to be put out! It's clearly over, but you refuse to do what is necessary and leave. And this is the predominant reason why it takes more time to recover because you stayed longer than you should have. There have been numerous times that I've had someone single tell me that God told them to leave a relationship, but all too often, they allow their emotions to govern their decisions and they remain in a relationship that is no good for them or is not going in the same direction of their destiny.

- There are singles that will get in or stay in a relationship because it's better than nothing. The biggest reason why many singles stay in toxic, passive, dead-end relationships is because staying is easier than going back to being single and alone. It is sad when someone would rather stay in a broken, toxic relationship than being in a solo relationship with themselves. They will stay in dead-end relationship because they don't want to go back to Friday nights alone; *that's probably because they had no life before them*. Holding on to someone just so you won't have an empty Saturday night will cost you in the long run. I'd rather sit on the couch at home alone on Friday night eating popcorn, watching old reruns of Laverne & Shirley and Gilligan's Island before I stay in a relationship with someone that's no good for me or settle for a substandard relationship! Never allow a relationship to define you; get a life and fill it with purpose before you enter another relationship and come to love your own company so that you won't settle for *any* company. It's easy to walk away from a substandard relationship when you love yourself!

- When you stay past the expiration date you will begin to rationalize bad behavior and make excuses for infidelity, their passive relationship with God, their inability to effectively communicate and manage relationships or their inability to hold down a job. One of the hardest things in a relationship is to be confronted with the realization that the person who you love should never have had access to your heart. To discover that they are not the person you thought they were and the dream of you two being together is more of a fairytale in your mind that is not going to happen is devastating. When the life you planned out in your head doesn't match reality it can be tough to let go. You've invested a lot of your time and your heart into the relationship, and though you know the relationship is over and it's not going to work, you stay, hoping it'll get better or they will change. It reminds me of something that my friend, Jamal Bryant said, "Some bad relationships are like bad movies: you won't leave because you keep hoping the next scene will get better." You end up staying several months, even years, wasting your life in a dead-end relationship that will inevitably crash and end. You tire yourself out trying to make something work that doesn't have the components or the capacity to work. Like an airplane waiting for permission to safely land, you circle the airport, using the relationship as a holding pattern while you run out of fuel, depleting yourself of your energy, your time, your self-worth, your purpose and your life. When men are in a bad relationship they lose 4 years of their lives, when women are in a bad relationship they lose 12 years of their lives.[2] I don't know about you, but I don't have that kind of time to waste.

While you hang in the balance of a decision, you've actually already made a choice. Postponing or delaying a decision is a choice in itself. "Wrong people never leave your life voluntarily; their survival depends on your patience."[3] The wrong person will not leave your life; they will stay as long as you allow them. When you stay in an unhealthy or substandard relationship you give people a blueprint of how to treat you. They will come to know that it's acceptable to persist in negative/destructive relational habits, passivity, and a lack of attention and commitment to the relationship as long as you will allow it. If you stay in a relationship where the other person is passive or half-hearted about you, treats you with disrespect, dishonesty, or abuse they're going to continue to treat you that way because you have shown that you don't require anything else. They realize that you don't value or respect yourself when you allow them to act this way in the relationship. Mike Murdock said it best,

"What you tolerate, you sponsor." When you refuse to tolerate unacceptable behavior by exiting the relationship, you show them that you value yourself more than what they are willing to offer.

You must exit the relationship before it begins to fester into an unhealthy attachment. When you stay past the expiration date, the relationship will become like a bad habit to break. It will become more of a habit than *meaning*. You end up staying now, not because you want to be with that person, but they have become a bad routine that you've become familiar with and can't, well...*won't* let go. The Bible says that slack habits and procrastination is equal to vandalism.[4] Vandalism means to willfully damage and destroy. That means that you are participating in the willful destruction of your life when you put off and delay leaving an unproductive, unhealthy or failed relationship. It's easier to "refund" an unproductive relationship at ten weeks verses ten months. And like any habit, it gets harder to break when it becomes a part of you too long. The longer you stay, the harder it becomes to leave. It's like picking a major and then you get into it and realize 'this is not what I want; I thought I did,' but you now know that you're not going to be in this field in the future. You then begin to think, 'I've invested so much into it," attention, time, and money and you feel you're obligated to stick with it. No, change your major; don't minor in people who you know are not going to be within your future or put a huge investment in something that is temporal and does not align with your purpose and destiny. When you know early on that a relationship does not have potential or that it is unhealthy, without hesitation, you need to put an end to it because that person is becoming a part of you and you carry that junk long after they leave. That's why it is important that you make a decision to let it go if it's not bearing fruit. When you see the relationship is going nowhere, cut your gain. Notice I said gain and not losses. Ask yourself, what will I gain when I lose this relationship?

- Unnecessary heartbreak often happens as a result of negligence, allowing someone to park in your life knowing they are not the one for you. Many heartaches could have been avoided if we simply leave unfruitful relationships but when you overstay your welcome in that kind of relationship you become emotionally toxic with resentment, unforgiveness, bitterness, anger, and regret. When we regret a relationship our automatic tendency is to be attracted to another person we will regret meeting. We will repeat the pattern, sending ourselves on an emotional roller coaster. Dr. John Gray said it best, "When we end a relationship with resentment or guilt, we are attracted to someone who will help us deal with unresolved feelings and issues." If you rebound into another relationship it will only act as anesthesia where you *unconsciously* engage in relationships in an unhealthy matter, but when you finally wake up, the anesthesia will wear off and the pain will resurface. Staying past the expiration date is like using painkillers to numb you of an incurable disease. You're holding on to an incurable relationship so the breakup is inevitable. No matter how you to try to hold on to it, glue it together or put tape on it to try and hold the seams together, the relationship will rip apart and end, and when it finally does, it's just going to be even more traumatic. You will end up having to choose between the pain of staying and the pain of leaving. When you drag the relationship along until there's no drop or ounce of anything left, unnecessary heartache will come as a result of you trying to give life to something that's dead. It's like a dead-end street; there's nowhere to go but the opposite direction: out of the relationship. I know you probably are delaying leaving because you don't want to deal with the pain, and the thought of now having to be without them kills you and it feels like you can't live without them, but remember this: you survived long before them and you'll be more than okay without them.

- We usually know early on that we should end a relationship but many people do not want to give up the relationship because the emotional high feels good. This is how unhealthy soul ties, unnecessary emotional attachments, and sexual falls and 'slip-ups' happen, but these are not accidental falls; there were sequential steps that led to the "fall" and it was only a matter of time before a sexual encounter would take place. All of the acts that preceded the fall was preparing and leading you to the bed to have sex. Neglecting to leave the relationship when you discovered that it was going nowhere, when you realized that it was an unhealthy and unproductive relationship, was the moment you prepared and set in motion the sexual fall. Now you will try to use more sex to keep the relationship glued together. Sadly, this is why you will find many single Christians with a trail or history of unhealthy soul ties. The best thing for you to do is repent, exit the relationship and run to God so that He can break the ties!

Dear Darla, I hate your stinking guts. You make me vomit. You're scum between my toes.
Love, Alfalfa
(Little Rascals 1994)

Payback
If you want the neck tie back you bought him, or you want to snatch the heart necklace off her neck that you gave her, if you want to bust the windows out of their car, put sugar in their gas tank, take Carrie Underwood's advice and dig your keys into the side of his pickup then you have proven that you are not truly prepared to pursue relationships because you lack one of the fundamental aspects of relationships: forgiveness.

> "When you forgive someone for hurting you, you perform spiritual surgery inside your soul; you cut away the wrong that was done to you." Lewis Smedes

I know, I know...they cheated on you, led you astray, did you wrong and you have every right to be hurt and upset, but besides temporary satisfaction and maybe a night in jail, what will busting their windows out of their car do? Bitter break-ups only keep you chained to the past and stuck in the relationship even though it has ended. You want sweet revenge? The best revenge is to take your life back and overcome the very thing that tried to bury you and take you out! Find the good in goodbye and begin to focus on fulfilling the life that you couldn't fulfill because that relationship hindered you.

The pain in your heart feels unbearable; you feel like you're going to die and you're never going to get over them. But I promise you, you will. Our Love Manual says that, "God heals the broken-hearted and binds up their wounds." (Psalms 147:3) Not only will God heal you, but no residue or remnants of the pain will be there. That word bind in the original translation means that your heart will be made new, back in its original state as if it was never broken. That means that your memory will be healed, your emotions will be healed, your broken spirit put back together again, giving you the ability to love like you've never been hurt.

- Heartache and grief is normal after a breakup; what is most important is how you handle it. Grab a box of tissue, get a good cry out and acknowledge your pain but don't use an ounce of your energy on retaliating or getting them back. Don't isolate yourself or go at it alone; find comfort in counsel and the shoulder of a good friend or prayer partner to help you get pass the pain. Not facing the pain can cause long-term damage but at the same time you must put an expiration date on breakup grief so that you won't allow the breakup to find itself in your future.
- Oftentimes, people compound their grief, even carry the pain and residue from previous relationships and do not adequately heal simply because they don't have the tools to help them overcome. I conducted a seminar on "How To Get Over A Broken Heart;" I highly recommend that you download it at www.iTy.TV and also seek counseling to help you overcome and get past the brokeness caused by the relationship.
- Whoever said, "The best way to get over an old man is to get under a new one," is a complete poptart! Don't believe them! If you go right into a relationship after ending one, you essentially place a comma there and continue the relationship; it's just the same person with a different face because you will only attract the previous relationship because its conditioning, mindset and residue is still on you. After a heavily involved or serious, long-term relationship, you need to allow roughly about six months for restoration and inner healing (and longer after a divorce). Resist the urge to fall in the arms of someone else to take the edge off the pain; rebounding is not an option. Fall into the arms of the Lord and allow space and time for Him to

heal and mend you from the relationship so that you will have the capacity to attract a wholesome relationship.

"As a dog returns to its vomit, so a fool repeats his foolishness." Prov. 26:11 NLT
"As a dog eats its own vomit, so fools recycle silliness." MSG

All Sales Are Final!
Denial is a common thread after breakups. Come to terms that the relationship has ended. Some people live in denial, thinking perhaps that the relationship didn't end and that they'll come back or perhaps you should give the relationship another try because you miss the comfort of the relationship. If the relationship has ended then make a clean break. Make up, then break up, then make up, then break up…that's reycyling foolishness. Keep your distance; don't visit Facebook pages or text late at night trying to muster up conversations about why the relationship ended or "just to see how they're doing" or to *pray with them*. Even if you find that you can be friends it is necessary to keep your distance after the breakup to allow both of you time to untie, mend and heal from the breakup. Don't allow your heart and your mind to stay in a relationship that's over; give it over to the Lord. Remember that when you allow God to heal you, He will remove every residue from the relationship and make you whole, completely.[5]

One of the main reasons why a dead relationship stays alive is because your memories will give it a heartbeat. Your feelings for that person will never die as long as you continue to feed it with old memories. Rehearsing the relationship over in your mind like a romantic Notebook movie will cause you to forget the reasons why you left the relationship. Don't allow an old relationship to rent space in your head for free! Kick it out! Every time you get the urge to reminiscence about the relationship cut it off and cast it down before it attempts to take up residence in your mind.[6] Read Luke 17:34. Go ahead and read it right now; I'll wait for you….(elevator music plays). What does it say? REMEMBER LOT'S WIFE! What did Lot's wife do? She looked back at the life God delivered and pulled her out of. When God delivers you out of something, don't you dare look back on what He allowed you to escape from! When you exit an unhealthy or unproductive relationship don't look in the rearview mirror. Looking back is for learning purposes only. Take inventory upon exiting the relationship, but don't stay there; move forward. Ask yourself what can you take away from the relationship? What have you learned about yourself? Taking inventory of the relationship can help you avoid relational mishaps in the future. Acknowledge and accept any personal responsibility in the failure or mistakes of the relationship as well. Learn from relational flaws and what contributed to the termination of the relationship but most of all forgive. A sign of a mature person is that they leave the relationship better, not bitter.

[1] James 1:17   [2] Dr. Mehmet Oz   [3] Mike Murdock   [4] Prov. 18:9 MSG   [5] Ps. 147:3   [6] 2 Cor. 10:3-5

DATING Addiction

Are you addicted to sex and love? Do you have a shopping addiction? Are you always shopping for a (wo)man, constantly in and out of relationships, and collecting emotional debts every time you get in a relationship? These are signs that you have developed negative or destructive patterns in your approach to love and relationships:

- You date a person or stay in a relationship that is substandard or no good for you.
- You often mistake a romantic relationship as "the one".
- You over spiritualize a relationship, calling it God, when it's your beguiled and superfluous emotions being camouflaged and laced with religion.
- You find yourself dating people who have different goals and values than you.
- You've been "in love" more than 4 times in your life.
- You often put more into the relationship than your lover does.
- Your last 3 relationships ended in heartache and/or depression.
- Your last 3 relationships became your sexual partners.
- After the first 2 or 3 dates you are fantasizing about wedding bells.
- You overcompensate or rationalize your date's inappropriate behavior, lifestyle, or warning signs.
- It's difficult for you to let relationships go even though they're no good for you or not going anywhere.
- You are "seeing" multiple people in that online dating site that you have an account with.
- You find yourself playing "house" with your boyfriend/girlfriend.
- You find yourself taking care of your lover financially, paying cell phone bills or helping him out on the rent or even allow him to move into your place for the sole purpose of keeping the relationship alive. (women)
- You make the first call after the first date because it's been days and he hasn't called or you consistently email and text him, and reach him to no avail. But after he finally calls, you accept his date and sexual advances. (women)
- You often find yourself hopping from one relationship to the next because you become easily dissatisfied.
- You are bored with one woman and can't seem to find what you need in one woman. (men)
- You romance a woman for the intent of having a brief sexual relationship with her. (men)
- You tell a woman that you love her when you really don't; you just have a strong sexual desire for her. (men)
- You are unable to commit to one relationship and have a few dating partners at one time.
- You throw caution to the wind and even your pre-marital sexual beliefs go out the window when you "feel" like he/she is the one.
- You stay in a relationship when you are being cheated on.
- You stay in a relationship even when you know that it's passive or at a dead-end.

10 Things That Destroys Relationships

1. Going against God's plan for relationships. The number one reason why relationships fail is because we go against God's plan. God's plan for relationships is clearly defined in the love manual He has given to us.

"Then the LORD God said, "It is not good for the man to be alone. I will make a helper who is just right for him." So the LORD God caused the man to fall into a deep sleep. While the man slept, the LORD God took out one of the man's ribs and closed up the opening. Then the LORD God made a woman from the rib, and he brought her to the man. "At last!" the man exclaimed. "This one is bone from my bone, and flesh from my flesh! She will be called 'woman,' because she was taken from 'man.'" This explains why a man leaves his father and mother and is joined to his wife, and the two are united into one. Now the man and his wife were both naked, but they felt no shame." Gen 2:18, 21-25

2. Eating knowledge from evil. God's plan for you was to never live or govern your life with knowledge outside of His already perfectly planned will for your life. It was never God's will for you to experience evil in your relationships.

"GOD commanded the Man, "You can eat from any tree in the garden, except from the Tree-of-Knowledge-of-Good-and-Evil. Don't eat from it. The moment you eat from that tree, you're dead." Genesis 2:15-17 MSG

"The serpent told the Woman, "You won't die. God knows that the moment you eat from that tree, you'll see what's really going on. You'll be just like God, knowing everything, ranging all the way from good to evil." Gen 3:4-5

3. Not resting and allowing God to prepare you for a relationship. In dating relationships, many couples simply jump into them without preparation.

"GOD put the Man into a deep sleep. As he slept he removed one of his ribs and replaced it with flesh. GOD then used the rib that he had taken from the Man to make Woman and presented her to the Man." Gen 2: 21 MSG

4. Staying in relationships that are not suitable. Many people get in and stay in relationships that are not suitable for them; wasting their lives aimlessly in relationships.

"Now the Lord God said, It is not good (sufficient, satisfactory) that the man should be alone; I will make him a helper meet (suitable, adapted, complementary) for him." Gen. 2:18 AMP

5. Getting naked without commitment, causing embarrassment and shame. God plainly laid out his plan for sex and when we deviate from His original plan, then sexual destruction is the result.

"At last!" the man exclaimed. "This one is bone from my bone, and flesh from my flesh! She will be called 'woman,' because she was taken from 'man.'" Now the man and his wife were both naked, but they felt no shame. Gen. 2:23-25 NLT

"And the man and his wife were both naked and were not embarrassed or ashamed in each other's presence." Gen 2:25 AMP

6. Not focusing on your purpose/life before getting into a relationship.

"God took the Man and set him down in the Garden of Eden to work the ground and keep it in order." Gen. 2:15 MSG

7. Allowing your emotions and desires to govern and make decisions instead of what God's Word says.
"The woman was convinced. She saw that the tree was beautiful and its fruit looked delicious, and she wanted the wisdom it would give her. So she took some of the fruit and ate it." Gen 3:6 NLT

8. Compromising and letting someone you're in a relationship influence you to go against what God says

When the Woman saw that the tree looked like good eating and realized what she would get out of it—she'd know everything!—she took and ate the fruit and then gave some to her husband, and he ate. Gen. 3:6 MSG

9. Blaming others and not taking responsibility for your own actions.

"The LORD God asked. "Have you eaten from the tree whose fruit I commanded you not to eat?" The man replied, "It was the woman you gave me who gave me the fruit, and I ate it." Then the LORD God asked the woman, "What have you done?" "The serpent deceived me," she replied. "That's why I ate it." Gen 3:11-13 NLT

10. Running and hiding from God when you make a mistake.

"When they heard the sound of God strolling in the garden in the evening breeze, the Man and his Wife hid in the trees of the garden, hid from God. God called to the Man: "Where are you?" He said, "I heard you in the garden and I was afraid because I was naked. And I hid." Gen 3:8-10 MSG

Chapter 17
Bodyguard

Quite often when singles come to me for counsel, they are often perplexed and confused as to why they find themselves folding under pressure and become prey to sexual temptation. They are shocked as to how their clothes even came off, they stand there with their shoulders shrugged and the "I don't know how it happened" look crookedly placed on their faces, "I went over just to have dinner and then the next thing I know, my clothes just somehow mysteriously came off my body!"

One particular evening, I was addressing this same issue to a large crowd of singles and I stretched my vocal chords as loud as I could and I started singing, "Pants on the ground, pants on the ground, lookin' like a fool wit 'cha pants on the ground..." On one of the seasons of the popular music reality show, American Idol, an elderly contestant boldly stepped on the stage and sang those lyrics in protest to the trend where many young men wear their pants sagging, almost down to the ground.[1] There's a real simple solution to their problem and yours; all you need is a belt! I know you're probably thinking, "I do have a belt but my clothes still came off!" Stick with me, my friend; I'm going somewhere.

> "Stand therefore [hold your ground], having tightened the belt of truth around your loins." Eph. 6:14 AMP

In this Scripture we've just walked in on Paul having a very important conversation about you. Close out your Facebook page from distractions right now and lean in because this is strategic, fail-proof, tactical instructions on how to combat satan's tricks. Paul says, listen, you're going to be put in situations where satan is going to try to trick you! Just as sure as he is a liar and a deceiver, trust that he will try to swindle you out of your clothes and how you're going to be able to stand against it is to put on a belt. Not just any belt, but the belt of truth! You must understand that one of satan's main schemes in attempt to destroy God's people is deception and the only thing that will annihilate that deception is truth!

> Finally, be strong in the Lord and in his great power. Put on the full armor of God so that you can fight against the devil's evil tricks. Our fight is not against people on earth but against the rulers and authorities and the powers of this world's darkness, against the spiritual powers of evil in the heavenly world. That is why you need to put on God's full armor. Then on the day of evil you will be able to stand strong. And

when you have finished the whole fight, you will still be standing. So stand strong, with the belt of truth tied around your waist Eph. 6:10-14

When Roman soldiers went into battle they put armor on to protect them and the belt that was a part of their armor was quite large in size where it covered much of the entire waist area and the loins, holding the entire armor in place, covering and protecting other parts of the body like vital organs, the spine, the pelvis and, yes, even the genitals. When Paul was addressing spiritual battles that we will encounter (like sexual immorality), he indicated that we must protect ourselves like Roman soldiers but our protection is the full armor of God. The first part of that armor is the belt of truth. This truth, my friend, is the Word of God. The Message translation says in this text that the Word of God is an "indispensable weapon!" With even more protection than a soldier's belt, our belt of truth is vitally necessary because it covers and protects us and gives us the ability to stand our ground against the enemy's tricks and deception. Just like a natural belt buckle holds things in place, our spiritual belt gives us the ability to do what many can't do in the natural. The problem with many single Christians is that they are spiritually naked. You are exposed and either don't put the armor of God on at all or perhaps have on other parts of the armor like righteousness and salvation (:14-17), but without the belt of truth, it does not hold the other parts of the armor in place. You can't keep your clothes on without having the belt of truth. Without the Word of God you will face many spiritual battles with great challenge and often defeated.

The belt of truth is a border that protects you from exposure. Remember we talked about borders early on and how they protect? The Word of God is your protection and you must buckle and fasten it on every day! This is the common thread that sews this entire book together. It is not enough to have a belt if you don't use it. You must apply it and use it in action. The Word of God must become a consistent fabric of your life. Because the Word, the belt of truth, is a border of protection that serves in helping you establish boundaries that safeguard sexual purity in your life. Using the Word as a guideline to establish these boundaries will set a purity border around you to prevent you from becoming subject to sexual calamity and temptation in your relationship. Without this parameter, you are exposing yourself to be an easy target for sexual sin.

Why set boundaries?
- Because the Lord uses your body as His residence; He lives in you. Your body belongs to the Lord and you have committed it to Him, so you will protect what is His. (1 Corinthians. 6:20, Romans. 12:1)

- Because you have a personal responsibility to manage and control your own body. (1 Thessalonians 4:4) You and God are partners in maintaining your sexual purity and you must be proactive in preserving and safeguarding your body from immorality.
- Do me a favor, pinch yourself; okay, just wanted to make sure you're alive. As long as you're in that skin, you're body is going to desire sex. With that said, it's not a matter of if, but when; you will face sexual temptation in your relationship. There are many singles that do not set boundaries because they think they are safe since they own a Bible and attend First Corinthians Zechariah Baptist Church, but I don't care how much you pray, what church you attend, or if you speak 10,000 tongues and can quote all sixty-six books of the Bible in your sleep: you're going to be tempted. Not one person holding this book is exempt from sexual temptation, including the person who authored it. Since no one is exempt then you must prepare and guard from it. To not set boundaries is to already make the choice that you're going to give in to sexual expression in your relationship. Without a plan for sexual purity, then by default, you plan to fall into sexual sin.
- There are some singles that are overly-confident because, "we're both Christians and should know what to do or expect," or they are a virgin or have been celibate so long that they think they are safe and exempt from falling. I've seen virgins and "second-time virgins" alike who had no intentions in falling but found themselves in situations that caught them off guard and they unfortunately had succumbed to the temptation because they didn't think it would happen to them. "The same thing could happen to us. We must be on guard so that we never get caught up in wanting our own way as they did…We must not be sexually promiscuous—they paid for that, remember, with 23,000 deaths in one day! These are all warning markers—danger!—in our history books, written down so that we don't repeat their mistakes…we are just as capable of messing it up as they were. Don't be so naive and self-confident. You're not exempt. You could fall flat on your face as easily as anyone else. Forget about self-confidence; it's useless. Cultivate God-confidence." (1 Corinthains. 10:6, 8; 11-12 MSG)
- "For I know that in me (that is, in my flesh,) dwelleth no good thing." (Romans 7:18) Your flesh does not care about your commitment to sexual purity. Your flesh has a mind of its own and does not want to live sexually pure and is silently calculating ways for it to be fulfilled. That is why you can't give it an ounce of sexual pleasure; it'll fool you into thinking, "just a little and I'll be satisfied." But a little allowances here and a little there, and bam! You're caught up in some sexual foolishness! We discussed previously that once your body gets inflamed in sexual arousal, you will abandon all common sense. You forget where all the fire exits are even though you went through the fire drill several times! It escapes your mind that you could be lying there with someone that is about to give you a sexually transmitted disease or how

about pregnancy, soul ties or a backslidden relationship with God; no, thank you! You cannot make any provisions for the flesh. (Rom. 13:14) So you need to set boundaries that protect you from you. You must protect you from your flesh; if you don't make boundaries, your flesh will make them for you. And if that happens, there will be no borders.

- Before you even begin dating you must establish what values you want to guide you and that will govern your relationships. These values will help you establish boundaries and those boundaries are guides/markers that will serve as a GPS into the right relationship and they will navigate you away from the wrong ones. When you establish boundaries, well before you even consider a relationship, they protect you from entering into futile, ineffective, useless, toxic or destructive relationships. You will be less likely to enter into relationships that are not healthy for you or one that is not going in the same direction. Your boundaries will aid you in making wise dating decisions and they will function as a security check system, preventing entry to anyone that does not align with or violates the boundaries that you've already set. When you establish personal boundaries before dating to govern and guide your own personal life, they will be independent of anyone else, so that when you enter into a relationship the boundaries are not subject or contingent on the relationship but your personal commitment to God and sexual purity.

How To Set Boundaries?

Zipped and belted

- Have a private moment alone where you sit before the Lord and right down your commitment to Him and your commitment to sexual purity. Your boundaries will be based upon your core values and streamline from your personal relationship with God, ensuring that He remains the center of your life and in the center of your dating relationship.
- Use your Relationship Manual as a guide, using Scriptures as a foundation to pattern and establish your boundaries. Psalms 119:9-11, 1 Corinthians 6:18, and Romans 12:1, 2 are good places to start. Go back through this book and highlight other Scriptures to set your plan in place.
- Set them and set them high! Since your commitment is birthed out of your relationship with God, you need to aim high, at the height of sexual purity and integrity. Don't aim low, trying to set the minimal level of sexual purity, operating with a low mentality that "I'm not going to sin *as bad* as I did in the past." No, reach for the Heavens! Stretch your capacity for purity and holiness! Go for absolute, total devotion and commitment to the Lord!

- Set clear boundaries with no shades of grey. Your vision of sexual purity should not be blurred with uncertainty, leaving room for compromise. 'I want to live sexually pure' is vague and leaves a margin for sexual error. Instead, detail what lines will not be crossed in the relationship. Don't forget emotional boundaries and even set "orange safety cones" around your personal challenges and areas of weakness:

    1. My body belongs to God so I will not allow heavy petting, fondling…
    2. I will not allow sexually charged conversations.
    3. I will not lie down in his/her bed.
    4. My curfew is at ____ o'clock.
    5. When I see even a small spark of temptation, I will _____.
    6. I will not remain in relationships that compromise my beliefs or that constantly cross boundaries.

    Etc, etc, etc. You see where I'm going? This is simply a guideline; you need to custom-design a boundary system that tailors your personal life.
- Many couples do not set boundaries until well after they've begun a relationship or find themselves in compromising situations, after they realize they've gone too far. Trying to find a Scripture in the book of Zechariah when you're in the heat of the moment is too late. It also makes it much more difficult to implement boundaries after you've already began dabbling in sexual activity versus if you would have established them up front. You need to establish what's too far before it gets too far. Don't just assume the person you're dating knows how to act or that they should know that you're not interested in fondling on the couch after dinner and a movie; clearly communicate your expectations and make an undeniable distinction between you and the average, typical Christian by your actions and your persona upfront. You give people a blueprint of how they should treat you by what you allow.

That is why when you begin any relationship you want to establish up front the values that you live by, what you will not allow in the relationship and what is inappropriate. When you set standards in the genesis of the relationship, you eliminate foolishness! And ladies, you get rid of the bumblebees. Do you want to know what a bumblebee is? He buzzes around trying to find what beautiful queen will give him some *honey*. You prevent getting stung by a bee when you swat him right in his tracks! You let him know right up front, "you're not getting any honey from the Queen bee!" You will know if you're off to a great start because a true man of God will ensure that the boundaries are established and held in compliance with integrity and righteousness.

- If you've had sex in your previous relationship and you're now entering a new relationship after having recommitted to celibacy, you must eliminate physical expression and place greater boundaries around the relationship. If you or your dating partner have had sexual struggles in your most recent past relationships then you need to set and ensure you pace the relationship with emotional and physical boundaries, (delaying emotional and physical expression) until you've had an chance to focus on developing the relationship properly. When I say physical expression, I am not talking about heavy petting because that's not an option at all. I am referring to cuddling and caressing. The chemical oxytocin releases during physical affection like kissing and hugging and so you want to place boundaries there in order to build on the relationship without bonding prematurely or setting a sexual environment that will set you up for failure and invoke temptation when you're newly recommitted to sexual purity.

Fantasy

In lieu of having sex or in attempts to avoid it, many singles will quench their sexual desires by retreating to sexual daydreams of them having sex with their dating interest. There are many of you that think it's safe gratification and that it it's no harm since you're not really having sex with them, but to produce an entire porn scene in your mind of you and your dating partner is the same thing as if you actually had sex with them. How? Because as a man *thinketh*, so is he! Without even touching them, you have already had sex with them.

"You have heard that it was said, 'You must not be guilty of adultery.' But I tell you that if anyone looks at a woman and wants to sin sexually with her, in his mind he has already done that sin with the woman." Matt. 5:27, 28 NCV

Your sexual fantasy of you and your dating partner is the same thing as the act of adultery. Essentially, your sexual thoughts are equivalent to the sexual act. Your mind has the propensity to sexually sin just like your physical body does. Therefore, mental sex and sexual fantasy is sexual sin; it is equal to adultery.

"Shun immorality and all sexual looseness [flee from impurity in thought, word, or deed]. 1 Corinthians 6:18 AMP

99.9% of single Christians would have 100% success in their life and relationships if they mastered and understood the importance of mental boundaries.

All battles are either won or lost first in the mind. If you find yourself sexually conquered then you were defeated in your mind first. That it is why it is fundamentally important that you control your thought life, resist, and stand firm against sexual fantasy. This subject matter is so important that I teach in depth on it in Single, Saved and Having Sex: The 30 Day Guide To Celibacy. We will revisit it and expound deeper in the next chapter as well so that your understanding will increase and give you the ability to conquer mental strongholds and sexual sin of the mind. You must resist the temptation to sexually fantasize about your date and safeguard yourself from sexually falling by guarding your thought life.

"Finally, brothers and sisters, fill your minds with *beauty and* truth. Meditate on whatever is honorable, whatever is right, whatever is pure, whatever is lovely, whatever is good, whatever is virtuous and praiseworthy." Philippians 4:8 Voice

The Christian Side Hug

Your eyes did not deceive you; that's an actual term that even made its way in the Wikipedia Encyclopedia. The side hug is the alternative to the front hug for Christians to put into practice while they are dating so that they do no ignite arousal or avoid sexual temptation. I shake my head at things like this. Instead of teaching God's people how to live holy and pure, there are some who will use legalism as a way of strong arming people into living sexually pure. Many times if a person can't handle a hug, they're dealing with deep-seated lust; telling them to do the Christian Side Hug only cosmetically covers the surface of sexual lust, but it does not get to the source of it. Setting boundaries is different from legalism. Unlike establishing borders that protect, legalism attempts to cover a problem rather than fix it. This Pharisaic approach to sexual purity, where you do rituals that appear to be pious and holy, will get you nowhere and only puts a band-aid on your lust wounds! Only a relationship with God and His Word will drive out lust, not some Christian Side Hug.

Chaperone

While I do believe that you need friends and mentors in your life to help you accomplish your relationship goals, you do not need to have a chaperone accompany you on a date. Although I understand the counsel of others who suggest this for dating, I believe that group dating is for teens, to protect those that are much younger. This book is not for teens; this book is for mature adults. What does a grown man or woman in their thirties look like going on a chaperoned date? You are not a toddler where your mom has to stand over you to make sure you don't eat all the cookies out of the jar at one time! By now, you should be able to go on a date unsupervised because you have learned to exercise self-control and integrity. I am not saying that you can't go on group dates; that's for fun and gives you an opportunity to observe him/her socially with friends, and in turn, your friends can get an objective eye. But to go on a group date every time you go out: INSANITY! Group dating does not give you an opportunity to grow on a deeper, intimate, pure level, where you personally get to know one another. And again, intimacy is not kissing, necking, and bumping and grinding. You are not qualified or ready to date if the Holy Spirit can't chaperone you and trust you to be alone with His son or daughter. One evening I walked into a restaurant and saw a young lady I knew on a date with some guy, acting inappropriately. She was embarrassed and ashamed that I saw her. With her hand over her mouth, signifying her shame, she started apologizing, as if I was Jesus. We should have more of a concern that our Father is watching us, and we need not any supervision, because we first and foremost, stand in His presence at all times and don't want to dishonor Him.

Covering your dating partner
"He or she made me do it" is unacceptable; you are ultimately responsible for your boundaries and control over your own body. However, you have the divine responsibility to cover your dating partner and to protect one another. When the other person is weak, the stronger one should cover the relationship that day. They'll be times when you're at a weak or vulnerable moment and there's nothing wrong with that, and your date should protect you. Part of protecting your dating partner and maintaining sexual purity in the relationship is knowing and understanding how the opposite sex is designed. God wired men and women differently. From the makeup of our bodies and our sexual drive, to the vast difference of our sexual stimuli, his response to touch exceeds hers by ten million yards! A man's sexual response is about three seconds; unlike hers, it takes twenty minutes or longer before she is aroused. Despite his best efforts to avoid sexual arousal, he can find himself sexually provoked without him even warranting or coercing it. A two-hour hug-a-thon on the couch will be romantic bliss for her, while he's in a sexually charged jungle the entire time! You two are sitting on the couch, the woman's soft skin on her arm unknowingly brushes against his and immediately he begins struggling to ward and fight off his arousal while she's sitting there as cool as a cucumber. She's in her own world and has gone on in another conversation about how her day at work went with her coworker having the audacity to wear the same Prada shoes as hers and has no idea that he doesn't hear a word she's saying because he's percolating like a hot coffee pot, fighting off thoughts of them on the floor *playing* their own version of the game, Twister!

A man is also stimulated by sight, so it would help him if the woman he is dating would dress in clothing that aid in protecting him. Since he is naturally aroused by sight, it does not help him that your shirt exposes cleavage or your shirt is so short and tight that the seams are about to burst! Before even walking out the door, stand in the mirror and ask yourself, "Does my dress preserve and protect his purity? Or will he be distracted all evening because his mind is battling with my see-thru dress?" Don't set relational boundaries but then sexually allure him; make sure that the boundaries you set have corresponding action. On the other hand, because a woman's arousal is much slower and she is more susceptible to verbal stimulation, the gentleman she spends her time with has the responsibility of protecting her emotions by not engaging those emotions at a high level. His conversation and choice words should safeguard her heart and emotional intimacy should be protected just like sexual intimacy. Because she is provoked by hugs and affection, and is stimulated by what she hears, holding her in your arms, enchanting her with your intimate words and whispering sweet nothings in her ear is an emotional cocktail that may have her heart intoxicated beyond the appropriate limits. For instance, while you're holding her hands on the couch, telling her how much you enjoy spending time with her, you glance down at her hands and notice how soft they are and how they pale in comparison to many other women you've met. You casually ask, "Wow! Your hands are so soft and small. What size ring do you wear?" Though it was a curiosity question for you and that conversation didn't even come across your thoughts again, she on the other hand is spending the next week thinking of names of your first child together, joining Weight Watchers and increasing her exercise regimen so that she can fit in her wedding dress! While there is nothing wrong with you expressing and communicating your feelings to her --and you should-- there must be balance, ensuring that you do not lead her on or leave her oriented like she just got off an emotional roller coaster. Are the things you're saying to her edifying her or arousing her to sexual intimacy? Are you leading her back to God or away from Him?

> "Hi, sweetheart, I know we were supposed to get together this evening but I've been on edge today and feeling a bit vulnerable all day. Though I was looking forward to us getting together for dinner, I think it would be better if we meet for breakfast instead."

At the end of the day, you must protect your dating partner, even from you. If you know that this evening you have plans to get together but you've been sexually agitated or in the "mood," postponing your date or time together until tomorrow when your emotions have settled is the sign of a mature Christian with integrity and one that has the desire to pursue the relationship authentically, and more importantly, honors the Lord.

> "Don't have sex through the phone, you could get hearing aids." Unknown

Sex Talk

There was this very attractive guy that had an interest in me. He began flirting and making his interest known and of course, he was a Christian, (I don't entertain or consider any other kind) and he was a minister and I thought, "If this goes real far we could find ourselves at a chapel and end up having some cute babies together." So we began building conversations by phone and email, and he would flirt, and I would flirt back. It started off cute and coy, but then our conversations began to escalate with some suggestive language. Each time that I would see hints of sexual pollution, I would steer the conversation back to a chaste tone, but anytime there was a slight door opening, he would try to see how far he could go and maneuver the conversation with sexual overtures. You know how in the beginning of a relationship you began to exchange and divulge things about your likes and interest? Well, in an earlier conversation he found out that I love country music, so he would call me up and say, "hey, cowgirl!" I'd respond, "hey cowboy!" Well, one day we got into a conversation where he teased me about being a black girl who loved country music. In my defense to the great sound of country music, I responded, "Well, if you hang around long enough, it won't be long before I have you at a country dance hall, line dancing, doing the boot scootin' boogie! Hahahaha!" You know when you're in the middle of a good laugh that someone can choke it by saying something downright stupid? Yes, this clown short-circuited my laugh and said, "Well, I know every cowgirl knows how to line dance, but they also know how to bull ride. I'd be more interested in you riding this bull!"

Immediately, I thought, "what the ham sandwich?!" I was appalled! If it had not been for the Lord, I would have flat lined right there and He would have had to resurrect me Lazarus-style! Before I could reply, this clown's crucifixion was delayed by a very important incoming call and I had to resort to making a critical mental note to have a conversation with him about unacceptable sexual advances! Before I could even follow up with a return phone call, he beat me to it with a text message saying, "Check your inbox and call me." When I received his text message, I happened to be pulling into my driveway, while listening to a worship CD he had given me. I didn't even turn off the ignition. I pulled up my email on my smart phone and clicked on the unread message from him. I expected a message with an apology from him for the sexual proposition, instead it was a picture of him in his birthday suit, wearing the same clothes he came into this earth with: NOTHING BUT SKIN! I screamed to the top of my lungs like I was at a rock concert!!!!!!!!!

I was in utter shock! I couldn't hit the "contacts" icon on my phone fast enough! He answered in a sexy, raspy voice, "Hi, cowgirl!" I wanted to vomit up that day's food intake! I was so disgusted! You guys would have been proud of me though; with great ease and control from backsliding into satan's language, in a Christian-like tone, I instead said, "It is ironic that I opened up your email while I'm sitting in my truck listening to the worship CD that you gave me. The lyrics in this song, "My heart belongs to You, Jesus," does not reflect the picture you just sent me. I apologize on my part for whatever I did that could have led you into believing that it would be acceptable for you to send me a naked picture of yourself. After our last conversation, I knew that it was necessary to have a conversation with you because I saw that sexual hints from you were going unchecked and each time that I spoke with you the sexual overtures would increase each time that we talked. I want you to know that virtuous women do not *ride bulls* and they certainly do not wish to see a man of God in ministry with his clothes off. I pray that Holy Ghost conviction would come upon you and that you would seek the Lord for healing to help you deal with this issue so that your religion and your service in ministry do not become worthless or barren."

"If anyone thinks himself to be religious (piously observant of the external duties of his faith) and does not bridle his tongue but deludes his own heart, this person's religious service is worthless (futile, barren)." James 1:26 AMP

"If you claim to be religious but don't control your tongue, you are fooling yourself, and your religion is worthless." NLT

"People who think they are religious but say things they should not say are just fooling themselves. Their "religion" is worth nothing." NCV

      Sitting on the phone at midnight, entertaining questions like, "So, what do you have on," or talking about what you want to "do" with each other is the conception of <u>sexual buttressing</u> and is not godly conversation fitting for those who desire to live sexually pure. I learned a valuable lesson that day: the moment there is the slightest hint of impure talk, you must check it! Not checking it only encourages and reinforces it. The first time there was suggestive language, I thought, "Maybe that's not what he meant." The next time he did it, I thought, "I don't want to seem kitschy or like I'm a plain Jane; it's just innocent flirting." The third time he dropped the "s" bomb, I thought, "I don't want to come across as a prude church girl. I don't want to run him off by *causing* him to think that I'm some granny." The next thing I knew, there were his "unmentionables" in my inbox! Boy, am I glad that I've spiritually matured and my worth is in Christ and I do not have to be validated by the thoughts of another man! Listen, they can think whatever the heck they want about you! Don't you accept any hint of sexual bullying or R.S.V.P to any sexual invitations! You have to be careful about your language and where you allow your conversations to go, the "s" bomb (sex talk) is banned! If you do not place a guard over your conversations, sexual overtures will escalate to full-blown phone sex! Avoid conversations with sexual language and do not sexually allure your dating partner with your words; whether by sexting, email or in conversation.

"Let no foul *or* polluting language, *nor* evil word *nor* unwholesome *or* worthless talk [ever] come out of your mouth, but only such [speech] as is good *and* beneficial to the spiritual progress of others, as is fitting to the need *and* the occasion, that it may be a blessing *and* give grace (God's favor) to those who hear it." Eph. 4:29 AMP

"Don't allow love to turn into lust, setting off a downhill slide into sexual promiscuity, filthy practices, or bullying greed. Though some tongues just love the taste of gossip, those who follow Jesus have better uses for language than that. Don't talk dirty or silly. That kind of talk doesn't fit our style. Thanksgiving is our dialect." Eph. 5:3-4 MSG

Home Security

Is your home lust-proof? Is it a pure environment or is it sexually charged? Because of my busy travels with speaking, I am rarely home on the weekends. Oddly, one Friday evening I found myself home alone with no plans. I sat on the couch in the silence of my home. It was so quite that the walls began to echo my thoughts, "Hmmmm…what should I do?!" A great idea popped in my head, "I'll go out on a date!" I got up from the couch went to the move rental place a mile up the street, stopped at the store and got a box of Goobers and popcorn, went back home and took myself out on a "movie date" on the comfort of my couch! Hey, don't judge me! Until you can enjoy your own company, you're not ready for someone else's company.

At any rate, it was well after midnight when I popped the movie in. Not even fifteen minutes into the movie there was a graphic scene building of this guy getting ready to have sex with two women! I couldn't believe it! My mouth peered wide open and I shouted, "The devil and his momma is a liar!" So much for PG-13; I got up from my couch and hit the eject button. I didn't care that it was almost one o'clock in the morning! With my pajamas and snuggie on, I slipped on my house shoes and drove back down the road and threw the movie into the return box! I was not waiting 'til morning; I didn't want that mess sitting in my house, making itself comfortable in my DVD player!

I have made a firm commitment to live sexually pure, so I don't allow an ounce of sexual sin to have a seat in my home! Nothing in my home or my environment does not feed or awaken me sexually. My entire house has a built-in security system that protects me from sexual contamination. This is already set-up without me even dating, so if someone comes in my home that boundary is already set in place and bolted down. You will not find me on the couch with some guy with the lights low, watching a sexually charged movie with erotic music on. There are some of you that will go on movie date or sit at home on the couch together and watch a sexually charged movie or turn the lights down while you allow music to play in the background with sexual content in it, talking about "what I wanna do to you…" The next thing you know, your body will be moving in harmony with that music. And then you wonder why you are not able to maintain sexual purity? Because you create an environment and an atmosphere for sex! Take inventory of your home and do a clean sweep; if there's anything in it that promotes or celebrates sexual sin: THROW IT OUT! Don't create an environment that stimulates and encourages sexual indulgence.

On the Couch

Are you a couch couple? There are many dating couples who spend far too much time on the couch together. You and your boo, nose-to-nose in the dark, sitting on the couch making out is not God's idea of how to develop a relationship. You've heard of the saying,

"Idle time is the devil's workshop." Well, your idle, isolated time on the couch is prime location for his workshop! Your objective when you spend time together should be finding ways to stay vertical as you grow the relationship. The more you allow yourselves to get in a horizontal position with one another, you increase your chances of sexual gratification. And if I'm trying to get you to get off the couch, then the bed is definitely not an option! Lounging in one another's beds should be prohibited. I just heard someone ask, "Why?" I'll tell you why: because the purpose of the bed is to sleep in or have sex in; neither of which you two should do together unless you get married to one another; so keep your bed sacred. You need to get creative with your time together and focus on becoming acquainted with one another through other activities that cause you to strengthen the bonds of the relationship; if not, you're flesh will gladly give you *something* to do. If you want to get physical, then get physical: get off that doggone couch and go hiking, bike riding, or dancing. Give your body something else to do other than touching one another's. I have started a list of date ideas and activities for you to do together besides the movies or sitting on the couch and making out. It's in the section, *Take Out*. So let's get off the couch and began implementing them!

KISSING
It is common practice for dating couples to express affection or feelings for one another with a kiss. I am often asked is this level of expression acceptable while dating or should it be prohibited. Well, let's explore it. Helen Fisher, an anthropologist at Rutgers University, is widely recognized for her study on the science of kissing, known as philematology. Fisher conducted a number of brain imaging studies and in her findings the kiss is linked to the sex drive, romantic love and attachment. Along with Fisher's study and other researches on the kiss, we find that:
- Kissing aids in mate assessment or helps you evaluate and appraise a relationship.
- Kissing releases endorphins and other hormones involved in pleasure, euphoria, and reward.
- Kissing triggers a chemical response that incites romantic or passionate love and promotes bonding and helps to prolong a relationship, or at least long enough to rear a child.
- Kissing activates chemicals that arouse areas of the brain used for sex and reproduction.
- The saliva has testosterone in it so it increases and revs up the sex drive when kissing.
- Known as the "love hormone," oxytocin promotes trust and attachment during a kissing session and is linked to feelings of sexual pleasure and bonding.
- Immediately following a kiss, cortisol levels drop, causing a relaxation effect.

- During kissing, your heart beats faster and your breathing becomes deep and irregular.
- While kissing, a surge of dopamine shoots through your body igniting the "kissing rush" feeling and giddiness.
- The lips have the slimmest layer of skin on the body and the most densely populated senory cells, making them highly sensitive to touch.
- The mouth is packed with nerve endings that send messages to the brain causing chemical changes in the body.
- During a kissing episode, your vulnerability heightens chemicals above their normal level, causing it to block other chemicals in the brain that prevent you from reasoning and exercising logic.
- These chemicals flood the area of the brain that keeps you coming back for more. So kissing plays a role in "falling in love."
- Kissing from Hebrew, nashaq, means to kindle. A kissing session can kindle, stir up, and ignite the body. It increases motivation to mate and provides sexual stimulation, and prepares the body for sexual pleasure and arousal.

Wow! All that happens with a kiss! Imagine what would happen if a girl kissed too many frogs…she would get too confused to know which if it's Prince Charming! Or suppose that you are in the beginning stages of a dating relationship and that person is not adequate or suitable for you or the relationship has all the components of an epic fail but you allow kissing in the relationship…then you've just kindled a chemical flood of deception in your brain and emotions that will bond you with someone that is not good for you, make you believe that you love him/her (when you don't), creating a euphoric bliss that tells you this person is wonderful for you (when they're not), and you bond with them though you don't want to be with them but your emotions keep pulling you back because the chemicals are telling you that you should because you feel a false sense of reward, safety and trust, revving up your sexual drive, cutting off your reasoning and logic, causing you to prematurely jump in the bed….all because of a kiss!

This is one of the reasons that many couples reserve kissing only for committed relationships, for that special someone that they're in a devoted, long-term relationship with and then there are some who have completely reserved it for their wedding. The nuptial kiss at the altar began during Roman times as a symbol of the spiritual union between the bride and groom. The kiss was symbolic of "the breath of life." The ceremony concluded with, "Now you may kiss the bride," signifying that after they have committed to one another for life in marriage, they *now* (at this point, not anytime before) are sanctioned and permitted to enjoy one another's body. Now in modern dating that kiss has dwindled to the front or back of the car or it seals the night with a kiss to show or represent that you like the person, or to indicate if you had a good time, but with all that you've just learned about what happens during a kiss, do you really want that with just anyone? I would invite you to explore and consider these questions to determine if you should reserve or exercise discretion with kissing:

⇒ Why do I kiss or want to?
⇒ It may be permissible but is it beneficial? Does it benefit my relationship or is it a disadvantage (1 Corinthians. 10:23)
⇒ What have my previous experiences with kissing been like or what has the outcome been?
⇒ Does it align with my core values and beliefs or does it contradict/conflict with them?
⇒ Is it affecting or hindering my relationship? The Bible says to lay aside the sin and the weights that easily besets or entangles us. Kissing may not be a sin but ask yourself, 'Is it a weight? Is it placing an unnecessary weight on the relationship or hindering it?"
⇒ Does kissing put my relationship in a compromising position?
⇒ Does kissing foster or promote lust in my relationship?
⇒ Does it sexually arouse me? Does it provoke me to engage in heavier forms of sexual expression?
⇒ Would reserving, postponing, or holding back kissing allow me to focus clearly on assessing the relationship for its true substance?

Greet each other with a holy kiss. [2]

If you open your relationship to this level of physical expression, then keep it holy. If kissing causes you to rev up the engine and you find that it is constantly putting you in a sexual compromise, then you should keep your choppers to yourself! Don't put your desire or pleasure above the protection of the relationship.

Triggers

You must come to know your own body, become more aware of your arousal clock or what causes your body to become aroused, recognizing sensitive times of the month, when you're stressed, feeling lonely and what triggers your sexual drive. Recognize when you're most vulnerable and times of weakness because it will give you the advantage of safeguarding your commitment to purity. When you identify sexual triggers, it will equip you with the ability to get control over destructive sexual proclivities and unhealthy relationship behavior before it has the opportunity to manifest itself in your relationship. Your body will let you know when you're crossing your boundaries, but you must listen to it and take heed. Your spirit and your conscience will have a conversation with you on the way to his/her house, "now you know good and well if you go over his house right now that your virginity will get hijacked!" That "inner voice" talks to us all the time and we ignore it, rationalize with it, or pretend like we didn't hear it, but we must become acquainted with it and heed its warning.

"When you are alone together and the moonlight is glistening upon your sweet love's face, it is quite unlikely that a prayer meeting will be taking place." Sex 101 Dr. Myles Munroe & David Burrows

Curfew and Sleepovers

When I was kid, I had a curfew; when the street lights came on I'd better be in the house or my momma would be standing at the door waiting for me with a belt! Why? Because bad things usually happen in the dark! That curfew and that belt protected me. For the flesh, the nighttime is the right time! You're at a greater risk to exposure of sexual pressure at night, you're more vulnerable, and your defense weakens. When the sunsets, your body naturally begins to wind down, you're reflexes are low and so does the ability to make rational decisions. You are more susceptible to giving into sexual pressure the later it gets. Don't fool yourself into thinking that you two can have Bible study late at your house; you and I both know that after while there will be no praying going on! So pack up your Genesis and Revelation and get home! There's nothing open late but a drive-thru! So, ladies it's time to close up shop; no one should be ordering off your menu, getting taste testers, or appetizers. Did you hear me? Close up shop and send him home! He will respect you more tomorrow morning; causing him to desire your company all the more, knowing that you have respect for yourself.

Gentleman, you have a responsibility to cover both you and her. Even if she says that it's okay for you to stay a little while longer so that you can read the book of Romans, you know that your flesh will want to roam instead. So kiss her on the forehead and moonwalk out the door! Or perhaps you two are out for the evening and the time has been well-spent and it is late. Instead of inviting him in for a cappuccino night-cap, allow the gentleman to simply escort you to the door and call it a night *because your Father is upstairs watching*. You and your date must set a decent time to end the night early enough to protect you and your date and to make sure that your relationship is pleasing to your *Father God*. And as for the sleepover, need I have to remind you about my story with Jonathan? I am often asked, "what about if the two of us are spending the night together when there's no sex involved. Is it ok if we're just up talking or sometimes we just fall asleep in each other's arms?" Well, let me ask you this, "Can a man hold fire against his chest and not be burned? Can a man scoop a flame into his lap and not have his clothes catch on fire?" [3] You're setting yourself up for sexual flames! I thought you guys learned not to play with fire when you were a child! There's no sex involved, right now, but there will be! The flesh will have you fooled into thinking you're safe, just long enough for you to let your guard down. Which is the direction you're headed if you continue to have your late night meetings in his bed. Sleepovers are not an option; even if there's nothing going on. I had a young lady insist that there was nothing going on during her sleepovers and that they were only up talking so there shouldn't be anything wrong with them spending the night together, right? Wrong! For some reason I think we believe that we can outsmart our flesh and we're wiser than God; He knows that a man can't handle hot fire in his chest without burning, but you, with your exempt self, think that doesn't apply to you; you must have some fire-proof vest on your skin or something? [3]

Plus, you're giving waaaaay too many privileges and access in the dating stage, ladies. You're creating a dangerous habit of sleeping in a man's bed that has not paid the price for that kind of access, *even if you're just sleeping*. When you do that, a man will keep you in girlfriend status or better yet, you'll end up an *ex* real soon after you two finally have sex at your harmless, innocent, little sleepovers. You must constantly keep in the forefront of your mind that you are a wife before you become one and you must act and respond accordingly. A wife would never give this kind of privilege to a man that has not made her *one*. If you want to protect your purity, then sleepovers are not an option.

Boy: "Your place or mine?" **Girl:** "Both, you're going to yours, and I'm going to mine!"

Crossing the lines

The Bible says "lay aside the weights and the sin that easily beset you." (Heb. 12:1) Some things may not be sin in your life, but could very well be weights. Weights are things that are heavy or they burden you or the relationship down. Yes, those things that you wouldn't necessarily classify as sin, but they hinder you. Take inventory of your relationship and ask yourself, "What lines have we moved or crossed? Is this behavior putting me in a compromising situation? Are we appropriating our time together properly? Is this a weight?" And if it is, then get rid of it. Identify weights in the relationship and remove them before they upgrade to sin. Don't minimize it or throw it off because it's small or appears as if it's 'not that bad.' If kissing always leads to heavy petting, or if every time you two sit down on the couch to watch a movie and it leads to a make out session, then you to need to tighten the security measures at "border patrol."

Small foxes spoil the whole vine! (SOS 2:15)

Small, unchecked breaches of your boundaries will, little by little, bit by bit, creep up and ultimately destroy a promising relationship. Once you cross the line and allow sexual gratification, you will start to compromise increasingly more and then move the borderline of protection and there will be a struggle to go back behind that line and stay there. Disinterest and a lack of satisfaction will set in the relationship because absent from the physical affection, the relationship itself will feel like it's not enough. That is why it's imperative that you do not jump that line! You must monitor your relationship and ensure that you maintain boundaries. Many times couples will lose ground and begin knocking over the orange caution cones, and instead of putting the cones back up around the relationship, they become more careless and continue to knock more cones over! If you begin to see a pattern leading up to a sexual fall, you must address it; don't ignore it. Ask yourself, "Are you making allowances for sexual expression in the relationship and allowing it to go unchecked? Are you compromising the boundaries that you've set and now you're beginning to move the lines?

Here are signs you're coming unbuckled:
- Every time you get together the boundary lines move and the sexual expression increases; last week you were kissing, now you're necking.
- You two have stopped talking about advancing the relationship and your conversations are more about sex.
  You're fantasying about undressing/having sex with them.
- If someone listened in on your telephone conversations, they'd think you were engaging in phone sex.
  You're spending more time horizontal than vertical.
- Every time you get together hands are roaming, there's groping, fondling, and heavy petting.
- You stop talking to your accountability partner or you're keeping secrets about the relationship.

Quick! If you sighed in agreement to any of these signs, then you need to run for the border! Roaming hands, *horizontal activities*, and sexually-charged conversations are high-risk behaviors and if you continue to keep putting yourself in compromising positions, testing the flesh, and pushing the boundaries, then you are setting yourself up for sexual failure! You are planting and sowing the seeds of lust into your relationship and soon it will harvest a crop of sexual sin in your life! It is vital that you sit down and address this immediately. You both must reinforce your commitment to sexual purity and structure a new plan that will protect you and the relationship. Apparently the one you have is not working or you're not implementing Godly principles in your relationship. You're trying to figure out how you keep falling; it's all a surprise to you. You're saying you don't want to have sex but you're doing everything contrary. You're only saying that you want to live sexually pure but you're not backing it up with your actions. It's not going to happen by osmosis or because you have the desire; you must put action behind what you believe.

"Have you pushed against any boundaries lately? If not, you're probably not accomplishing much." Phil Cooke
NO!
"No" is a complete sentence. If the person you're dating persist in crossing or violating the boundaries you've set and continue to pressure you for sex after you've said no to their sexual advances, then they clearly do not respect and honor you, your God, nor your commitment to sexual purity and the relationship should be terminated! Staying says, "my commitment to sexual purity and to God is negotiable, your influence in my life is greater than God's, and I'll remove the boundary line for you; my no really means yes, I'm just playing hard to get and if you stick with it, I'll eventually give in." If you allow sexual advances without stern consequences, then it will only serve as a welcome sign to persist until you give in. A no-compromise clause must be understood at day one and the moment they cross it: Iammdonewithyou.com!

Give the gift of your absence to the person who doesn't appreciate your abstinence.

Why even further the relationship if the person you're dating does not hold the same tenacity and fervency for sexual purity as you do or one that does not have the same mindset concerning sexual boundaries? I'm not talking about someone that comes face-to-face with temptation and then battles or perhaps war with it. If you have someone that is warring with sexual temptation, then there should be signs of conviction or remorse should they have challenges or stumble. A person that loves God, and you, will not delight in sin, and when they face temptation they will walk in repentance and make the necessary corrections to align their lives to come in right standing with the Lord. If they're okay with sin and lust, pushing boundaries, and justifying their "need" to fulfill their sexual desire, then you should take the first exit out of the relationship; right now! If you're the only one resisting or bearing the responsibility of withholding, then you're going to have a big problem on your hands: their hands will end up on you. You're already fighting against satan and your flesh, the last thing you want is to have to fight against the person you're dating. You want someone on your side helping you fight, not pulling you in the ring! It's much easier to maintain sexual purity when you entertain a relationship with someone that you don't have to constantly say no to because he/she will be the man/woman who is guarding himself and placing boundaries on his life that not only protects himself, but you also. Your commitment to God will only work with someone that shares in the same goals of maintaining sexually purity. You must be in agreement about refraining and equally responsible for safeguarding the relationship. This kind of relationship will help you keep your vow to God because he/she will have the same aspiration for sexual purity and living a life that's pleasing to the Lord.

Unlimited pleasure

As the relationships grows, so will your feelings for one another and therefore your commitment to sexual purity will be tested. The more you grow in a relationship the desire for sexual expression will increase. There will be temptation to compromise or alter the boundaries, but you must make a firm pact with yourself and God that you will not move the borders based on feelings. Don't allow your feeling to override what is right. I strongly advise that you be even more solicitous in maintaining purity during every stage of your relationship. Enforce the boundaries that you've set because they are set in place to safeguard you from falling prey to sexual temptation and from destroying a potentially successful relationship. And once you have set them, don't move the margin the closer the two of you become. A real man or woman of God will respect you more when you uphold your convictions and your love for God more than your desire to please them. Take your vow to God and cement it in the foundation of your heart, affirming that there will be no alterations on your vow to purity. You must reaffirm your commitment and fortify its purpose, constantly putting its value, benefits, and the rewards it will produce before you. And every time you think of even remotely caving in, remind yourself that the temporal, short-lived pleasure is not worth you forfeiting the unending bliss that awaits you! ♥

Why is it important to have boundaries in your personal life and your relationship? _____
_____
Why is it important to place boundaries on your mind and your conversations? _____
_____
What does the belt of truth mean to you and how can you apply it to your everyday life? _____
_____
My personal commitment to God is _____
_____
_____
My personal commitment to myself is _____
_____
_____
These are my boundaries and I will not compromise them _____
_____
_____
Is your behavior aligning with the boundaries you've set? _____
_____
I am finding it (easy), (challenging) or (difficult) to withstand temptation or stick to the boundaries I set. If you answered challenging or difficult, what adjustments do you need to make in your relationship to

make it easier for you to withstand temptation? _____

What do you believe are triggers to your sexual arousal? What steps or measures do you have in place when these triggers arise? _____

Is there anything in your home that you need to remove to maintain a pure environment? _____

What are you doing to ensure that your conversations are not sexually charged? _____

What are your views on kissing? Is this a safe expression of intimacy in a dating relationship, why or why not? _____

What are your thoughts on the Christian Side Hug? _____

What ways can you guard and protect your dating partner? _____

How can using the Take Out Menu help you and your date become acquainted/grow in a relationship? How does it help you minimize opportunities for sexual temptation? _____

What steps can you make to ensure that your relationship is pleasing to God? _____

[1] General Larry Platt 2010 [2] 2 Cor. 13:12 [3] Prov. 6:27,28

Chapter 18
How Far Is Too Far?

What if you were given a new walk-in closet full of three hundred pairs of designer shoes, all for free? Cool, right?! There's only one thing: you wear a size eight and all three hundred pair of those new designer shoes are a half size off; it's a size seven and a half! It's only a half size; should be no problem, right? I think you and I would agree that a half size less does matter. Try wearing a half size less than your shoe size; that would be quite painful! That'll little pinky toe of yours would be hurting so bad by the middle of the day!

It's interesting how we can see the problem and the pain associated with wearing a half size less than our shoe size but not see the problem and the pain that comes as a result of someone engaging in "half sex." BUT THE CONSEQUENCES ARE MUCH MORE PAINFUL. Is there even such a thing as having half sex? Like, can you have half of an orgasm and if you do have ½ of an orgasm, does that mean you haven't had sex? That's like saying if you have sex with half of your clothes off, you're not having sex. Yet, there are many single Christians who think they are safe and that it is acceptable to indulge in a fraction of sexual pleasure by not going "all the way." There are many singles who want to engage in sexual pleasure and get as close as they can to sexual intercourse without culminating the "full" act. Many Christians try to get as close to sin and hell as they can without burning. That's like playing with matches; you'll start a fire that you can't extinguish.

Many single couples will awaken and arouse the body by engaging it in aggressive levels of foreplay and then attempt to back off and extinguish the sexual flames they've ignited through as much of a preview to sex as they can; as though it's a taste test, attempting to get a sample of sex as opposed to the "full course." I get many emails from singles echoing the same question, "How far is too far? Like, how far can we go with sex and get away with before it's actually considered sex?" So they'll sit on the couch and canoodle (I like saying that word), and they'll engage in heavy petting, groping, grinding, dry humping, and tongue strangle one another with deep-throat kissing that's so deep that they touch their dating partner's tonsils! And dry humping? Do twenty, thirty and forty year-olds still do that? That should have gone out of style when you were in your teens! But rumor has it, there are many grown adults still dry humping. ☹ And not only dry humping but engaging the body in high levels of sexual arousal through foreplay; using oral sex, masturbation, and heavy fondling as sexual outlets as the means for not going "all the way." I don't know if you know this or not but I have a major announcement to make: YOU'RE HAVING SEX! You think that you're not having sex because you don't go "all the way" or there's no penetration, but you're having sex because foreplay is simply "outercourse."

    Foreplay is stimulating the body for sexual arousal or pleasure and the means by which you prepare the body for sexual intercourse. When you touch or stimulate the body you are revving up the body's number one sexual organ: the brain. When you begin to stimulate the body, your brain sends your body parts a message back saying, "It's time to have sex." You'll find that trying to quench your sexual desire by attempting to cool it off with a little sex or *half of sex* only inflames it; not extinguish it. The body aggressively begins to prepare itself and when the body becomes aroused, the flesh doesn't want it to stop, it doesn't care that you're a Christian and that you're a member of the Greenway Super Second Corinthian Apostolic Baptist Church. The sensations your body will experience is going to cloud your spiritual vision and you'll forget where the book of Genesis is. Your commitment to sexual purity will go right out the window when your flesh becomes inflamed.

"Put no confidence in the flesh." Philip. 3:3 NIV

    Many people underestimate sexual arousal and think there's nothing wrong with having a full "make out session" on the couch but then send me an urgent email of how shocked they are that they went all the way! But what did you expect when you aroused the body to have sex? I know, you were just only kissing, then all of a sudden...! I hear it all the time, "We didn't intend on having sex; things just got out of hand!" ...Yeah, your hands... You can't put yourselves under volatile sexual pressure and not expect your body to send you a-must-attend-invitation to sex. Sex is progressive in nature and that's how the body is designed. You think that as long as I don't touch the "major parts" that we'll be safe, but arousal is not just limited to the genitalia. There are erogenous zones, areas on the human body, like the neck, the arm, the thighs, and even the lips, when stimulated can incite sexual arousal. You only intended on kissing, but kissing led to necking, then necking led to touching, touching went to fondling...the entire time you're stimulating the body, it's sending messages to your brain to prepare it to have sex. The brain then sends messages back to the body, causing it to sweat, expand, sweat, and pulsate, while the heart rate, blood pressure and breathing accelerates, all during your "little harmless half sex make out session." Your brain doesn't distinguish the difference between oral sex, masturbation, heavy petting and fondling, or intercourse; it all equates to sex in your brain.

Once you raise the body to this level of arousal it becomes more difficult to resist. You can pray and rebuke it all you want! Your body is not going to make a spiritual decision; it's going to make an arousal decision: it wants to have sex! You can't play "sexual roulette" with your body and think there will not be any repercussions. Sexual frustration comes in when you engage the body in high levels of arousal and then back out of it and you then begin to develop an unhealthy, love-hate relationship with sex because God didn't create your body to be awakened by sexual arousal and then it not be fully fulfilled. Your half sex mentality distorts the original plan for sex because God created sex and orgasm to go hand-in-hand; not for you to prematurely engage in sex and then back out of it. The body knows that it's supposed to have intercourse when it is aroused and stimulated but you arouse it and then disconnect it from the culmination state. Your body then is forced in constant disarray; you're confusing your body and placing it in an unhealthy imbalance. You make out on the couch with your date with tongue kissing and grinding, indulge in sex by yourself through masturbation or pornography, perform oral sex or do heavy fondling with your dating partner, and then you stop, just short of the culmination of the sexual act. You thrust the body into a state of sexual confusion.

Many singles never develop a healthy relationship with their sexuality while they're single because of the constant sexual confusion that you put the body in and then when you get married there's guilt associated with pleasure. When you're finally in a position to fulfill the complete sexual act, guilt, shame and confusion then shows up in your marital bed. Guilt comes with achieving an orgasm because throughout your years as a single man/woman you develop an unhealthy disconnect between sexual arousal, pleasure and the orgasm. All while you're single you a play a game with your sexuality in the *Minor Versus Major Sin League*, where you develop the mentality that heavy petting, making out, oral sex or a little masturbation is not as bad as sexual intercourse. Now, touch, oral sex and mutual masturbation can't be enjoyed in marriage, because the relationship with sexual intercourse/penetration had a battle between good versus evil in your singleness. Getting the body ready for sex when you can't go all the way with it is insanity! It's marring and tarnishing the beauty of sex; it's sexual vexation at its worst!

Several years ago in my beginning days as a Christian, I started dating this guy who was also a Christian. "Jonathan" was his name and he had been a Christian much longer than I had been; let's just say he was "robbing the cradle" because he was an "adult Christian" and I was a baby Christian and I had no business dating during that time. I was fresh out of a relationship with satan and anything could send me running back to my "ex." Well, Jonathan and I started getting real close because we were spending a lot of time together and I was always over to his house probably about four or five of the seven days in the week. When the weekends came I would stay over to his house until the wee hours of the morning since neither of us had to go to work. We would sit on the couch all night, talking, watching movies, kissing and caressing a bit but we never would go "too far" before one of us would pull back and stop it; *we had things under control,* especially since I would leave before sunrise so we wouldn't call it "spending the night." At first I would leave by midnight, then the midnight curfew went to 2 a.m., and sometimes I would fall asleep in his arms and wake up and find its three-thirty in the morning! I'd jump up and go home and just go back in the middle of the day on Saturday and that cycle would repeat itself. The more time I spent with Jonathan, the closer we became and I would feel *safer,* causing me to stay longer each time I would go over to his house.

      The so-called security the relationship was building even allowed for movie time to go from the couch to his bedroom. Watching movies while lying across his bed was no threat to us because we always made sure that we didn't go too far and since there now was a "security blanket" in the relationship, it was safe to let our guards down because we knew we would stop from going all the way every time we had our intimate moments. When I would wake up and find that I had slept too long, I would sit up to make my way out of the bed and Jonathan would pull my arm back and ask me not to leave. I would stay because we proved that we were not going to have sex and that we could handle ourselves. Now sunrise on the weekends would be spent waking up to Jonathan. The more comfortable we became with one another, the more we would let our guards down and allow for more sexual expression but stop in the "nick of time!" Because that would happen several times, we trusted that we were strong enough and had the ability to go far and put the brakes on, but one too many times with revving up the engine and one night we found ourselves not being able to stop and gave into the heightened sexual pressure. The first time it happened we were in complete, utter shock; just flabbergasted! Like, how could this have happened?! We couldn't believe that we had sex! We repented and promised that we would not have sex again, but we had developed a cycle of letting go, sexually relieving and pacifying ourselves with sexual favors that it happened again! "Why does this keep happening to us," clueless, as if there was some conspiracy against us! We thought that because we were able to stop before going all the way, that surely we would be able to stop again, but now we had no strength in us to say no because every time you give into sexual favors you weaken your ability to say no to sex the next time. And as we established in the previous chapters, when you operate in sexual sin and lust you program the brain to operate in a sexual cycle independent and contrary to your spirit and your desire to live sexually pure. So even though you know what is right or even desire to do what's right, you create a battle or struggle within to prevent you from living right.

      "Make no provision for the flesh, to fulfill its lusts." Rom. 13:14 NKJV

Sex became normal and it was happening on such a regular basis with Jonathan and I that we were having sex like we were married! We no longer wrestled with it and the more we had sex the guilt and conscience level would weaken; we started to see nothing wrong with it and even justified it. We weren't bad people, we were not out being sexually promiscuous and sleeping around with different people; we were two people who had affection and *love* for one another and we paid our tithes and still attended church on Sunday morning after having "relations" the night before on Saturday. That's what sexual sin will do; it will numb you and your conscience will become seared, and what you once thought was impure and wrong you'll begin to make right and acceptable. Heavy petting, kissing, and fondling may seem small but they are the very sparks that start a forest fire. This is why you must make no provision for the flesh. Don't provide it with sexual pleasure at all! The moment you begin making allowances for your flesh to indulge in sexual favor, you open the gateway for more sexual indulgence.

Did you know that oral sex is not a safe alternative? Virtually all STD's can be transmitted through oral sex and some STD's, including genital Herpes, Syphilis, and Chlamydia, are easily spread through oral sex as well.

Many singles allow sexual fondling because it's an excuse that "as long as I don't go 'all the way,' I'll be fine." But sexual release without penalty is impossible when you don't have a legal right or access to it. Heavy petting and necking is just another term for foreplay and a cute way of getting away with sexual pleasure. Since sex is a gift for married couples, then unwrapping it while you're single is ruining the surprise and wow factor of sexual intimacy. Sexual stimulation without the covenant of marriage is dangerous because you put yourself in a constant state of sexual pressure and tension but then leave your body and spirit in a volatile condition, vulnerable and open to impulsive and erratic sexual behavior. Not only do you lose objectivity but it violates the conscience. Don't fool yourself into thinking you are safe because you are not going "all the way." The sexual ruining of many great men and women began in the small stages of foreplay. Many of you who truly desire to live sexually pure while dating do not purposely set out to fall sexually, but you allow gradual progression of sexual gratification to take place, destroying a promising relationship with sexual favors. Don't put yourself in sexual danger; reserve sexual stimulation for marriage so that you can enjoy sexual freedom without the consequences. Sexual expression of any kind is for marriage, period! Pointblank.com!

½ OFF SALE

- **Pornography** does not increase sexual satisfaction, it decreases it. It is dangerous because it leads to an unrealistic, view of sexual expression. Viewing pornography detaches you from the "real world" and real relationships with people. People who routinely view pornography have to eventually get more and more increasingly hard-core pornography to get sexually stimulated. Porn has the ability to physiologically change the mindset of the viewer because it triggers sexual responses that are instinct and your brain and eyes do not make a distinction between sex on a computer or a TV screen and sex in real life. So the affect is as real as actually being in the act; the brain programs and transmits it as an actual sex act on the body. The body then substitutes arousal through illusion, fantasy and a 19" monitor for a real relationship. Pornography in essence, becomes nothing more than a sexual mirage; it impacts the body in such a way that it believes it's actually having sex.

Pornography tarnishes sexuality. Pornography use, whether by men or women, leads to a distorted perception of sexuality as a whole. Porn nurtures sexual dissatisfaction among men and women and it leads them to believe that promiscuous behavior is a healthy form of sexual expression, resulting in the diminished value of marriage. Porn users are more likely to trivialize not only marriage and commitment, and should they marry they will tarnish and mar their marital bed because of pornography.

"One of the most important questions you must ask a guy when you are dating him is, "DO YOU LOOK AT PORN?" Mark Gugnor

Pornography is an emotional affair. When a person watches porn and/or comes to an orgasm as a result of it, their brain releases the same chemicals (dopamine, oxytocin, testosterone, vasopressin) that stimulate sexual arousal, pleasure and bonding hormones that cause strong emotional attachment in human relationships. the brain doesn't make a distinction between the computer and a real person, thus bonding, falling in love, or attaching itself with the act as if it is a "real" experience. Pornography is a virtual, emotional affair and though it camouflages itself behind a screen, pornography is just another form of adultery and if it is not broken, single men will simply get married and transfer that into marriage.

"...Anyone who even looks at a woman with lust in his eye has already committed adultery with her in his heart." Matthew 5:28 NLT

"If u think that masturbation is consdiered a form of "waiting" then porn is just an appetizer for married couples" Ty Adams

Pornography is **artificial, fake, counterfeit sex.** Pornography is the biggest lie because it leads people to believe that is the way that sex really is. Sex is nothing remotely close to the concepts depicted in porn! It is utter and complete deception!

Pornography is the twin devil of masturbation because it almost always accompanies and fuels the addiction of the other. Pornography forces and compels the body to have sex and unfortunately it's usually sex with yourself, since isolation and secrecy is the only wardrobe to cover-up with and you're often alone when you are watching porn.

- **Masturbation:** the excitation or erotic stimulation of one's own or another's genitals to achieve an orgasm by practices other than coitus/sexual intercourse, by instrumental manipulation, usually manually, occasionally by sexual fantasies or by various combinations of these agencies. Self-gratification, autoeroticism, self-abuse. From the Latin word masturbatus and manstupare, meaning to stir up, to defile oneself, to dishonor, to stupefy.

I have heard it said by many, even by some "Christians," that masturbation is not sex and it's acceptable to do as long as you don't lust; PURE FOOLISHNESS! Even if you don't have a third grade education, you can clearly see that masturbation is sexual gratification. But many like to use that as an excuse to do it so that they can get a little sex without going "all the way." But whether you have sexual intercourse or sexually manipulate your own genitals to achieve an orgasm or to incite sexual pleasure, you are having sex. The reason why you masturbate is for sexual pleasure and to experience an orgasm. An orgasm is the culmination, the climax of any sexual act, whether it's with a partner(s) or sex with yourself. And that's exactly what masturbation is: solo sex; it is sexual release through self-stimulation, but God never created sex for you to engage in sex with yourself. Yet, many have justified masturbation because they don't see a Scripture that says, "Thou shall not masturbate." Well here is your scripture for it, allow me to echo the words of God:

"Now the body is not for fornication, but for the Lord; and the Lord for the body." (1 Cor. 6:13)
Fornication (Greek word porneia, meaning: harlotry, adultery, incest, and to indulge in unlawful lust).

Fornication is not simply limited to sexual penetration/intercourse, but it's any indulgence in sexual pleasure that God does not stamp His approval on. Why? Because anytime you have any sexual act, God is in that sexual act, because He lives in of us (*if Jesus is your Lord*). And every time you, as a Christian, masturbate, you take Jesus' body into that sexual act and the Lord cannot remain in a body that is full of sexual contamination and sin.

> "Do you not know that your bodies are members of Christ? Shall I then take the members of Christ and make them members of a harlot? Certainly not! Or do you not know that he who is joined to a harlot is one body with her? For "the two," He says, "shall become one flesh." But he who is joined to the Lord is one spirit with Him." I Cor. 6:15-17 NKJV

- Masturbation is what I'd like to call, tormenting pleasure. The three-second blissful orgasm achieved by masturbation offers more torment than it does pleasure. Masturbation often promises the pleasure but can never fulfill your inward void. And the many people that have been imprisoned by its nonthreatening lure come to find that the trap is not worth the three seconds it took to get it. Two things I've come to know about masturbation is this: it brings shame and it is addictive. Most people who have engaged in masturbation know that the culmination of this sexual act ends in shame. During a TV appearance on TBN's Praise The Lord, I dealt with the effects of masturbation. After the airing of that broadcast, we had an influx of calls to my office from people wanting prayer about their struggle with masturbation. A gentleman in his fifties called my office weeping. He used masturbation as a means of "keeping himself" until God would bring him a wife. Instead of it keeping him, it caused sexual addiction and perversion. In the beginning, he would fantasize about having sex with a woman. The more he indulged in self-sex, the fantasies escalated to more perversion without his own provoking and his sexual fantasies spiraled with him with several women simultaneously, then intensified with him having sex with other men. He wept profusely as he described the shame and emptiness it left him in. There's thousands of emails that have landed in my inbox with the admittance to the shame that masturbation riddles its victims with. If you've ever been bound by it you know all too well that it'll leave you curled up in a fetal position, crying, pierced with guilt. It'll promise fulfillment but your bed is emptier and you're even lonelier than you did before you violated yourself because lust doesn't stop until it kills its victim.

"But every person is tempted when he is drawn away, enticed and baited by his own evil desire (lust, passions), then the evil desire, when it has conceived, gives birth to sin, and sin, when it is fully matured, brings forth death." James 1:14, 15 AMP

If you think you're quenching your sexual flame with masturbation, you've got another thing coming. It only ignites it; it intensifies the flame and frustrates your sexual drive all the more because it's not fulfilling your sexual desire: *it's corrupting it*. Masturbation is saturated with lust; it's virtually impossible to engage in it without lusting. Because of the lust, impure thoughts and sexual fantasies that accompany masturbation you develop a distorted view of sex. Many men begin to view women in that distortion and no longer respect the beauty of a pure woman and ruining your pure appetite for sex; you'll take the shame, the guilt and the addiction right into marriage with you like a gentleman who emailed with his frustration about his masturbation addiction that followed him into married. He sent me an email because he thought marriage would now quench his sexual thirst and he would no longer have to masturbate but three years into the marriage he was still being controlled by the grip of masturbation. Many people who in engage in sex don't understand what happens in their body. He was mastered by masturbation because the more a man masturbates the more his body increases his desire to do it more. His addiction to masturbation in his singleness followed him into his marriage and now his wife couldn't compete with his abnormal appetite to release.

> Self abuse from the 1605 Etymology dictionary says that it is self-deception, a synonym for masturbation or self pollution. The American Heritage Stedman's Medical Dictionary says it is the abuse of oneself or one's abilities.

The dictionary defined masturbation as self-abuse: the miss use of self; it's the mistreatment, the manipulation, the exploitation of YOU. And if that's not already agonizing, it's a never-ending cycle that you habitually become dependent upon, like a drug. And like any other drug, you can never achieve the high you're looking for...Because MASTERbation will MASTER you! You enter into a contractual agreement with it and it will govern your life sexually. It will rule and control your life...it taps you on the shoulder three o'clock in the morning even when you don't want it. You want to stop but you can't. You cry, you repent and say you won't do it anymore but you find yourself molesting yourself again. When will it ever end? I'm here to tell you that cold showers don't work and saying, "you won't do it anymore," won't either, because masturbation will become your MASTER. Its appetite is ferocious and it will not end until it dominates. Its three- second ecstasy will put you in a stupor and numb your faculties, your senses, your receptivity and emotional response. It will control your intellect, your reasoning, your judgment of things, and your own significance and leave you trapped in a mind full of warped sexual fantasies. It will overpower, subdue and suppress you, hold you back, paralyze your forward movement and hinder you from walking in what God has for you. Is having sex with yourself even worth it? I didn't think so... The only way to come out of the chains of masturbation is to dethrone its power by allowing God to become the MASTER over your sexual drive and appetites. Make a decision that you will not be mastered and brought under the power of anything! Do you hear me, woman of God? Not by another man or my own hands! No sex means: no sex!

There may be others that are gratifying their flesh, indulging and sampling sex but I have made a decision that I will glorify God with my body and live in complete purity.

"I have the right to do anything," you say—but not everything is beneficial. "I have the right to do anything"—but I will not be mastered by anything." 1 Cor. 6:12 NIV

So, if you are trying to determine how much can you do or how far you can go, or how much sexual pleasure you can, have here it is:

ZERO! ZILCH! NADA! NOTHING!

- If mental sex is a sin, how much more the physical acts? (Matt. 5:28) Since God even widens sexual sin to include the mind as well, then acts like pornography and fantasy are illicit and sexually immoral. Which then includes masturbation since fantasy accompanies it. If God does not even want our minds to indulge in sexual sin, he certainly does not want our bodies in it. Matthew 5:28 proves that sexual sin/immorality is more than just sexual intercourse.
- There is no provision for sexual expression for singles because it's a gift that is reserved and only to be opened in marriage. 1. Cor. 7:1, Heb. 13:4
- Since there is no provision for sexual expression, sexual acts like masturbation and oral sex are forbidden. The word fornication in its original and complete definition is not limited to sexual intercourse, but these acts as well. Hence, masturbation and oral sex is fornication.
- Because the word "masturbation" does not appear in the Bible or the commandment, "Thou shalt not masturbate" is not in the 10 commandments, it does not give an approval to the act. In our Sex and Relationship Manual, the phrase, "such like," actually substantiates and confirms that this sexual act is forbidden. (Gal. 5:19, 21)

"The works of the flesh are manifest, which are these: adultery, fornication, uncleanness, lasciviousness…and such like." KJV
"Now the doings (practices) of the flesh are clear (obvious): they are immorality, impurity, indecency…and the like." AMP
"When you follow the desires of your sinful nature, the results are very clear: sexual immorality, impurity, lustful pleasures…and other sins like this." NLT

"…Let me tell you again, as I have before, that anyone living that sort of life will not inherit the Kingdom of God" and therefore settles that not only is masturbation a prohibited sexual act among singles but also other sexual expressions.

- Even beyond sexual acts like oral sex and masturbation, there are other sex acts (anal sex) being devised by society that singles should forbid expression of in their relationship. The Bible says that those who are in sexual perversion are "inventors of new forms of evil." (Rom. 1:30) The book of Romans and Galatians would have been eight hundred more pages if God would have listed the forbidden, perverted and evil sexual acts. Because "new forms of evil" and sexual sin is being conceived the phrase "such like" and "forms of evil" would be categorized with any acts similar or that imitates sexual sin. SO if society concocts another sexual act, then that act would be included as well.

- "Not a hint" makes it clear that any expression of sex while you are single is considered sexual immorality. It is not even fitting for people who are called to live a holy and consecrated life for God. Eph. 5:3 NIV

Shun immorality and **all** sexual looseness [flee from impurity in thought, word, or deed]. I Cor. 6:18 AMP

This word, shun, means to deliberately avoid it and make no contact with it at all. Are bodies are not to be used as an instrument of evil, but to glorify God in every area: in our thoughts and actions. That is why we are not to have any affiliation with masturbation and pornography because it consumes and contaminates our minds. That is why you can go half way and still be impure; that is the difference between sexual abstinence and sexual purity. It means nothing to refrain from sexual intercourse, yet you engage in oral sex; you're still sexually impure. There are far too many single Christians who are accustomed to sexually exploring that nothing is pure; exchanging oral sex is on the same level as a kiss with many singles. You want your mouth pure when you kiss your husband or wife on your wedding night; not riddled with contamination from oral sex that you performed on others while you're single.

See how one man's act with oral sex destroyed him in my book, "Single, Saved, & Having Sex."

This means that you may have to end relationships that hinder you from accomplishing that. If the person you are dating is insisting on engaging in sexual acts or require that you have to at least "put out" with some form of sexual pleasure in order for the relationship to exist then I suggest you put one foot in front of the other and walk out of that relationship. I have had singles tell me that their dating partner justified their masturbation and porn activity because it was a prevention method for not going outside the relationship to seek pleasure or these sexual acts were withholding measures that helped them from engaging in sexual activity with one another. That's not sexual withholding; many single Christians use masturbation as a form of abstinence, as if it's a means of waiting for marriage or holding out until you can "legally" have sex; but masturbation is not waiting. Do you hear me, man of God? Do you hear me, my sister? Engaging in sexual expression or activity is <u>not</u> celibacy or sexual abstinence.

> "You can't pick and choose in these things, specializing in keeping one or two things in God's law and ignoring others. The same God who said, "Don't commit adultery," also said, "Don't murder." If you don't commit adultery but go ahead and murder, do you think your non-adultery will cancel out your murder? No, you're a murderer, period." Jam. 2:10-11 MSG

We attempt to put sin on a scale where one is worse than the other, but not in God's eyes: if you're a masturbator, you're a fornicator. If you're having oral sex, you're fornicating. You can't separate sin from sin; it all comes from the same vile pit and they're all deemed sexual immorality and one is not any less sin than the other. When you operate in any sexual activity you violate God's original plan for sex. Many single Christians are focusing on what they can get away with and how much they can sexually please themselves and their sex partners instead of setting their hearts on how far away they can get from sin to get closer to God's heart. Christians who are trying to figure out what sexual sin they can get away with don't have a love relationship with God, because you will protect anything that will violate or hinder that relationship because your heart is set on pleasing Him more than your sexual desire. As you develop a consistent, unwavering commitment to God, it gives you the ability to live completely in sexual purity, and not just half way; there's no such thing as half pure. Make a firm decision that you will not allow any sexual activity, on any level, during your single life. Instead of trying to think of how you can satisfy your sexual desire, throw yourself into finding ways to please the Lord with your life.

"Do not let sin control the way you live; do not give in to sinful desires. Do not let <u>any part</u> of your body become an instrument of evil to serve sin. Instead, give yourselves completely to God, for you were dead, but now you have new life. So use your whole body as an instrument to do what is right for the glory of God." Romans 6:12-13 NLT

If you're struggling with masturbation and/or pornography, I would strongly encourage you to read and meditate on the chapter, *Pants On Fire*, in the pages ahead. In addition to reading *Single, Saved and Having Sex*, I have an audio series entitled, *Mastering Masturbation* on my website available for download in which I share effective tools to finally master and conquer the addictive stronghold of masturbation. www.iTy.TV

Why is the going "half way" mentally a fallacy? _____
_____
_____
Why is going "half way" equivalent to foreplay? _____
_____
How do singles develop destructive sexual patterns when they engage in sexual activity? How does it

affect marital sex? _____
_____

How can the progression of sex mislead you into thinking you're safe with sampling sexual arousal?
_____
_____

How does a series of going half way progressively weaken your conscience and your strength to withstand sexual pressure? _____

Are there relationships that you've been in that had a promising future but was destroyed because of sexual involvement? How did it affect it? _____

Why are acts like oral sex and masturbation considered fornication? _____
_____

What does the Bible say about sexual expression outside of marriage? _____
_____

Instead of using your body to fulfill sexual lust, in what ways can you use your life to please the Lord?
_____
_____

Chapter 19
Pants On Fire

I just finished Single, Saved and Having Sex and just wanted to say Thank You for letting God use you. When I accepted Christ 11 years ago as a single man I knew I had to change the way I lived but was not sure how. My church family was able to tell me what not to do but I was left with a lot of questions about how to live single and saved. I still had the same sexual urges and the desire for female companionship but no way to deal with them. After vowing to not have sex again until I got married, I found myself time and again back in the same dating lifestyle that I lived before I was saved complete with lust, fornication and self-pleasure. Having been taught, "it is better to marry than to burn," I married. The marriage, which should have never been in the first place, has ended. Now I am a divorced father with a one-year-old and facing the single life again. Having read your book, I feel better prepared to succeed in saving myself until my God-sent bride is revealed to me. I am really excited about your follow-up book, which addresses how to date as a single believer. I have dubbed your books "The Power Pack" and I'm giving them to my single friends. Again, thank you for allowing yourself to be the vessel.

Signed, Mike

Most dating couples will face sexual pressure and temptation, for some, that pressure may be more intense, unbearable at times, as if "My skin will peel off or I'll pass out and die if I don't have it," admitted one sexually tortured man who found it difficult to refrain from having sex with his girlfriend. I can almost positively say that no one has ever died from not having sex, but even Paul, a eunuch, described it as a torturing burn.

> "But if they have not self-control (restraint of their passions), they should marry. For it is better to marry than to be aflame [with passion and tortured continually with ungratified desire]." 1 Cor. 7:9 (AMP)

> "But if they (unmarried and widows) can't manage their desires and emotions, they should by all means go ahead and get married. The difficulties of marriage are preferable by far to a sexually tortured life as a single. (MSG)

"Inflamed, tortured continually with ungratified desire, and a sexually tortured single life?" That would make any single want to extinguish the flames and run to Vegas; or shucks, take the short cut and just run down stairs in your house and do a basement wedding! No wedding dress, no flower girls, skip the invitations and reception, grab some aluminum foil and concoct a wedding ring out of it, and Skype your licensed-minister-cousin via iPad to officiate the ceremony! Sometimes, in the middle of sexual arousal that's how you feel, because when you're sexually provoked you think stupid! This Scripture, erroneously interpreted, has put many people into marriages that they were never supposed to be in; all so that you can have some sex! If you are being ruled and governed by uncontrolled passion, then your flesh is making your marital decision and whatever you birth in the flesh, *you have to maintain in the flesh*. Here's the problem with that: I've never seen sex sustain a marriage. You're in for a rude awakening if you allow sex to be the determining factor by which you choose to marry someone because you will come to find that a climax will not fix the other issues you'll face. But when you believe that the only way to put a burning flesh out of its misery is to run and get married, after having sex, you will roll over and realize after the thrill is gone you're stuck with "Mr. or Mrs. What In The Hello Kitty Was I Thinking?!" I've seen many people unhappily married to someone that is unstable, insane, relationally ignorant, abusive, a masquerading Christian, financially irresponsible, unfaithful, drug and sexually addicted, and spiritually cancerous, but oh, can give you some amazing sex! Ha! Who cares about six seconds of temporal pleasure when I have to spend my life living tortured, day-by-day in my home with such a person? A sexually tortured single life is not sounding all that bad right about now…

Many singles, filled with sexual lust or longing, are burning to a crisp and they attempt to put the fire in their flesh out by taking a forward dash into marriage but find that the flame only got hotter! Then we get a choir of disappointed people who end up singing a sad song that marriage doesn't work. Well, I have an announcement to put in the church bulletin: marriage is not going to cure or stop the burning; it will only amplify it. If you struggle with maintaining sexual purity, uncontrolled lust and desires, it will follow you into marriage. Getting married is not a cure for sexual integrity. In fact, the opposite happens because marriage will only expose your struggle. After appearing on television in an interview about singles and their sexual struggles, a young man in his early thirties who saw the broadcast contacted my office for counseling because he struggled with masturbation while he was single so he got married thinking it would cure his struggle; it increased, in high levels, to the point that he was having more sex with himself than he was his wife. In his words, "I now have a beautiful wife to enjoy lovemaking with but can't because I'm trapped and bound by masturbation." Sexual sin and perversion is multi-layered, carrying the seeds of other sexual traps. If you find it difficult to stop masturbating, then pornography will be waiting for you in marriage. If you find it difficult to manage and control your sexual drive now, then adultery will be waiting for you when you get married. Masturbation and fornication while single is only the metamorphosis of pornography and adultery coming into full maturity in marriage. Whatever sexual struggles you have prior to marriage will just follow you into it and what was once a sexual struggle in your singleness turns into sexual dissatisfaction in marriage because marriage is not a "healing ministry" that will magically remove what you have neglected to deal with while single. I know, many people have preached in error and prescribed "it's better to marry than burn" as the cure for singles who can't manage sexual desire and have justified the hijacking of marriage to hose down sexual flames, but if we subscribe to that theory then we usurp God's will for singles:

> "For this is the will of God, that you should be consecrated (separated and set apart for pure and holy living): that you should abstain and shrink from all sexual vice, that each one of you should know how to possess (control, manage) his own body in consecration (purity, separated from things profane) and honor. Not [to be used] in the passion of lust like the heathen, who are ignorant of the true God and have no knowledge of His will…For God has not called us to impurity but to consecration [to dedicate ourselves to the most thorough purity]." 1 Thess. 4:3-5, 7 AMP

> "God wants you to keep clear of sexual sin so that each of you will marry in holiness-not in lustful passion in ignorance of God and His ways." 1 Thess. 4:3-5 TLB

Here's the problem with that: the flesh is perishing day-by-day and therefore doesn't have the capacity to sustain a marriage. (2 Corinthians 4:16) That is why in the genesis of God's mind, marriage originates or is birthed in the spirit. (Genesis 2:21-24) Therefore, if you are ever going to possibly have a great, lasting marriage, it's going to be predicated on the condition and spiritual health of your spirit and your flesh in your single state. With that said, you have to get to the place where you celebrate your sexuality, where you love and live passionately without burning.

Fire Hydrant
Abstinence and cold showers don't work! Abstinence is not sexual purity and neither is it deliverance. Throwing a teaspoon of water on a flaming body is not going to put any blazing flame out. Make shift remedies, knowing the 'do's and don'ts of Christianity' and doing religious activities will not put an end to your sexual struggle. Some of the fire rescue efforts that I've seen many Christians attempt are merely temporary mirages that appear as sexual wholeness. That is why you can find yourself back into sexual bondage because you were never delivered. You just lacked opportunity. But soon as the opportunity arises, a new relationship or the cycle of sexual temptation comes, you fall prey to it because abstinence and cold showers are only temporary vacations from sex. But God is calling us to be chaste and pure. Just because a person is not having sex doesn't mean that they are pure. I've seen many impure virgins. Chaste means to be pure from unlawful sexual intercourse both in thought and in action; not merely abstaining from sex, but having a chaste mind and chaste eyes. "But among you there must not be even a hint of sexual immorality, or any kind of impurity." (Ephesians 5:3 NIV) The Bible says that the Word is itself will wash us and

cleanse us; it is like a fire hydrant that will cleanse us from sexual sin. If you want to live sexually pure, then you have to develop a daily relationship with the Word.

Fire Drill

I remember when we were kids in school we had to do fire drills to practice and prepare, in case there was a fire. We'd go through a drill just as if there was a fire. The fire alarm would sound, often in the middle of doing schoolwork, but that didn't matter; we would have to drop our pencils and stop whatever we were doing and evacuate the building just as if it was an actual fire. There were certain factors during the fire drill that are vividly etched in my mind: remember the exit routes, never take the elevator, always use the stairs, go away from the smoke and the time in which we exited the building was always an important factor. Though there was never a fire, there were safety measures taken just in case. The problem with many singles is that they do not **practice** fire drills *in case of sexual fires*. Waiting until you're in one another's arms and your clothes are set ablaze is far too late to figure out an escape plan!

Whenever I conduct a seminar for singles, I have them implement the exercises that I've shown you in this chapter and the previous chapter, Pants on the Ground, in which you prepare for what you will do should you face sexual temptation. But I also want to show you another purity management application that I've created that I want you to put into practice. It's called Fast Forward where you are offered an opportunity or an invitation to engage in sex, inappropriate sexual behavior, or any temptation to go against God's will for your life. Before you accept the invitation, you need to first consider the outcome or the consequences if you were to accept the invite. Most often, almost all of those who stop and consider the cost will decline the offer when they see that the price tag of sin or going against God's plan for their life is not worth it. Usually when temptation comes, we do not consider or see the immediate consequences so we enjoy the temporal gratification without factoring the long-term cost. When dealing with sexual temptation, I *fast-forward* the scene to see the conclusion and the outcome of me giving into the temptation, and when I look ahead to see the consequences, I think to myself, "thanks, but no, thanks! I'll pass on that one!" Okay, so let's try it:

For example:
     You meet someone who is very attractive, has everything on your list, but one problem: he/she is borderline Christian. Ask yourself, "If I get into a relationship with this person, what would happen? Fast-forward to what your life would be as a result of you accepting the invitation to be in a relationship with this person:

                       The pure lifestyle that I live now will change
                       My relationship with God will be destroyed

> My prayer life will fall off
> Church attendance dwindles or dissipates
> I'll end up on Maury Povich trying to figure out who's the father
> I married this crazy person and I live in a house with a person that I didn't have nothing in common with but cute and I can't stand them!
>
> _____
> _____ (insert yours here)

Let's try another one:
> You're on the couch, you and your boyfriend/girlfriend are watching TV and you began kissing. It gets hot and heavy, your clothes come off and…fast-forward:
>> I'm not able to finish school because I have to raise a baby now
>> The role in my church or my community is now affected because I can't lead without being an example
>> My dream of becoming America's next Top Model or the next Steve Jobs has been severely compromised!
>> I got pregnant by someone that turned out to be a short-term fling and now my child has big ears and looks like a cross between Lil Wayne and Joan Rivers, but I didn't see that when I was intoxicated by lust.
>> _____ (insert yours here)

I think you get where I'm going with this. I know the combination of Lil Wayne and Joan Rivers is not a good sight but in all seriousness, the point I'm making is that you need to step back and consider the outcome of poor relational or sexual choices whenever the invitation to sin shows up. Counting up the cost, planning an escape route, and implementing prevention measures will help you avoid the pitfalls that so many singles easily fall for.

Escape routes
Whenever single couples tell me that they fell into sexual temptation, I always ask, "What exit route did you fail to take? What exit sign did you ignore?" I am 100% confident that whenever there is sexual temptation, there is always an option out of it, and if a couple falls prey to it then they simply ignored or disregarded it.

> "For no temptation (no trial regarded as enticing to sin), [no matter how it comes or where it leads] has overtaken you and laid hold on you that is not common to man [that is, no temptation or trial has come to you that is beyond human resistance and that is not adjusted and adapted and belonging to human experience, and such as man can bear]. But God is faithful [to His Word and to His compassionate nature], and He [can be trusted] not to let you be tempted and tried and assayed **beyond your ability**

and strength of resistance and power to endure, but with the temptation **He will [always] also provide the way out** (the means of escape to a landing place)." 1 Cor. 10: 13 AMP

God will always send you a text message alerting you of impending danger, providing you with an escape route to ensure that you do not fall prey to temptation. God is faithful to Himself! He will not allow you to be put in a situation where you cannot escape sexual destruction. No one can ever say that they didn't have a way out, ever! You can never use the excuse that the temptation overtook you or that the sexual arousal was stronger than you and *you couldn't help it* because God will give you strength that is stronger than the temptation. I've heard the church mother say, "God'll keep you if you want to be kept!" You can trust that God is going to do His part; the question is, "Do you want to be kept?" There are many times that I can account where God pulled me out of compromising sexual situations, where I had the heart and desire to maintain sexual purity, but didn't know how I was going to get myself out of that fine mess. But, God! If it had not been for Jesus I would have fallen! This is why your strength alone cannot help you; even with the best intentions.

> "And Abraham said of Sarah his wife, She is my sister. And Abimelech king of Gerar sent and took Sarah [into his harem]. But God came to Abimelech in a dream by night and said, Behold you are a dead man because of the woman whom you have taken [as your own], for she is a man's wife. But Abimelech had not come hear her, so he said, Lord, will you slay a people who are just and innocent? Did not the man tell me, She is my sister? And she herself said, He is my brother. In integrity of heart and innocency of hands I have done this. Then God said to him in the dream, Yes, I know you did this in the integrity of your heart, for it was I Who kept you back and spared you from sinning against Me; therefore I did not give you occasion to touch her." Gen. 20:2-6 AMP

You need to know that I just stood up and did a cartwheel praise on that right there! My Lord! Are you guys getting this? Abimelech brought Sarah into his palace to *have at her* but God sent a text message to him in his sleep and told him, "You're as dead as a doorknob! You're dead as an iPhone without a charger! You're as dead as an all-beef special patty from Mickey D's!" God will not let you lie in sin without saying anything to you! He'll text message you, speak to you in a dream, place a roadblock on the route to the hotel, or blow out your tire on the way to their house before He stands back and just let you land in sin without a warning and an opportunity to exit! Abimelech was like, "Lord, please, I didn't know! In the integrity of my heart, I would not have done this!" Okay, now this right here is my absolute favorite part and you guys might as well get ready to do another cartwheel-praise with me! I can imagine how God checked him, "I know your intentions were pure. I know you're a king and rule over palaces, but don't think you're that royally strong that you could lie in the bed all night with Sarah in your palace and not have sex with her; IT WAS I WHO KEPT YOU FROM SINNING AGAINST ME! I DIDN'T GIVE YOU AN OCCASION TO TOUCH HER!" Somebody better stop right now and bless God for blocking a sexual fall! You mean to tell me that Abimelech didn't have an "occasion?" No, he had every opportunity to sin because he was with her in the bed throughout the night but God blocked it!!!

I don't care who you are, how saved you are, and how strong you think you are, you're best intentions and willpower alone with not keep you! You need to rely on the power of God to keep you! Even in your best efforts, you can find yourself falling short. I've seen many people attempt to fight sexual sin on your own and come up short every time. Paul attempted the same thing and look where it got him.

> "But I need something more! For if I know the law but still can't keep it, and if the power of sin within me keeps sabotaging my best intentions, I obviously need help! I realize that I don't have what it takes. I can will it, but I can't do it. I decide to do good, but I don't really do it; I decide not to do bad, but then I do it anyway. My decisions, such as they are, don't result in actions. Something has gone wrong deep within me and gets the better of me every time." Rom. 7:18-20 MSG

Many of you are trying to use willpower instead of God's power! As you come face-to-face with sexual temptation you will come to realize that your willpower will have little power. Does that negate your responsibility? Absolutely not! This doesn't give you the liberty to purposely sin or put yourself in sexual compromise and let Sarah lie in the bed all night with you *because God is going to do the work of keeping you sexually pure.* Don't just throw yourself in the bed with your boo and hope for the best! Can a man take fire in his bosom and his clothes not be burned? (Proverbs 6:27) Let's make this plain and simple: can a man and a woman spoon and not catch fire and burn? Can a man and a woman dry hump and not catch fire? Can they make out on the couch and not get burned? The Word makes it clear that if you play with fire, you're going to get burned. Again, don't purposely put yourself in compromising positions and then make excuses for "falling" into sin because God's got your back. God's grace is not liberty for us to live in sin.[4] That grace gives us the liberty to tap into God's strength to live a life of righteousness. We are in partnership with Christ as He works in us His power to live right. "I can do all things through Christ who gives me the strength."[5] In fact, your weakness is the place in which God's strength is most effective; it's the place where He rest His strength in.

> "But He said to me, My grace (My favor and living-kindness and mercy) is enough for you [sufficient against any danger and enables you to bear the trouble manfully];

for My strength and power are made perfect fulfilled and completed and show themselves most effective in [your] weakness." 2 Cor. 12:9 AMP

Sadly, I see far too many Christians who do not understand that God is the best place to drop your weakness at. Many are afraid to admit their weaknesses or struggles that they have to a God that has the unlimited power to change it. Samson had a weakness for ungodly women and struggled with living sexually pure. Samson's enemies knew his weakness better than he did, which gave them the upper hand and the ability to take him out![6] Let me ask you this, does satan know your struggles and weaknesses better than you do? Does he know what to lure and bait you with? Satan knows how to ensnare you in a sexual trap because he knows your sexual weakness better than you do. I know the things I can't touch; I won't even go near it! And I don't have a problem with admitting that! Admitting my weaknesses does not make me weak: <u>it empowers me!</u> Many of you are afraid to face, acknowledge or admit your weakness and you attempt to avoid them and that is why you are powerless over them. Instead of giving it to God, there are some of you that try to carry it or bury it in shame and attempt to overcome your struggles on your own because you're afraid to expose your weakness to the Lord. One evening during an altar call at a church I was ministering at, I was led to deal with those who were carrying shame and guilt and afraid to release it to the Lord; the altar was full that night. I remember this young lady who wept in my arms at that altar because she was so afraid to come to God, thinking He would turn her away because of her sins that she struggled with. This is one of the reasons why so many singles struggle so long with sexual sin because they carry the sin instead of giving that struggle to the Lord. If there's only one thing that you remember that I've said in this book, let it be this: I don't know what you struggle with, what sins you've been battling, what mess you're in, or how bad you've sinned, don't allow none of them or let no one ever stop you from coming to God. You have every right and access to the presence of God because Jesus paid the price for you to have that access. In fact, God says you can boldly come to His presence for help.

> "For we do not have a High Priest Who is unable to understand and sympathize and have a shared feeling with our weaknesses and infirmities and liability to the assaults of temptation, but One Who has been tempted in every respect as we are, yet without sinning. Let us then fearlessly and confidently and boldly draw near to the throne of grace (the throne of God's unmerited favor to us sinners), that we may receive mercy [for our failures] and find grace to help in good time for every need [appropriate help and well-timed help, coming just when we need it]." Heb. 4:15-16 AMP

Jesus understands every weakness and struggles that you have. The Word says that He was tempted in ALL points, without the sin. So He understands the sexual temptation that you face, your loneliness, your battle with maintaining sexual purity, the inner war that some of you have with masturbation, the disgust and the hate you have for your pornography addiction, the empty longing you have for a mate…Jesus says that weakness is the place that I want my strength to rest in and when you face those struggles you have every right and access to fearlessly, confidently, and boldly come to the throne of grace to receive the grace and mercy, and to help you in the time of need. I don't know about you, but that gives me confidence in knowing that I'm going to be all right! That whatever temptation I face, it will not triumphant over me! So right in the middle of temptation, right when you're tempted to log on to sin, or sexual arousal has taken over you and you find yourself in a sexual compromise with your boyfriend/girlfriend, boldly call on God for His grace and strength, and watch the power to overcome stand up strong in you! Draw from the power of the Holy Spirit; sin and temptation is not match for it!

> "We don't have a priest who is out of touch with our reality. He's been through weakness and testing, experienced it all-all but the sin. So let's walk right up to Him and get what He is so ready to give. Take the mercy, accept the help." MSG

Fire Extinguisher My mind wants to have sex!
In order for you to control your desires, we have to go to the seat of your desire. Desire, arousal, sexual longing and urges, all initialize in the brain. Sex is chemical and it begins in the brain long before it shows up in your bed so if we are going to control the burning we have to put out the fire in your brain and stop your mind from having sex; well, at least until you get married. Many of you don't intend to give into your sexual desires, but your actions somehow get disconnected from your intentions. Actions are only thoughts in motion. You can get back the power by simply getting control over your thoughts. Thoughts are chains, links of events, patterns, images, words, and imaginations. Once these links are sequential, practiced and patterned, they become automatic reactions: habits. Now it appears that your sexual burning is a bad habit that you can't seem to break, but that's furthest from the truth; you didn't all of sudden wake up burning in passion. Your mind will have you thinking that this is a part of your nature and you can't "help" it. But your mind had practice in having sex, and after enough sex rehearsals, the stimulation of those thoughts began to show up in your life. By repeated gratification of desire, you've formed a sexual habit. And as the saying goes, 'practice makes perfect.' You practiced and practiced and practiced; then perfected the sin.

Don't allow your mind to make you think you're prone to sexual impurity, subject to nature that can't be controlled. No, just like you've developed this habit of giving in to your sexual cravings, you can break the habit by redeveloping and redirecting the thought patterns: mental discipline. Mental discipline is vital for anyone who wants to reclaim sexual integrity. Unless the mind is strengthened with new thought patterns to master and thwart the impulses of sexual longing, you'll constantly lack control and you will be subject to erratic sexual behavior. Reassigning new images, words, events and imaginations, and breaking the chains of your old thought patterns will give you the ability to produce new actions. Romans 12:1, 2

Forest Fire
If you've ever seen a forest fire you know they are extensive in size and quite dangerous. They are susceptible to start in hot climates and whenever a forest fire has the potential threat of even coming near residential communities, you can be assured there will be a mandatory evacuation because its speed has the capacity to spread quite rapidly and its potential to change direction unexpectedly causes uncertainty for anyone near its path. That's just how your flesh is when it catches a sexual fire!

- It's dangerous!
- It's susceptible and prone to hot climates
- Sexual arousal spreads rapidly and changes directions unexpectedly
- Requires a mandatory evacuation

Not only do some of us think we can outsmart our flesh but we must think we are wiser than God. A forest fire will catch fire to you and your little puss in boots on the couch and you'll sit there and negotiate with your flesh! No, here's a better one: you'll both sit there and try to pray it out! Oh, you want to try and act deep and super-spiritual right now and pray? It's not praying time, it's running time! When there's a forest fire in your flesh, God calls for a mandatory evacuation! Listen, He is the designer of sex and understands how sexual passion is and if our wise God thought that prayer was the solution to a sexual fire, make no mistake about it, He would have said, "pray!" But no, my little sizzlin' hot cakes, prayer is not the antidote, fleeing is!

"Flee fornication."
"Flee also youthful lusts."

I would say, "RUN, FOREST, RUN," but Forest Gump wasn't running fast enough! Running is too slow; God says, "Flee!" You see, running is just a faster pace of walking and it can imply that there is no sense of urgency. Fleeing is much different! Fleeing means you run away from impending trouble or danger like you're running for your life! If you want to take a chance at getting caught up in sexual temptation, then you run like Forest; but if you want to save your life, then you flee like Joseph!

"The Lord was with Joseph, and he became a successful man. He lived in the house of his master, Potiphar...so Potiphar was very happy with Joseph and allowed him to be his personal servant. He put Joseph in charge of the house, trusting him with everything he owned…Now Joseph was well built and handsome. After some time the wife of Joseph's master began to desire Joseph, and one day she said him, "Have sexual relations with me." But Joseph refused and said to her, "My master trusts me with everything in his house. He has put me charge of everything he owns. There is no one in his house greater than I. He has not kept anything from me except you, because you are his wife. How can I do such an evil thing? It is a sing against God." The woman talked to Joseph every day, but he refused to have sexual relationship with her or even spend time with her. One day Joseph went into the house to do his work as usual and was the only man in the house at the time. His master's wife grabbed his coat and said to him, "Come and have sexual relations with me." but Joseph left his coat in her hand and FLED[1] out of the house." Gen. 39:2-12 NCV

Joseph had the favor of God all over his life! Everything he touched prospered, even catching the attention and favor of his boss where he made Joseph head over his palace! Not only was God's favor on Joseph's life, he had the nerve to be the best eye candy you've ever seen! He was fine, built and God-fearing! Whewwww, Lord, help me! Even his boss's wife found him to be irresistible! Joseph would mind his own business and do his work, but his boss's wife would stand there giving him the side eye, looking at him like she could sop him up with a buttermilk biscuit! I can just imagine how she probably would walk around the palace with a Victoria Secret nightie on in the day time, purposely trying to get Joseph's attention. But he was not paying her any attention! Her tacky Desperate Housewife of Egypt self just came right out and asked him to have sex with her! Just when I thought that Joseph couldn't get any finer, he not only refused to sleep with her, but he checked her and said, "My boss, who just happens to be your husband, trusts me with everything in this palace. I have access to everything in here, except you! I could have you if I wanted to *but I don't want it*; and furthermore, I wouldn't do something so wicked and sin against my God!" Kahboom! Pie all in her face! You would think after he turned her down she would go and sit down in a corner somewhere, but she kept taunting him! Every day she would try to get him to have sex with her but Joseph didn't bend; he avoided her like she was a plague! She couldn't take it anymore! Like a lioness in heat, she grabbed him by his coat and was gonna just take *it* from him, demanding, "You're going to have sex with me if it's the last thing I do!" Joseph tore himself away from that crazy chick and fled the scene like OJ Simpson fled the cops! Joseph was trying to get away from her so fast that as he was snatching himself away, she was holding on to his coat to try to stop him from getting away, but he was fleeing from her so fast that he tore out of his coat and left her holding it! The Road Runner, Usain Bolt (the world's fastest man), Superman or a speeding bullet didn't have anything on Joseph!

As God-fearing and the praying man that he was, note that Joseph didn't stick around to share his faith and try to get her saved, or "lay hands" on her and pray that seductive, sex demon off of Potiphar's wife; instead, he got out of dodge! Because the remedy for sexual temptation is to flee; Joseph ran, but David watched. Did you hear me? Your response to sexual temptation will determine your victory or defeat over sexual sin. Joseph became governor,[2] while David committed murder, adultery and he impregnated a woman that he was not married to. You mean the king demoted himself down to a baby daddy?

> "One evening David got up from his bed and walked around on the roof of the palace. From the roof he saw a woman bathing. The woman was very beautiful, and David sent someone to find out about her. The man said, 'She is Bathsheba, the wife of Uriah.' Then David sent messengers to get her. She came to him and he slept with her. Then she went back home. The woman conceived and sent word to David, saying, 'I am pregnant.'" 2 Sam. 11:2-5 NIV

To all the men reading this book: you're a king, not some baby daddy! Let the king inside of you rise up! You can lie there in the bed and negotiate with sexual temptation and desire if you want, but know that destruction is brewing while you're trying to dillydally with it. The Word already forewarns us and attempts to protect us from sexual destruction, proving that Matthew five and twenty-eight has every ounce of truth in it when it states that sexual lust in the mind is equal to adultery. David let his eyes govern him and he watched a bit longer than he should and adultery was the inevitable outcome. Just like David played with sexual desire, the same was the case with Samson as he laid in the bed fancy-footing and hair frolicking with Delilah and he lost his strength and his eyes were gouged out of him![6] If you find yourself in the heat of the moment with your (boy)girlfriend, you need to take off running! Again, temptation is not your problem, not fleeing is…temptation is not a sin, but playing with it is.

- If you're getting hot and heavy and your boyfriend does not make you leave, then we have a problem, Houston! He's not planning on running for the border and either somebody's eyes are getting ready to get gouged out or someone is going to get impregnated with consequences.
- If you are constantly putting out fires--sexual fires--then you need to examine the relationship, because the people in it are mismanaging desire and have proven that you do not know how or refuse to govern yourselves. If you're struggling with sexual purity, you should make a decision to pull back from dating until you can get yourself together, rather than using someone as target practice.
- If you find yourself constantly "falling" even after sincerely putting effort in maintaining sexual purity, then I strongly suggest that you seek counseling.

Sometimes counseling and therapy are frowned upon among some Christians because it somehow signifies that 'you don't believe God or don't have enough faith' or maybe 'you just need to pray harder or make another visit to the altar.' Neither is the case; in fact, not seeking help is an injustice and could very well be an assassination against your faith without having the help you need to assist you in overcoming your sexual struggles. There are many people in the pew that have deep-seated wounds and sexual tragedies from their past that they are carrying, and prayer, accompanied with professional help, (sound, Biblical) counsel and direction can help you overcome your struggle.

Smoke Screen
Why are there so many people who have called on Jesus Christ to be Lord still bound by sexual sin? I believe the greatest reason is because they don't truly believe in the power of the One they call Lord. I believe that many people have minimized the power of God. Though they've called on Him to be their God, they deny His Presence, The Holy Spirit. The manifested presence of God has the power to break any sexual stronghold if only we would allow Him access. The Bible says that Lot lived in an environment engrossed with sin. In fact, the Bible says that Lot was VEXED in his soul because of the overt sin he was subjected to everyday. (Gen 20:1-8, Gen 19)
Okay, maybe you don't get it. This man was barricaded by sexual perversion and thousands of homosexual men who were going to take his life, but escaped it! Why? Because the presence of God blocked it! *THE LORD KNOWETH HOW TO DELIVER THE GODLY OUT OF TEMPTATION! (2 Peter 2:9)* **How** is that a woman addicted to men, with a history of sleeping with several of them that would not even marry her, walk away from a history of sexual entanglement, become an evangelist and never go back to it? Because with one introduction of God's presence, He blocked her past from taking possession of her future! (John 4:1-41) Listen, my friend, the presence of God has the power to fireproof you! (Daniel 3:25 NLT) When you allow the Lord's Presence to stand at the entrance of your life, you don't have to burn with passion or be held hostage to it, or struggle with sexual sin, ever again! He's already proven Himself to be a smoke screen when He took your place in fire. Now all you have to do is live in His presence..♥

2) Gen. 39:26   4) Romans 6:1,2   5) Philippians 4:13   6) Judges 16:1-21

Myths About Singles
Who Are Waiting Until Marriage to Have Sex

The Ugly Myth
The only reason why a person would wait until marriage to have sex is because they're ugly, unattractive and can't get a date. No one would try and have sex with them so it's easy for them to refrain from sex.

The Truth
That's actually hilarious and holds no truth whatsoever because, what someone considers attractive is relative to one's own preference or what they deem to be beautiful. Beauty comes in all forms and different degrees and there are kahzillions of "attractive" people that are waiting until marriage to have sex because they believe it's a beautiful thing to preserve lovemaking for the one that finds their sexual purity and their commitment to the Lord as the highest level of beauty. The ugly truth is that if a person believes that their outward appearance holds its value for the exchange of sex, then if they hold a mirror facing inward, what would glare back will be quite unattractive.

The No Desire Myth
People who are waiting have little to no sexual desire. They probably have some weird, hate thing about sex and think that it's nasty or disgusting because no one with a normal sex drive would wait.

The Truth
Singles who are waiting actually have the opposite point of view about sex. They, we, place a higher regard and value on sex and believe it's a beautiful expression of love with someone you have committed your life to in marriage, and that person is the only one worthy of it. We have a normal, healthy sex drive that we have put in reserve for our future spouse, in which we'll freely rev up the engine and put it in gear and put on a life-long cruise control from our honeymoon forward. There's no need to test-drive our sexual drive and put a lot of mileage and wear and tear on it. While we await that blissful time, we honor our bodies for the Lord and preserve it so that we can have the ultimate pleasure without the emotional scars that are left by uncommitted sex. Instead, we focus our drive and energy in our God-given purpose and no longer allow our sexual drives to control us or direct our lives.

The Age Myth
Only teenagers, who are forced by their parents, are waiting to have sex. Adults are cable of making grownup, responsible decisions about sex; waiting is for young teens.

The Truth
Did you say grownup and responsible decisions? The highest number of those who don't use contraceptives and are contracting sexually transmitted diseases and have unintended pregnancies are adults.* That is one reason teens are not the only ones waiting. Many single adults have made a commitment to wait until marriage to enjoy sex without the destructive consequences. Many adults have come to realize that the lie they bought into from society of the "just do it, one-night stands, multiple partners, unbridled sex life" is not what it cracked up to be and that it leaves them with more sexual and emotional baggage than they can afford to carry.

The Miserable Life Myth
If I wait until marriage to have sex, I'm not going to have any fun in life or relationships.

The Truth
Satan is such a liar! He tries the same stunt on you, that he tried on Eve: "your life will surely suck if you live your life God's way; you mean to tell me you're going to believe *this Guy*? He's trying to steal all your fun and suck the life out of you!"[1] No, truth is satan is the one that comes to kill, steal and destroy. Jesus came to give us life, overflowing, in abundance![2] True freedom and real life doesn't begin until you start living your life according to God's plan for it! I used to think the same thing, "My life will suck if I start living like a Christian! I'm going to pass out if I don't have sex! There's nothing wrong with having sex outside of marriage; nothing bad is going to happen. And besides, what am I supposed to do in a relationship if we don't have sex?!" Blah, blah, blah, blah, blah! If I would have shut the devil's yakking up a long time ago I would've enjoyed life much sooner and experience abundant joy and peace that comes with living pure! And let me tell you the real truth! I was living a life of turmoil while I was engaging in premarital sex. I was fooled into believing that was the extent of fun, but no, my friends! Once I dedicated to sexual purity I came to know the truth! Life doesn't begin until you fully jump in it with God!

The Boring Myth
If you marry a person that is waiting to have sex until marriage, your marital sex life is going to be totally and utterly boring!

The Truth
Truth is, that actually is what happens to those who don't wait until marriage. Their sex life is boring because they treated their bodies like a roller coaster in an amusement park, allowing a long line of waiting riders to get on, twist, roll and shout, and now they're left with nauseating (e)motion sickness to even enjoy it in their marriage. They've ransacked their single life with too many sex partners, preventing them from enjoying it with their

spouse. Too much experience makes for a boring, marital sex life. But when you wait, you come to the marital bed without sexual residue, giving you the ability to create fresh, new, unique, untainted sexual experiences with your spouse.

The Virgin-Only Club Myth

Waiting is for people who are virgins and have not already had sex. If you've had sex, it's too late; you've already messed up.

The Truth

It's never too late! No matter how bad you've messed up, God can and will forgive you. There are many people who have rededicated to celibacy, allowing God to heal them and make them whole again. This is not a virgin-only club, it's a pure club; because you can be a virgin, but not a pure one. Purity is not just in body, but mind, soul and spirit. A virgin is no greater than a person that has recommitted to sexual purity, because in God's eyes *we all needed to be purified*. And that is what God wants: to heal and purify us completely so that we can experience love and sex the way He designed it to be.

The Willpower Myth

It's impossible; they must have stronger willpower or magical powers or something! I don't know how they're doing it; I don't know how they're able to withhold or deny something so strong as sex!

The Truth

I know, it looks like we have superhuman strength, but don't be fooled. Truth is, we can't take credit. We're weak without God and totally rely on His strength. If we relied on our own strength and willpower then expect a sexual fall because even the strongest willpower is not enough to sustain you. With our best intention, will, and determination we are subject to fail.[3] Let me let you in on our secret: It is God working in us to do His will.[4] It is God's keeping power that is keeping us and giving us the ability to live sexually pure! And no matter how impossible it seems, anyone can wait until marriage if you simply give your life to God.

*Guttmacher Institute December 2013 [1]Genesis 3:4-5 [2]John 10:10 [3]Romans 7 [4]Hebrews 13:21

Is He (or she) the One?

"Every good and perfect gift comes from the Father" James 1:17

- ✓ We are equally yoked/compatible in foundational areas of a relationship
- ✓ In this relationship I feel God's love chasing after me through them
- ✓ We support one another
- ✓ My mate is sensitive and attentive to my needs
- ✓ Our relationship is God-centered
- ✓ My mate and I pray together, as we strive to be God-led in our decisions
- ✓ We are both open and honest with one another
- ✓ I can just be happy doing nothing with them
- ✓ I'm at peace
- ✓ Our future plans and goals are similar and I feel secure in building a family and a future with my mate
- ✓ Our relationship glorifies God
- ✓ My mate truly cares for me
- ✓ Our family and friends support and approve of our relationship
- ✓ We communicate well with one another
- ✓ We resolve or come to a medium with disagreements and forgive one another when we've fallen short or have made mistakes
- ✓ My mate makes this relationship important and a priority
- ✓ My relationship with God is growing
- ✓ My mate and I strive to have a relationship that mirrors a Biblical blueprint where we sacrifice, honor, submit, and serve one another
- ✓ I feel safe with them
- ✓ My mate speaks kind to me
- ✓ My life has improved since I've been in this relationship
- ✓ This relationship challenges me and causes me to become more life Christ
- ✓ My mate is faithful and committed
- ✓ I can spend the rest of my life with them!

YOUR DATE'S HISTORY
His story, her story

A comprised list of what you should know about the history of the person you're dating:

Spiritual
- Who is God to you?
  When and how did you come to know the Lord?
- Describe your relationship with God and how it has evolved.
- On a scale from 1 to 10, how strong is your commitment to Christ?
- Have you ever been in a backslidden state or have left the Lord? Explain
- Define what it means to you to be a Christian.
- Describe your life as a Christian.
- What does it mean to follow Christ?
- Describe what it means to be led by God?
- What are your fundamental beliefs?
- Describe your prayer life?
- How often do you pray and ready your Bible?
- How is the Bible relevant to today/the present? How is it relevant in your life?
- How do you apply the Bible in your life?
- What areas of the Bible do you find hard to implement in your life?
- What areas do you need to grow in spiritually and/or in your relationship with God?
- Which areas are you most/least strongest in: love, joy, peace, longsuffering/patience, gentleness/kindness, goodness/kindness, faith, meekness/humility, temperance/self-control?
- Who do you have in your life that helps you grow in your faith?
- Do you know your spiritual gifts and what capacity do you serve with them?
- Are you a member at a church? Where and how long?
- How often do you attend church?
- What are your beliefs and thoughts on worship?
- How would you describe your style or form of worship?
- If you did not have God in your life, how different would your life be?
- What was your life like before Christ and how different is it after having Him?
- If you died, are you sure that you would go to Heaven?

Mind, Intellect
- Where/who do you gain wisdom and knowledge?
- How important is education to you?
- Is continuing education important to you?

- What was your grade point average in school?
- Did you attend college? Why or why not? If so, describe your experience?
- Do you have any education loans/debt? If so, how are you eliminating that debt?
- Do you like to read? What do you read and how often?
- Do you have a mentor? If so, who, and what wisdom do they provide?
- What type of activities/event do you use to enhance/expand your mind/intellect?
- Explain how you reason, rationalize or make daily decisions? How does God play apart in your choices/decision-making?

Family
- What does family mean to you?
- What was your upbringing like?
- If you could change anything about your upbringing, what would it be?
- What are your fondest memories growing up?
- What are your most painful memories growing up?
- Have you gone to counseling/therapy for familial or childhood problems?
- Do you have family issues that are unresolved?
- Describe your relationship with your parents growing up? How is your relationship now?
- What is your relationship like with your siblings?
- Do you ever want to have children? If you are a parent now, describe your parenting and your relationship with your children.
- If there is anything from your childhood that you would do different with rearing children, what would it be?
- What have your parents taught you?
- What did you learn from your parents about love, relationships, and sex?
- Describe what it is like to spend the holidays with your family?

Lifestyle/Social
- Describe your personal lifestyle?
- What areas are you most disciplined in? Undisciplined?
- What are daily habits? What are your best habits? Bad habits?
- Who are your closest friends?
- What would your top 3 friends say about you?
- Who do you share your secrets with?
- How do you typically spend your day? Weekends?
- What are your hobbies? How much time do you spend in those hobbies?
- What is entertainment for you?
- What kind of music do you listen to? Movies?
- What are your views on alcohol, wine, and social parties/night life?
- Describe your social media habits.

Personality

- Describe your personality.
- Describe your usual temperament/disposition.
- Are you an introvert or extrovert?
- Dependent or independent?
- Reserved/laid back or high-energy?
- Spontaneous or planned?
- Organized or free flowing?
- Conservative or liberal?
- Traditional/old-fashioned or modern/contemporary?
- Flexible or firm?
- Social, reserved, bold, or shy?
- Talkative or quiet?
- What type of personality are you attracted to?
- What type of personality do you clash with?

Emotions

- What makes you happy/sad?
- On a scale from 1 to 5, how well do you manage your emotions?
- What makes you angry and how do you handle anger?
- How do you respond to disappointment or failure?
- How do you manage/handle stress?
- How do you feel about forgiveness?
- What areas do you find it hard to forgive?
- Is there anyone that has done something wrong to you that you find it hard to forgive?
- Do you or have you ever struggled with depression?
- What emotional trauma have you faced?
- Have you sought counseling or therapy for emotional trauma?

Health

- What is your regular diet?
- What areas do you struggle with in food/diet?
- On a scale from 1 to 5, how important is a healthy diet to you?
- How often do you exercise?
- Have you ever experimented with drugs, alcohol, smoking?
- Do you or have you ever had any addictions?

- How do you feel about your body image?
- On a scale from 1 to 10, how happy are you with your body?
- Do you have a sickness or illness you are facing?
- Do you or have you ever struggled with a mental disorder?
- Have you ever had to take prescription drugs for an extended length of time?
- Do you regularly have health examinations?
- Do you have health insurance?

Ethics/moral/character

- How do you determine right from wrong?
- In what areas do you refuse to compromise in?
- What areas do you battle with standing firm on?
- What does integrity mean to you?
- What do you believe is unethical?
- Define honesty?
- What does it mean to be trustworthy?
- In what instances is it okay to lie or tell a white lie?
- If your family, friends, or coworkers were interviewed, how would they describe your character?
- Have you ever committed a crime?
- What are your views on politics, justice, activism, abortion, gay marriage?

Communication

- How do you handle conflict/disagreement?
- Explain how you resolve disagreements?
- Do you feel that yelling is acceptable in a conversation or disagreement?
- On a scale from 1 to 5, how well do you think that you listen?
- On a scale from 1 to 5, how well do you allow equal exchange in a conversation?
- Do you think that swearing or profanity is acceptable?
- Do you repress how you feel in a conversation?

Money

- What is the first thing that comes to mind when you think of money? Why?
- What are your challenges with money?
- What do you spend most of your money on? Describe your spending habits.
- Do you maintain a regular/consistent budget?
- Are you financially prepared for the future? What plans are in place or in the process?
- Do you regularly tithe, give, or donate?
- Do you save or invest money? How?

- If you were married, who would be best at managing money?
- Do you think a married couple should have separate/same accounts?
- What have you learned about money, investing and saving?
- What is your credit score?
- How many credit cards do you have?
- How much debt do you have and how are you resolving the debt?

Career

- If you could choose any job/career, what would it be?
- Are you in the career you love/enjoy? Why or why not?
- What factors are considered in your career choice: location, income, benefits, passion/purpose?
- Have you ever had a difficult time in maintaining a job/career?
- What are your work ethics?
- Does your career require lengthy travel?
- What are your plans for retirement?

Purpose

- Why were you born?
- What do you believe is your purpose in life?
- How are you pursuing your purpose?
- What are you most passionate about?
- What do you value most in life?
- What is the most important thing you would like to do before you die?

Goals

- What are your dreams and aspirations?
- What plans do you have to accomplish them?
- Do you maintain a daily or weekly to-do list?
- Where do you expect to be in 5-10 years from now?
- On a scale from 1 to 10, how close are you to achieving those goals?

Personal image and esteem

- What do you like most about yourself?
- What areas do you want to improve in?
- What do you like about your personal style? What would you change/improve?
- How important is personal image to you?

- If you could change anything on your body, what would it be?
- What is unique about you?
- What are your fears?
- What are you most confident about?
- What do you think God thinks of you?

Sex
- How do you feel about sex?
- How did you first learn about sex?
- What do you believe is the purpose of sex?
- What are your personal beliefs on sex before marriage? Sex within marriage?
- What forms of sexual expression is acceptable before marriage in a dating relationship?
- What are your views on pornography? Masturbation?
- What are your personal struggles with sex and how are you working on those struggles?
- Have you ever dealt with a sexual addiction?
- Have you ever dealt with sexual trauma?
- Have you ever contracted a disease?
- When was the last time you've had a sexual health test/report?
- What does sexual purity mean to you?

Relationship
- What do you define as attractive?
- What qualities are most important to you in a mate?
- What is your definition of love?
- What is the difference between lust and love?
- How do you express and communicate love?
- How do you define affection? What forms of affection is acceptable in a dating relationship?
- How do you know if you're in love?
- What is a committed relationship?
- Is it acceptable to date more than one person at a time?
- What are your expectations of your partner?
- How do you determine or know if someone is right for you?
- What is most important to you in a relationship?
- What are your strengths/weaknesses in relationships?
- What are your concepts on gender roles?
- Have you ever dealt with domestic violence? Explain
- How do you define infidelity?
- What are your beliefs on divorce? When is divorce acceptable?
- Have you ever been married? How did it impact your life and what have you learned from it? How have you healed from it?

- Does God play a role in mate selection?
- How does God play a role in your relationship?
- What does a successful relationship look like to you?
- Why do you believe you are not married now?
- What does marriage mean to you? Do you ever want to marry, why/why not?

Chapter 20

Pizza & A Date!

Meat Lovers

There's something to be said when you have a relationship or a connection with someone who you can take a casual Saturday afternoon, grab some take out or order up a Veggie pizza with extra cheese, add pineapples, but hold the zucchini, over conversation about zilch and do nothing with and still find the simplest joy in just enjoying one another's company. But what if there's more to it than that? What if your relationship is more than it being about a pizza and a date, perhaps a deeper dish of connecting beyond what you are accustomed to in relationships? What if there's something more that goes beyond your weird, mutual liking for anchovies and horseradish on pizza? God wants you to have more than just a slice of causal, cookie cutter, average boy meets girl, I like you, you like me, let's go out on a few dates until the life seeps out of it, then we break up and go on to the next soon-to-be ex. What if your relationship was actually different, not the typical passive, go-with-the-wind default relationship but actually has a deeper meaning, with the commitment of a glacier extending to the bottom of the deepest depths, measuring the sky's length, resembling oxygen's life, with the carbon copy of Christ's love, that mirrors His sacrifice, that emulates His compassion, that photocopies His pursuit, a replica of His forgiveness that has the audacity to bring glory to God's name?! Imagine that…two lovers meet and they actually layer their relationship with God's fail-proof recipe for love, allowing Him to be the center…being an example of what He intended for love to be.

Many people desire this; they say they want it and that they're tired of substandard, defective, broken, undersupplied relationships but continue to relate and engage on that same level. You were not made for average or poor quality relationships but you've been settling for mere cheesy relationships, undercooked with no substance but God's plan is for you to only experience love on His level, but it's not going to come by osmosis or hoping and wishing, waiting for it to be delivered to your doorstep. I will give you the ingredients, but you're going to have to jump in here and personally hand toss God's recipe for yourself and be willing to stretch like mozzarella cheese! Yes, if you want this God-kinda love then you're going to have to stretch and widen your capacity to give love and receive love on this level. You're going to have to be willing to come off of baby food, grow up, and prepare and train your palate for meat! Yes, even you 'vegetarian Christians' who only pick and choose some parts of God's word to live by, taking off the toppings that you don't like. You have to eat the whole pie! You have to apply God's entire truth to your relationship in order to yield these results. You're going to have to change your appetite and desire for the ultimate relationship by becoming a meat lover! Yes, devour God's Word, allowing it to become the truth by which you live and apply it to every area of your life and your relationship.

> "You have been Christians a long time now, and you ought to be teaching others, but instead you have dropped back to the place where you need someone to teach you all over again the very first principles in God's Word. You are like babies who can drink only milk, not old enough for solid food. And when a person is still living on milk it shows he isn't very far along in the Christian life, and he is still a baby Christian! You will never be able to eat solid spiritual food and understand the deeper things of God's Word until you become better Christians and learn right from wrong by practicing doing right." Hebrews 5:12-14 TLB

The Crust
I love pizza! Ooey, gooey, cheesy pizza! Like who in the world doesn't?! Whether you're in Italy, Australia or the good ole USA, pizza is an international food loved by many around the world! From the meat lovers, to all veggies, even seafood; the variations of toppings are endless: pepperoni, sausage, shrimp, olives, mushrooms, tomatoes, bacon, ham, pineapples, green peppers…it doesn't matter! You can suite it to your taste and add whatever toppings you like just as long as the crust is great! Whether it's thin crust or deep-dish, everyone knows that the pizza is not good -no matter what toppings you put on it- unless the foundation of the pizza, THE CRUST, is fantastic!

It's the same with relationships, it doesn't matter what your "type" is or what you're attracted to: short, tall, dark, light, slim, chunky and huggable, blonde, brunette, bald, thinning around the edges, educated, blue-collar, successful, rich, zany, nerdy, interracial. It doesn't even matter what the structure of your relationship will look like: get married and have two kids with a big white house and picket fence or buy a farm and raise chicken and pigs on it…it doesn't matter, as long as the foundation of that relationship is God. If God is not what upholds the relationship, I don't care what you layer on top; the relationship will sink and fall apart! No matter how you slice it, your life and your relationships are nothing without God! The success of your relationship is going to be predicated on you allowing God to start out as the foundation and remaining that throughout it.

Toppings
Many single couples start out by going out on dates, spending time with one another, catching a movie, dinner, and start piling on the toppings on a crustless pizza by adding one another to their life routines and launch into a deep-dish relationship without ever establishing the relationship's purpose or inviting God in the groundwork of it.

"And Isaac went out to meditate and bow down [in prayer] in the open country in the evening; and he looked up and saw that, behold, the camels were coming. And Rebekah looked up, and when she saw Isaac, she dismounted from the camel. For she [had] said to the servant, Who is that man walking across the field to meet us? And the servant [had] said, He is my master. So she took a veil and concealed herself with it...And Isaac brought her into his mother Sarah's tent, and he took Rebekah and she became his wife, and he loved her." Genesis 24:63-67 AMP

Deep-dish Prayer

An overwhelming number of dating Christians do not pray before entering into a relationship, nor do they pray with their dating partner; they are simply leading themselves into relationships and hoping interaction alone with their dates will reveal to them what they need to know about them. This method has proved to be an epic fail! The failure-proof formula is to allow intimate prayer with God to be the catalyst of dating matchmaking! If you look at the text of Scripture above, you will see that Isaac was in prayer when Rebekah was led to him. If finding the right person is a result of prayer, then I would get down on my knees like Isaac and pray if I were you! Integrating prayer in the foundation of your dating relationship serves as a GPS (God's Positioning System), a guiding system to navigate you to the right person, insight on the person you share your time with and the source in which to determine if you should even marry that person.

Make a commitment to spend time in prayer with your dating partner and the Word of God for direction and wisdom as to what areas you and/or your dating partner needs to be covered in:

Wisdom in the relationship
The Will of God
Sexual purity
Pray for balance with your schedule and time management
Where you can help your dating partner most
Pray about obstacles or challenges he/she may be facing
Pray against spiritual attacks Pray for his/her relationship with God
Then spend time in worship daily♥

The spirit of your relationship is the lifeline of it. If you are not connecting with your dating partner on a spiritual level on a regular basis, then the spirit of your relationship will die. When you keep God out of the center of your relationship you are signing up for the execution of it because God can't bless a relationship that He's not in. We want the blessings of God, but not His way; it doesn't work like that. You must keep your relationship God-centered, incorporating prayer and the Word of God. *Couples that do not pray together, are simply a ticking explosive, waiting to explode;* **because the only way to achieve a healthy, lasting relationship is to have God as the sustainer of it.**

"How can a young person stay on the path of purity? By living according to your word. I seek you with all my heart; do not let me stray from your commands. I have hidden your word in my heart that I might not sin against you." Psalms 119:9-11 NIV

Oven-baked Word

Incorporating the Word of God in your dating relationship is fundamentally necessary to help you and your dating partner maintain character and integrity, direction and even peace. Just as much as you make plans to go out on dates and dine, you need to make plans and set apart time where you spend time reading and studying God's word together. You can't simply live off the emotional, mental or physical part of the relationship, the spiritual aspect of your relationship should be the most central and significant part. Spending quality time in God's Word with your dating partner will keep you both focused on what's important in your relationship and will serve as a barrier and protection against falling prey to sexual temptation and even relationship idolatry.

A FALSE balance and unrighteous dealings are extremely offensive and shamefully sinful to the Lord, but a just weight is His delight. Prov 11:1 AMP

Slice it

All too often many couples begin to place an imbalance in the relationship where they begin to put their entire focus on the other person causing the relationship itself to become an idol. A healthy relationship should have balance where your life is not completely hidden in the relationship. You both need space and time apart to miss each other and for your own personal development; nothing grows in the shade. Spending time apart is just as important as being together where it allows you to have a healthy, proportionate slice of time where you are able to maintain your own personal relationship with God, your career/purpose, personal interest, family and friends. Maintain yourself and your identity in Christ.

Thank you

My Lord and Savior, Jesus Christ, who is my first Love. Nothing compares to Your Love…I adore You. It brings me to my knees, in total adoration, knowing I get to spend forever loving and worshipping You. I am simply nothing without You and I will spend the rest of my days telling the world of Your amazing, unconditional, life-changing Love!

To my daughter, Heaven: You are the love of my life! I absolutely love and adore you. My every moment is consumed and filled with how I can love you more and more each day. I will spend my entire life doing that; making sure I put a smile on your face and your heart every day. Your love for God is amazing and I honor you for commitment to live for Him and to live pure. God has given you so many gifts and talent! I know that you will accomplish all of your dreams; I will make sure that happens! I love you, L.A!

To my family, my Mom, I love you soooo much; you are my heart! To my dad, Dadda, thank you for being there for me, especially when I needed you most. Toy, my sister and best friend, nothing can ever separate our love. My heart beats for each of you: Prena & Promise, Man, Kinya and the girls (Elec, Zhona, Jalaunda, Diamond, Autumn, lil AJ), my God-daughter, Rachel, Samia, Samquavis, Kay, Kayonna, Tori, Lil Man, Scottie & Sabastian, Samiah & Mariah, Sarah, LaRon, Raheen Stroud, the entire Adams, Curry, and Phelan Family, and a special note to my cousin, Ray Ray, love you all so much!

Dad & Mom~Papa Myles & Ruth Munroe, you have impacted my life, undeniably for the Kingdom of God. I am honored to call you my spiritual parents.

Marlon Hines, with tears in my eyes as I type this, I am eternally grateful for your sacrifice to not only this ministry, but to me and Heaven. You have been there for me when all hope was out of sight, when there was lack, hardships…I marvel at your generosity, unwavering commitment and love for us and the Lord. For every TV production and box office film, you will share in the harvest of it all.

To my staff, team and volunteers: Marlon Hines, Glendon Dixon, Elisabeth Johnson, Jessie Davis, Shamalia Mali Willis, Kourtnee Swafford, LaShawn England, Alicia Hill, Jamaal Hines and a host of volunteers who serve, give of your time and substance to this ministry, your labor for the Lord is not in vain and will be rewarded greatly. Rasean & Winter Reeves

Bahamas Faith Ministires, Northridge Church Family, Word of Faith, to my best friends: Melanie Few, Medina and Orrin Pullings, Scott Hughes~love you beyond words, Jillian (love you Jill Jill!) and the Blackwell family, Michelle Wilson, Amy Basel, Pam Perry, Kiana Kiwi Dennis, Gayle & Shaunee Brannan/VEC Family, Neechy, Bethany Ann and Rachel Roughley, Morod 'Mo' Zayed, Tiphani-Tip & Paigey, Michelle Black & family, Deleah Sharp, Ayanna Thomas, Devon Franklin (We will do box office movies together), Jor'el Quinn, Sonya Eppes, Heather VanSweringen, Aneesa Francis, Arian Simone, Joseph Bachota, Nellie Abraham & my small group family, Marianne Marsh, Pas. Tim Alden, Cedrina Davis Family, Mabel Pena, Robert/Stephanie Jones, Kenneth Sean "Holiness Is The New Sexy" Daly, Jeff Taylor, Carlos Peanut Butter Faison, Bishop Wayne T. & Beverly Jackson, Rochelle Mann, The Coopers, Renda Horne, Marlin Reid, Keenann Knox, Angelo B. Henderson, James Riley, Corey Coco Brother & Rosann Condrey, Glenda Gadie, Lee/Lashell Griffin, Horace H.B. Sanders, Dr. Jamal Bryant, Kevin Redd Felder…I'm running out of space here…To all the supporters of Ty Adams Int'l and to every who picks up this book to defy the odds and the stats, thank you. Stay committed to Christ.

Start A Dating Revolution!

Imagine what it would be like if each one of us began pursuing relationships the way that God intended? Well, we can!

1. Starting with you! As you travel through the pages of this book, make a dedicated commitment to begin approaching and pursuing relationships the way that God designed it.
2. Then start a ripple, domino effect: share God's plan for relationship with someone else and before you know it, there will be millions of singles doing love and relationships God's way! Imagine that! There will be more qualified and whole singles, providing a pool of quality options in a mate; even causing the divorce rate to diminish! Yahooo!
3. Share this book with your pastor or single's ministry and ask if the single adults can do a study group with the book to empower the singles in your church.
4. Order books and start your own single's book party for six weeks, meeting weekly in your home or clubhouse! The book party guide comes with a guide, complete with challenges, obstacles, discussions and fun assignments for your group to do. What a party that'll be! You can download the Dating Bible Book Party guide at www.TyAdamsTV.
5. If you are currently dating, get an extra copy for your dating companion and journey through this book together.
6. Buy extra copies and give it to your friends, family members, or co-workers.
7. Post it on your Facebook page or tweet about it on Twitter using the hash tag: #DatingBible #HowToDate.

Thank you for your support and doing love God's way!